German

FOR

DUMMIES®

2ND EDITION

German

FOR

DUMMIES®

2ND EDITION

by Paulina Christensen, Anne Fox,
and Wendy Foster

John Wiley & Sons, Inc.

German For Dummies,® 2nd Edition

Published by
John Wiley & Sons, Inc.
111 River St.
Hoboken, NJ 07030-5774
www.wiley.com

For general information on our other products and services, please contact our Customer Care Department within the U.S. at 877-762-2974, outside the U.S. at 317-572-3993, or fax 317-572-4002.

For technical support, please visit www.wiley.com/techsupport.

Wiley also publishes its books in a variety of electronic formats. Some content that appears in print may not be available in electronic books.

Library of Congress Control Number: 2010942180

ISBN: 978-0-470-90101-4

ISBN 978-1-118-01846-0 (ebk); ISBN 978-1-118-01847-7 (ebk); ISBN 978-1-118-01848-4 (ebk)

Manufactured in the United States of America

10 9 8 7 6 5 4 3

WILEY

About the Authors

Paulina Christensen has been working as a writer, editor, and translator for almost ten years. She holds a degree in English and German literature and has developed, written, and edited numerous German-language textbooks and teachers' handbooks for Berlitz International. Her work as a translator ranges from new media art to science fiction (*Starlog* magazine). She occasionally works as a court interpreter and does consulting and interpreting at educational conferences, as well as voice-overs for educational videos and CD-ROMs. Dr. Christensen received her M.A. and Ph.D. from Düsseldorf University, Germany, and has taught at Berlitz Language Schools, New York University, and Fordham University.

Anne Fox has been working as a translator, editor, and writer for the past twelve years. She studied at Interpreters' School, Zurich, Switzerland, and holds a degree in translation. Her various assignments have taken her to outer space, hyperspace, and around the world. She has also taught at Berlitz Language Schools and worked as a legal and technical proofreader in the editorial departments of several law firms. Most recently she has been developing, writing, and editing student textbooks and teacher handbooks for Berlitz.

Wendy Foster has been working as a teacher, writer, editor, and translator for longer than she can remember. She holds a degree in German from the Language and Interpreting Institute, Munich, Germany, an M.A. in French from Middlebury College, and a public school teaching certificate for German and French. She studied in France for two years, and then settled in Munich, Germany, where she worked in various teaching and writing capacities at various institutions, including Siemens, Hypovereinsbank, Munich Chamber of Commerce, and a number of publishers. She recently returned to her New England roots, where she works from her home overlooking a spectacular salt marsh that constantly beckons her to go kayaking, swimming, walking, and bird watching.

Berlitz has meant excellence in language services for more than 120 years. At more than 400 locations and in 50 countries worldwide, Berlitz offers a full range of language and language-related services, including instruction, cross-cultural training, document translation, software localization, and interpretation services. Berlitz also offers a wide array of publishing products, such as self-study language courses, phrase books, travel guides, and dictionaries.

The world-famous Berlitz Method® is the core of all Berlitz language instruction. From the time of its introduction in 1878, millions have used this method to learn new languages. For more information about Berlitz classes and products, please consult your local telephone directory for the Language Center nearest you or visit the Berlitz Web site at www.berlitz.com, where you can enroll in classes or shop directly for products online.

Acknowledgments

Wendy: I must thank Paulina Christensen and Anne Fox, who put so much time, effort, and knowledge into the first edition of this book. Thanks also to the editorial staff at Wiley for their unwavering support and to the technical reviewers, Tom Beyer and Chris Bellmann, who provided invaluable assistance. Finally, I would like to thank my friends at Fisherman's Cove for their friendship, patience, and humor, especially Phil, Crista, and Kitty.

Publisher's Acknowledgments

We're proud of this book; please send us your comments at http://dummies.custhelp.com. For other comments, please contact our Customer Care Department within the U.S. at 877-762-2974, outside the U.S. at 317-572-3993, or fax 317-572-4002.

Some of the people who helped bring this book to market include the following:

Acquisitions, Editorial, and Media Development

Project Editors: Corbin Collins, Tracy Barr

(Previous Edition: Mary Goodwin)

Acquisitions Editor: Michael Lewis

Copy Editor: Christine Pingleton

Assistant Editor: David Lutton

Technical Editors: Thomas Beyer, Christian Bellmann

Assistant Project Manager: Jenny Swisher

Associate Producer: Josh Frank

Quality Assurance: Doug Kuhn

CD Producer: Her Voice Unlimited, LLC

Editorial Manager: Jennifer Ehrlich

Editorial Assistant: Jennette ElNaggar

Art Coordinator: Alicia B. South

Cover Photo: ©iStockphoto.com / ihoe / Brian Chase / Amanda Cotton

Cartoons: Rich Tennant (www.the5thwave.com)

Composition Services

Project Coordinator: Sheree Montgomery

Layout and Graphics: Mark Pinto, SDJumper, Christin Swinford

Proofreaders: Linda Seifert, Dwight Ramsey

Indexer: Potomac Indexing, LLC

Illustrator: Elizabeth Kurtzman

Publishing and Editorial for Consumer Dummies

    Diane Graves Steele, Vice President and Publisher, Consumer Dummies

    Kristin Ferguson-Wagstaffe, Product Development Director, Consumer Dummies

    Ensley Eikenburg, Associate Publisher, Travel

    Kelly Regan, Editorial Director, Travel

Publishing for Technology Dummies

    Andy Cummings, Vice President and Publisher, Dummies Technology/General User

Composition Services

    Debbie Stailey, Director of Composition Services

Contents at a Glance

Table of Contents

Introduction

We are the players in a fascinating era, one that interconnects us with others all around the world. With globalization and technology as the driving forces, we find ourselves getting in closer and closer contact with more and more people. As a result, knowing how to say at least a few words in a language such as German is becoming an ever-more-vital tool.

Our natural curiosity to find out about other cultures motivates us to hop on a plane and find out firsthand what everyday life is like in the German-speaking regions: Germany, Austria, Switzerland, South Tyrol in northern Italy, Luxembourg, and Liechtenstein. Conducting international business in an increasingly competitive market necessitates personal contact; hence, more businesspeople are traveling overseas to countries like Germany, which has the largest economy in the European Union. On a more personal level, you may have friends, relatives, and neighbors who speak German, or you may want to get in touch with your heritage by learning a little bit of the language that your ancestors spoke.

Whatever your reasons for wanting to learn some German, *German For Dummies,* 2nd Edition, is a terrific choice because it gives you the skills you need for basic communication in German. We're not promising super fluency here, but if you want to know how to greet someone, purchase a train ticket, or order food from a menu in German, you need look no further than this book.

About This Book

German For Dummies, 2nd Edition, is set up so that you can use it any way you want to — as a reference to dip into for specific questions you have about German, as a means of gaining knowledge of German in a systematic way, or just for the fun of getting the feel for another language. Perhaps your goal is to learn some words and phrases to help you get around when you travel to a German-speaking country. Maybe you simply want to be able to say "Hello, how are you?" to your German-speaking neighbor. At any rate, you can go through this book at your own pace, reading as much or as little at a time as you like. You don't need to plod through the chapters in order, either; you're welcome to read the sections that interest you most.

Conventions Used in This Book

To make this book easy for you to navigate, we've set up a few conventions:

- German terms are set in **boldface** to make them stand out.

- Pronunciation is set in parentheses following the German terms, and the stressed syllables are italicized.

- English translations are italicized. You'll find them set in parentheses following the pronunciation of German terms or sentences.

- In some cases, German speakers use the same pronunciation as English speakers for words, many of which are borrowed from English or other languages. When such words are pronounced the same way in German as in English, you'll see the English word in the pronunciation followed by the notation "as in English" rather than the usual phonetic pronunciation. Of course, if the pronunciation differs between the English and German, we include the German pronunciation as usual.

- Verb conjugations (lists that show you the forms of a verb) are given in tables in this order:

  - The "I" form

  - The "you" (singular, informal [or sing. inf.]) form

  - The "you" (singular, formal [or sing. form.]) form

  - The "he, she, it" form

  - The "we" form

  - The "you" (plural, informal [or pl. inf.]) form

  - The "you" (plural, formal [or pl. form.]) form

  - The "they" form

  Pronunciations follow in the second column. The example shown uses the verb "to be." The conjugation starts with the German equivalent of "I am, you are," and so on.

Conjugation	Pronunciation
ich bin	iH bin
du bist	dooh bist
Sie sind	zee zint
er, sie, es ist	êr, zee, ês ist

Conjugation	*Pronunciation*
wir sind	veer zint
ihr seid	eer zayt
Sie sind	zee zint
sie sind	zee zint

To help you make fast progress in German, this book includes a few elements to help you along:

- ✔ **Talkin' the Talk dialogues:** The best way to learn a language is to see and hear how it's used in conversation, so we include dialogues throughout the book. The dialogues come under the heading "Talkin' the Talk" and show you the German words, their pronunciations, and the English translations.

- ✔ **Words to Know blackboards:** Acquiring key words and phrases is also important in language learning, so we collect these important words in sections that resemble chalkboards, with the heading "Words to Know." *Note:* In the pronunciations given in these sections, the stressed syllables are underlined rather than italicized.

- ✔ **Fun & Games activities:** If you want to flex your new language muscles, you can use the Fun & Games activities to reinforce what you learn. These activities are fun ways to check your progress.

Also note that, because each language has its own ways of expressing ideas, the English translations that we provide for the German terms may not be exactly literal. We want you to know the essence of what's being said, not just the meanings of single words. For example, the phrase **Es geht** (ês geyt) can be translated literally as *It goes,* but the phrase is actually the equivalent of *So, so,* or *Okay,* which is what you see as the translation.

Foolish Assumptions

To write this book, we made some assumptions about who you are and what you hope to gain from this book:

- ✔ You know no German — or if you took German somewhere in your deep, dark past, you don't remember much more than **Ja, Nein, Kindergarten, Guten Tag,** and **auf Wiedersehen**.

✔ You're primarily interested in communicating verbally in German, not in reading or writing German.

✔ You're definitely not looking for a ho-hum textbook that puts you to sleep, nor do you want to plod through monotonous language exercises that drill German into your brain. You just want to know some practical words, phrases, and sentence constructions so that you can communicate basic information in German — with confidence.

✔ You have no interest in memorizing long lists of bookish-sounding vocabulary words or a bunch of boring grammar rules.

✔ You're excited about German and are looking forward to having some fun as you pick up a bit of the language.

If any or all of these statements apply to you, you've found the right book!

How This Book Is Organized

This book is divided by topic: first into parts and then into chapters. The following sections tell you what types of information you can find in each part.

Part 1: Getting Started

This part gets you acclimated by providing you with some German basics: how to pronounce words, how to form sentences, and so on. You find a wealth of basic survival-type expressions such as greetings and numbers. We even challenge you to boost your confidence by activating some German words that you probably already know. Finally, we outline the basics of German grammar that you may need to know when you work through later chapters in the book.

Part 11: German in Action

In this part, you begin learning and using German. Instead of focusing on grammar points as many dull, dusty language textbooks do, this part focuses on communicating effectively in everyday situations, such as shopping, asking for directions, going to a museum, dining, phoning, and lots more.

Part III: German on the Go

This part gives you the tools you need to take your German on the road, whether you're looking to change money, find a place to stay, plan a trip, or take public or private transportation. There's even a chapter on handling emergencies.

Part IV: The Part of Tens

If you're looking for small, easily digestible pieces of information about German, this part is for you. Here, you can find ten ways to learn German quickly, ten useful German expressions to know, and more.

Part V: Appendixes

This part of the book includes important information that you can use for reference. Appendix A is a handy mini-dictionary in both German-to-English and English-to-German formats. If you encounter a German word that you don't understand or you need to know a specific word in German, you can look it up here. Appendix B features verb tables that show you how to conjugate both regular verbs and those verbs that stubbornly don't fit the pattern. Appendix C gives you the answer keys to all of the Fun & Games activities that appear in the book. Finally, Appendix D provides a listing of the tracks that appear on the accompanying audio CD so you can find out where in the book those dialogues are and follow along.

Icons Used in This Book

You may be looking for particular information while reading this book. To make certain types of information easier for you to find, the following icons have been placed in the left-hand margins throughout the book:

This icon highlights tips that can make learning German easier.

This icon points out interesting information that you won't want to forget.

Languages are full of quirks that may trip you up if you're not prepared for them. This icon points to discussions of important grammar points.

If you're looking for information and advice about culture and travel, look for these icons. They draw your attention to interesting tidbits about the countries in which German is spoken.

The audio CD that comes with this book gives you the opportunity to listen to real German speakers so that you can get a better understanding of what German sounds like. This icon marks the Talkin' the Talk dialogues that you can listen to on the CD.

Where to Go from Here

Learning a language is all about jumping in and giving it a try (no matter how bad your pronunciation is at first). So take the plunge! Start at the beginning, pick a chapter that interests you, or use the CD to listen to a few dialogues. Before long, you'll be able to respond, "**Ja!**" (yah) (*yes*) when someone asks you **Sprechen Sie Deutsch?** (*shprêH-en zee doych?*) (*Do you speak German?*)

Note: If you've never been exposed to German before, you may want to read the chapters in Part I before you tackle the later chapters. Part I gives you some of the basics that you need to know about the language, such as how to pronounce the various sounds, some basic expressions and words, and the fundamentals of German sentence structure.

Part I
Getting Started

The 5th Wave   By Rich Tennant

"Here's something. It's a language school that will teach you to speak German for $500, or for $200 they'll just give you an accent."

In this part . . .

You have to start somewhere, but we bet that you know a lot more German than you think. Don't think so? Then check out Chapter 1. Chapter 2 covers some nuts-and-bolts grammar info that, well, you need to absorb. But don't worry — we make it fun. The other chapters get you up to speed with some basic expressions and vocabulary you can use right away, such as saying hello and goodbye, expressing numbers, time, and measurements, or talking about your family. **Jetzt geht's los!** (yêtst geyts lohs!) (*Here we go!*)

Chapter 1

You Already Know a Little German

*T*he best way to learn a new language is to jump right in — no pussyfooting around. In this chapter, you get a head start in German by seeing some of the language you're already familiar with. You also find out some popular German expressions, and you get the hang of why you need to be careful with what are called "false friends," that is, words that seem to be the same in both languages but actually have different meanings.

The German You Know

Because both German and English belong to the group of Germanic languages, quite a few words are either identical or similar in both languages. Words that share a common source are called *cognates*. Another group of words common to German and English stem from Latin-based words that English speakers are familiar with. Many of these have direct equivalents in German, for example, nouns that end in "-tion."

Friendly allies (perfect cognates)

The following words are spelled the same way and have the same meaning in German and in English. The only differences are the pronunciation, as shown in parentheses, as well as the fact that in German, nouns are always capitalized. In addition, German nouns have one of three genders, as seen on this list by the words **der** (masculine), **die** (feminine), and **das** (neuter) in front of each noun. See Chapter 2 for details on what gender is all about and go to Chapter 3 for information on the pronunciation key for each word presented in this book. In a few instances, the German and English pronunciation for the word is the same, so you'll see the English word in the pronunciation (followed by the notation "as in English.")

- der **Arm** (dêr ârm)
- der **Bandit** (dêr bân-*deet*)
- die **Bank** (dee bânk)
- die **Basis** (dee *bah*-zis)
- **blind** (blint)
- die **Butter** (dee *boot*-er)
- **digital** (di-gi-*tâl*)
- **elegant** (êl-ê-*gânt*)
- die **Emotion** (dee ê-moh-tsee-*ohn*)
- **emotional** (ê-moh-tsee-oh-*nahl*)
- der **Finger** (dêr *fing*-er)
- die **Hand** (dee hânt)
- das **Hotel** (dâs hotel [as in English])
- die **Inspiration** (dee in-spi-râ-tsee-*ohn*)
- **international** (in-ter-nâ-tsee-oh-*nahl*)
- **irrational** (ir-râ-tsee-oh-*nahl*)
- **legal** (ley-*gahl*)
- **liberal** (lee-bêr-*ahl*)
- der **Mast** (dêr mast)
- die **Mine** (dee *meen*-e)
- **modern** (moh-*dêrn*)
- der **Moment** (dêr moh-*mênt*)
- die **Motivation** (dee moh-ti-vâ-tsee-*ohn*)
- das **Museum** (dâs mooh-*zey*-oohm)

- der **Name** (dêr *nah*-me)
- die **Nation** (dee nâ-tsee-*ohn*)
- **normal** (nor-*mahl*)
- die **Olive** (dee oh-*lee*-ve)
- **parallel** (pâr-â-*leyl*)
- das **Problem** (dâs proh-*bleym*)
- der **Professor** (dêr professor [as in English])
- das **Radio** (dâs *rah*-dee-oh)
- die **Religion** (dee rey-li-gee-*ohn*)
- das **Restaurant** (dâs rês-tuh-*ron*)
- die **Rose** (dee *roh*-ze)
- der **Service** (dêr *ser*-vis)
- das **Signal** (dâs zig-*nahl*)
- der **Sport** (dêr shport)
- die **Statue** (dee *shtah*-tooh-e)
- der **Stress** (dêr shtrês)
- das **System** (dâs zers-*teym*)
- das **Taxi** (dâs *tâx*-ee)
- der **Tiger** (dêr *tee*-ger)
- **tolerant** (to-lêr-*ânt*)
- die **Tradition** (dee trâ-di-tsee-*ohn*)
- der **Tunnel** (dêr *toohn*-el)
- **wild** (vilt)
- der **Wind** (dêr vint)

Kissing cousins (near cognates)

Many words, like the ones shown in Table 1-1, are spelled almost the same in German as in English and have the same meaning. Table 1-1 also shows you something about German spelling conventions, which include:

- The English *c* is a **k** in most German words.

- The *ou* in English words like *house* or *mouse* is often equivalent to **au** in German words.

- Many English adjectives ending in *-ic* or *-ical* have an **-isch** ending in German.

- Some English adjectives ending in **-y** are spelled with **-ig** in German.

- Some English nouns ending in **-y** have an **-ie** ending in German.

Table 1-1	Words Similar in Meaning, Slightly Different in Spelling
German	*English*
die Adresse (dee ah-*drês*-e)	*address*
der Aspekt (dêr âs-*pêkt*)	*aspect*
der Bär (dêr bear [as in English])	*bear*
blond (blont)	*blond(e)*
die Bluse (dee *blooh*-ze)	*blouse*
braun (brown [as in English])	*brown*
die Demokratie (dee dê-moh-krâ-*tee*)	*democracy*
direkt (di-*rêkt*)	*direct*
der Doktor (dêr *dok*-tohr)	*doctor*
exzellent (êx-tsel-*ênt*)	*excellent*
fantastisch (fân-*tâs*-tish)	*fantastic*
das Glas (dâs glahs)	*glass*
das Haus (dâs hous)	*house*
hungrig (*hoong*-riH)	*hungry*

(continued)

Table 1-1 *continued*

German	English
die Industrie (dee in-dooh-*stree*)	*industry*
der Kaffee (dêr *kâf*-ey)	*coffee*
die Komödie (dee koh-*mer*-dee-e)	*comedy*
die Kondition (dee kon-di-tsee-*ohn*)	*condition*
das Konzert (dâs kon-*tsêrt*)	*concert*
die Kultur (dee kool-*toohr*)	*culture*
logisch (*loh*-gish)	*logical*
das Mandat (dâs mân-*daht*)	*mandate*
der Mann (dêr mân)	*man*
die Maschine (dee mâ-*sheen*-e)	*machine*
die Maus (dee mouse [as in English])	*mouse*
die Methode (dee mê-*toh*-de)	*method*
die Mobilität (dee moh-bi-li-*tait*)	*mobility*
die Musik (dee mooh-*zeek*)	*music*
die Nationalität (dee nât-see-oh-nahl-i-*tait*)	*nationality*
die Natur (dee nâ-*toohr*)	*nature*
offiziell (oh-fits-ee-*êl*)	*official* (adjective)
der Ozean (dêr *oh*-tsê-ân)	*ocean*
das Papier (dâs pâ-*peer*)	*paper*
das Parlament (dâs pâr-lâ-*mênt*)	*parliament*
perfekt (pêr-*fêkt*)	*perfect*
politisch (poh-*li*-tish)	*political*
potenziell (po-tên-tsee-*êl*)	*potential* (adjective)
praktisch (*prâk*-tish)	*practical*
das Programm (dâs proh-*grâm*)	*program*
das Salz (dâs zâlts)	*salt*
der Scheck (dêr shêk)	*check*
sonnig (*zon*-iH)	*sunny*
der Supermarkt (dêr *zooh*-pêr-mârkt)	*supermarket*
das Telefon (dâs *tê*-le-fohn)	*telephone*
die Theorie (dee tey-ohr-*ee*)	*theory*
die Tragödie (dee trâ-*ger*-dee-e)	*tragedy*
die Walnuss (dee *vahl*-noohs)	*walnut*

False friends

As does every language, German contains some false friends — those words that look very similar to English but have a completely different meaning. As you read the following list, you can see why you should treat any new German word with kid gloves, especially if it looks like an English word, until, that is, you find out for sure what it means in English.

- **After** (*ahf*-ter): If you want to avoid embarrassment, remember the meaning of this word. Its German meaning is *anus* and not *after.* The German word for *after* is **nach** (nahH) or **nachdem** (nahH-*deym).*

- **aktuell** (âk-tooh-*êl*): This word means *up-to-date* and *current,* not *actual.* The German translation for *actual* is **tatsächlich** (tât-*sêH*-liH).

- **also** (*âl*-zoh): This one means *so, therefore,* or *thus;* not *also.* The German word for *also* is **auch** (ouH).

- **bald** (bâlt): This word means *soon* and is not a description for someone with little or no hair. The German word for *bald* is **kahl** (kahl) or **glatzköpfig** (*glâts*-kerpf-iH).

- **bekommen** (be-*kom*-en): This verb is an important one to remember. It means *to get* and not *to become.* The German word for *to become* is **werden** (*vêr*-den).

- **Boot** (boht): This is a *boat* and not a *boot,* which is **Stiefel** (*shteef*-el) in German. A *sailboat* is called a **Segelboot** (*zey*-gêl-boht).

- **brav** (brahf): This word means *well-behaved* and not *brave.* The German word for *brave* is **tapfer** (*tâp*-fer).

- **Brief** (breef): This is a noun and means *letter,* not *brief.* The German translation for the English adjective *brief* is **kurz** (koorts), and, for the English noun, **Auftrag** (*ouf*-trahk) or **Unterlagen** (*oon*-ter-lah-gen).

- **Chef** (shêf): This is the German word for a person you take orders from, your *boss* or *supervisor,* not someone who's in charge of the cooking. The German word for *chef* is **Küchenchef** (*kueH*-ên-shêf) or **Chefkoch** (*shêf*-koH). Otherwise, a plain *cook* is called a **Koch** (koH) in German.

- **eventuell** (ey-vên-tooh-*êl*): This one means *possible* or *possibly,* not *eventual* or *eventually,* both of which would be **schließlich** (*shlees*-liH) in German.

- **fast** (fâst): This is an adjective that means *almost* — not the speeds at which Formula One drivers race. The German word for *fast* is **schnell** (shnêl) or **rasch** (râsh).

- **genial** (gê-nee-*ahl*): This adjective describes an idea or person *of genius* and has nothing to do with *genial.* The German word for *genial* is **heiter** (*hay*-ter).

✔ **Gift** (gift [as in English]): The German meaning is *poison,* so when you're giving your German-speaking host a *present,* you should say you have a **Geschenk** (gê-*shênk*), that is, unless you really are giving something like weed killer or a green mamba.

✔ **Kind** (kint): This is the German word for *child.* It has nothing to do with the English *kind,* which is **nett** (nêt) or **liebenswürdig** (*lee*-bens-vuerd-iH) in German.

✔ **Komfort** (kom-*fohr*): This word means *amenity,* for example, the amenities you expect in a five-star hotel, not *comfort.* The German verb meaning *to comfort* [someone] is **trösten** (*trers*-ten).

✔ **kurios** (koohr-ee-*ohs*): This word means *strange,* not *curious.* The German word for *curious* is **neugierig** (*noy*-geer-iH).

✔ **Mist** (mist [as in English]): Be careful not to misuse this word that actually means *manure* in German! It doesn't describe heavy moisture resembling a fine rain, which is called **Nebel** (*ney*-bel) or **Dunst** (doonst).

✔ **Most** (most): This is the German word for unfermented fruit juice, and in southern German-speaking regions, a young fruit wine. The German word for the English *most* is **das meiste** (dâs *mays*-te); for example, **die meisten Leute** (die *mays*-ten *loy*-te) (*most people*).

✔ **ordinär** (or-di-*nair*): This word means *vulgar* rather than *ordinary.* The German word for *ordinary* is **normal** (nor-*mahl*) or **gewöhnlich** (ge-*vern*-liH).

✔ **pathetisch** (pâ-*tey*-tish): This one means *overly emotional,* not *pathetic,* which, in German, is **jämmerlich** (*yêm*-er-liH) or **armselig** (*ârm*-zey-liH).

✔ **plump** (ploomp): The German meaning is *clumsy* or *tactless,* not *roundish,* which in German is **rundlich** (*roont*-liH).

✔ **Präservativ** (prê-zêr-vah-*teef*): Another embarrassing moment can be avoided when you know that this word means *condom* in German. The German equivalent of *preservative* is **Konservierungsmittel** (kon-sêr-*yeer*-oongs-mit-el).

✔ **Provision** (proh-vi-zee-*ohn*): The meaning of this word is *commission,* not *provision.* The German word for *provision* is **Vorsorge** (*fohr*-zor-ge) or **Versorgung** (fêr-*zohrg*-oong).

✔ **See** (zey): This word means *lake* or *sea.* In German, the verb *to see* is **sehen** (*zey*-en).

✔ **sensibel** (zen-*zee*-bel): The meaning of this word is *sensitive* rather than *sensible,* which translates as **vernünftig** (fêr-*nuenf*-tiH).

✔ **sympathisch** (zerm-*pah*-tish): This word means *likeable* or *congenial,,* not *sympathetic.* The German word for *sympathetic* is **mitfühlend** (*mit*-fuel-ent).

Lenders and borrowers

A few German words have been adopted by the English language and have retained their meaning, such as **Kindergarten** (*kin*-der-gâr-ten), **Angst** (ânkst), **kaputt** (kâ-*poot*), **Ersatz** (êr-*zats*), **Sauerkraut** (*zou*-er-krout), **Zeitgeist** (*tsayt*-gayst), and **Wanderlust** (*vân*-der-loost).

However, the number of these German words is minimal compared to the English words that have made their way into the German language. At times, the combination of English and German makes for somewhat curious linguistic oddities. For example, you may hear **das ist total in/out** (dâs ist toh-*tahl* in/out [as in English]) (*that's totally in/out*) or **Sie können den File downloaden** (zee *kern*-en deyn file [as in English] *doun*-lohd-en) (*You can download the file*).

The following is a list of German words that have been borrowed from the English language. Note that they all retain their English pronunciations, with a slight exception: The borrowed verbs are "germanified," which simply means they combine the English verb, such as *kill* or *jog*, with **-en**, the German suffix that creates the infinitive form (*to kill* and *to jog*). Go to Chapter 2 for more on German infinitives:

- ✔ der Boss
- ✔ das Business
- ✔ das Catering
- ✔ die City (German meaning: *downtown*)
- ✔ der Computer
- ✔ cool
- ✔ das Design
- ✔ das Event
- ✔ Fashion (used without article)
- ✔ das Fast Food
- ✔ das Feeling
- ✔ flirten (*to flirt*)
- ✔ der Headhunter
- ✔ Hi
- ✔ hip
- ✔ der Hit
- ✔ das Hotel
- ✔ das Internet
- ✔ das Interview
- ✔ der Jetlag
- ✔ der Job
- ✔ joggen (*to jog*)
- ✔ killen (*to kill*)
- ✔ managen (*to manage*)
- ✔ der Manager
- ✔ das Marketing
- ✔ das Meeting
- ✔ Okay
- ✔ online
- ✔ outsourcen (*to outsource*)

- ✔ die Party
- ✔ pink
- ✔ das Shopping
- ✔ die Shorts
- ✔ die Show/Talkshow
- ✔ das Steak
- ✔ **surfen** (*to surf waves or the Internet*)

- ✔ das Team
- ✔ der Thriller
- ✔ der Tourist
- ✔ das T-Shirt
- ✔ der Workshop
- ✔ Wow

Finally, a few English terms have different meanings in the German language. For example, the word **Evergreen** refers to a *golden oldie*, **Handy** means a *cellphone*, **Mobbing** means *bullying* or *harassing*, **Oldtimer** refers to a *vintage car*, and **Wellness-Center** means *spa*.

Talkin' the Talk

Read the following conversation with a grain of salt — and a smile. It gives you an idea of how many words have slid into German. However, you're not likely to overhear this many examples of mixed language in a single conversation. In this scenario, two friends, Claudia and Jana, meet on the street. Notice how some terms have a slightly different meaning in German.

Claudia: **Hi Jana, wie geht's? Wie ist der neue Job?**
Hi [as in English] *yâ*-nâ, vee geyts? vee ist dêr *noy*-e job [as in English]?
Hi Jana, how are you? How's the new job?

Jana: **Super! Heute war meine erste Presentation vor meinem big Boss, und er war total cool.**
super [as in English]! *hoy*-te vahr *mayn*-e êrs-te pre-zen-tât-see-*ohn* fohr *mayn*-êm big boss [as in English], oont êr vahr toh-*tahl* cool [as in English].
Super! Today was my first presentation in front of my big boss, and he was totally cool.

Claudia:	**Wow! In meinem Office gibt es nur Stress. Mein Boss kann nichts managen. Mein Kollege checkt nichts, und denkt, er ist ein Sonnyboy, und alle anderen spinnen.**
	wow [as in English]! in *mayn*-êm office [as in English] gipt ês noohr shtrês. mayn boss kân niHts *mân-â*-gen [*g* as in English]. mayn kol-*ey*-ge checkt niHts oont dênkt êr ist ayn sonny boy [as in English], oont *âl*-e *ân*-der-en *spin*-en.
	Wow! In my office there's nothing but stress. My boss can't manage anything. My colleague isn't "with it," and thinks he's a hot shot , and all the others are crazy.
Jana:	**Ich gehe shoppen. Kommst du mit?**
	iH *gey*-e *shop*-en. Komst dooh mit?
	I'm going shopping. Do you want to come along?
Claudia:	**Nein, danke. Gestern war ich in einem Outlet und habe ein T-Shirt in pink und eine Jeans im Boyfriend-Look gekauft. Ich gehe jetzt joggen. Bye-bye!**
	nayn, *dân*-ke. *gês*-têrn vahr iH in *ayn*-em outlet [as in English] oont *hah*-be ayn T-shirt [as in English] in pink [as in English] oont *ayn*-e jeans [as in English] im boy-friend-look [as in English] ge-*kouft*. iH *gey*-e yêtst *jog*-en [*jog* as in English]. bye-bye [as in English]!
	No, thanks. Yesterday I went to an outlet and bought a pink T-shirt and a pair of jeans in boyfriend look. I'm going jogging now. Bye!
Jana:	**Schade. Bye-bye!**
	shah-de. bye-bye!
	Too bad. Bye!

Using Popular Expressions

Just like the English language, German has many *idioms,* which are expressions typical of a language and culture. If you translate these idioms word for word, they may sound obscure, silly, or just plain meaningless, so you definitely need to find out what they really mean in order to use them appropriately.

Some expressions may have an English equivalent that's recognizable, so it's easier to get the hang of using them. For example, the German idiom **ein Fisch auf dem Trockenen** (ayn fish ouf deym *trok*-ên-en) literally translates into *a fish on the dry,* which somewhat resembles the English *a fish out of water.* On the other hand, if you were to take apart the German expression **Da liegt der Hund begraben** (da leekt dêr hoont be-*grah*-ben) word for word, you'd probably feel sorry for the poor dog, because in essence, it means something like *That's where the dog is buried.* However, the English equivalent is *That's the heart of the matter.*

A few other typical German idioms are

Die Daumen drücken. (dee *doum*-en *druek*-en.) (*Press the thumbs*). The English meaning is *Keep your fingers crossed.*

Wo sich Fuchs und Hase gute Nacht sagen (voh ziH fooks oont *hah*-ze *gooh*-te nâHt *zah*-gen) (*where fox and hare say good night to one another*), which means *in the middle of nowhere,* or *in the sticks.*

Ich bin fix und fertig. (iH bin fix oont *fêr*-tiH.) (*I'm quick and ready.*) This means *I'm wiped out,* or *I'm exhausted.*

Du nimmst mich auf den Arm! (dooh nimst miH ouf deyn ârm!) (*You're taking me on your arm!*), meaning *You're pulling my leg!*

Das ist ein Katzensprung. (dâs ist ayn *kâts*-en-shproong.) (*That's a cat's jump.*) The English meaning is *It's a stone's throw away.*

Schlafen wie ein Murmeltier (*shlâf*-en vee ayn *moor*-mel-teer) (*sleep like a woodchuck [marmot]*). In English, you say *sleep like a log.*

Apart from such idioms, many handy and frequently used German expressions are easy to learn. Here are some of them:

Prima!/Klasse!/Toll! (*pree*-mah!/*klâs*-e!/tôl!) (*Great!*)

Fertig. (*fêrt*-iH.) (*Ready./Finished.*) This can be either a question or a statement.

Quatsch! (qvâch!) (*Nonsense!/How silly of me!*)

Einverstanden. (*ayn*-fêr-shtând-en.) (*Agreed./Okay.*)

Vielleicht. (fee-*layHt.*) (*Maybe./Perhaps.*)

Mach's gut. (vîrt ge-*mâHt.*) (*Take it easy.*) This is a casual way of saying *good-bye.*

Wie, bitte? (vee *bi*-te?) (*[I beg your] pardon?/What did you say?*)

Macht nichts. (mâHt niHts.) (*Never mind./That's okay.*)

Nicht der Rede wert. (niHt dêr *rey*-de vêrt.) (*Don't mention it.*)

Schade! (*shah*-de!) (*Too bad!/What a pity!*)

So ein Pech! (zoh ayn pêH!) (*Bad luck!*)

Viel Glück! (feel gluek!) (*Good luck!*)

Oder? (*oh*-der?) (*Isn't that true?/Don't you think so?*)

Bis dann! (bis dân!) (*See you then!*)

Bis bald! (bis bâlt!) (*See you soon!*)

Chapter 2

The Nitty-Gritty: Basic German Grammar

In This Chapter

▶ Identifying parts of speech

▶ Combining words to create sentences

▶ Talking in terms of the past, present, and future

▶ Making a case for cases

*W*hen you think about grammar, imagine a big dresser with lots of drawers. Instead of being filled with all kinds of clothing, these drawers contain different types of words, called parts of speech: nouns, verbs, adjectives, adverbs, and so on. Each part of speech is in a separate drawer.

Now imagine it's early morning and you're about to utter your first German sentence of the day. To begin, you reach into the noun drawer and pull out the word **Socken** (*zok*-en) (*socks*). Next, to describe your socks, you reach into the adjective drawer and pull out two words, **neu** (noy) (*new*) and **schwarz** (shvârts) (*black*). To indicate what you do with your new black socks, you fish through the verb drawer and pull out the verb **anziehen** (*ân*-tsee-en) (*to put on*). And because you're running late, you dive straight into the adverb drawer and grab the word **schnell** (shnêl) (*quickly*). Now, to construct a whole sentence, you need another item, this one from the pronoun drawer: **ich** (iH) (*I*). Before you know it, you've pulled a complete sentence out of the dresser: **Ich ziehe schnell meine neuen schwarzen Socken an** (iH *tsee*-he shnêl *mayn*-e *noy*-en *shvârts*-en *zok*-en ân) (*I quickly put my new black socks on*).

To construct a correct sentence, you need to know how to string all these words together, and that's what grammar is all about. This chapter makes using grammar as easy as getting dressed in the morning. With a few basic rules in your back pocket, you'll be using grammar with confidence in no time. So arrange your thoughts, grab the words you need, and before you know it, you'll be out the door and speaking — **auf Deutsch** (ouf doych) (*in German*).

Getting a Handle on Parts of Speech

To construct a simple sentence, you need a certain number of building blocks, the parts of speech. The most essential of these are nouns, articles, pronouns, verbs, adjectives, and adverbs. The following sections give you the lowdown on each of these.

Nouns

A rose is a rose is a rose, right? Well, a rose is also a noun, and nouns aren't exactly the same in German and English. Although nouns in both languages name things (people, places, objects, concepts, and so on), the difference is that all German nouns are capitalized and have one of three genders: masculine, feminine, or neuter. The following sections go into more detail on gender and how to make singular German nouns plural.

Understanding a noun's gender

As mentioned previously, German nouns have gender. That is, they are one of the following: masculine, feminine, or neuter. Unfortunately, the meaning of a noun isn't usually much help in predicting its grammatical gender. You need to keep in mind that in German, grammatical gender is an element of German grammar, and it's not related to the meaning of the noun. Instead, it's a kind of marker that identifies how the noun fits into a sentence. Sorry, no easy way out. You simply have to memorize the gender that belongs with each noun. However, a few guidelines can get you started:

- ✔ Nouns for male persons, cars, nationalities, occupations, seasons, days, and months are usually masculine.

- ✔ Nouns for most female persons, many flowers, and trees are feminine.

- ✔ Nouns beginning with **Ge-** are usually neuter.

- ✔ Nouns ending in **-ist**, **-ich**, **-ismus**, and **-ner** are usually masculine.

- ✔ Nouns ending in **-heit**, **-keit**, **-ik**, **-schaft**, **-ei**, **-tät**, and **-ung** are usually feminine.

- ✔ Nouns ending in **-chen**, **-lein**, **-ium**, **-um**, and **-tum** are usually neuter.

Knowing a noun's gender becomes even more important when the noun is plopped into a sentence. How's that? Well, depending on the role the noun plays in the sentence, the three definite articles **der** (dêr), **die** (dee), and **das** (dâs), all of which translate to the English *the,* can go through all kinds of spelling gyrations, and sometimes even the noun's spelling is altered. Same with the indefinite articles **ein** (ayn), **eine** (*ayn*-e), and **ein** (ayn), which correspond to the English *a* and *an.* In fact, because you can't really talk about German nouns without talking about the articles that accompany them, we devote a whole section to the topic. The key to all this morphing is what's known as case. Read the section "Putting the Language in the Proper Case" later in this chapter to shed more light on how to put German nouns and articles into sentences.

Making singular nouns plural

Throughout this book, you encounter nouns in their singular and/or plural forms. You may notice that in German, there are several ways to change a singular noun to its plural form.

Two groups of words are easy to deal with:

- ✔ **The group of nouns that are the same in both the singular and plural forms, like the English noun "sheep."** Many of the nouns in this group are masculine- and neuter-gender words ending in **-er**, like **das Fenster/ die Fenster** (dâs *fens*-ter/dee *fens*-ter) (*window/windows*), and **der Amerikaner/die Amerikaner** (dêr â-mey-ree-*kah*-ner/dee â-mey-ree-*kah*-ner) (*American/Americans*).

- ✔ **The group of nouns that are mostly of foreign origin:** The plural form of these nouns has an **-s** ending, for example **das Radio/die Radios** (dâs *rah*-dee-oh/dee *rah*-dee-ohs) (*radio/radios*) and **das Café/die Cafés** (dâs café [as in English] /dee cafes) (*café/cafés*).

Other plural form patterns include nouns that add **-e**, **-er**, or **–en**; nouns that add an umlaut (represented by two dots over a vowel, as in ä, ö, and ü); or a combination of both. Following are three examples: **der Vater/die Väter** (dêr *fah*-ter/dee *fai*-ter) (*father/fathers*), **die Lampe/die Lampen** (dee *lâm*-pe/dee *lâm*-pen) (*lamp/lamps*), and **das Buch/die Bücher** (das booH/dee *bueH*-er) (*book/books*). Sound complicated? You're right, so do try to make a point of remembering the plural form of a noun (and its gender!) when you first incorporate it into your active vocabulary.

Articles

Nouns often appear in the company of a sidekick: a definite article (**der, die,** and **das**, which correspond to the English *the*) or an indefinite article (**ein, eine,** and **ein**, which correspond to *a* or *an*). Read on for more.

The definite articles ("der," "die," and "das")

Here's where German gets sticky. While the definite article *the* has only one form in English, in German, it has three forms: **der** (dêr) (masculine), **die** (dee) (feminine), and **das** (dâs) (neuter). Which form you use depends on the gender of the German noun. **Der** is the definite article used with masculine nouns, **die** is used with feminine nouns, and **das** is used with neuter nouns.

When meeting a new noun, find out whether its definite article is **der**, **die**, or **das** — in other words, determine the gender of the noun. For example, memorize **der Garten** (dêr *gâr*-ten) (*the garden*) rather than just **Garten** (*gâr*-ten) (*garden*), **die Tür** (dee tuer) (*the door*) rather than **Tür** (tuer) (*door*), and **das Haus** (dâs house [as in English]) (*the house*) rather than **Haus** (house) (*house*).

For plural nouns, things are comparatively easy. The definite article for all plural nouns, regardless of gender, is **die** (dee). And, as in English, the indefinite article *a* just vanishes in the plural: *a garden* becomes *gardens*. (The next section explains indefinite articles in more detail.)

The indefinite articles ("ein," "eine," and "ein")

In English, you use the indefinite article *a* or *an* when you want to specify one of a particular thing. Because you're dealing with three different genders in German, you also have to use three different indefinite articles. Luckily, the indefinite article for masculine and neuter nouns is the same:

- ✔ **For masculine nouns:** You use **ein** (ayn), for example, **ein Name** (ayn *nah*-me) (*a name*), **ein Mann** (ayn mân) (*a man*), and **ein Berg** (ayn bêrg) (*a mountain*).

- ✔ **For neuter nouns:** You use **ein** (ayn), for example, **ein Problem** (ayn pro-*bleym*) (*a problem*), **ein Museum** (ayn moo-*zey*-oom) (*a museum*), **ein Bier** (ayn beer) (*a beer*).

- ✔ **For feminine nouns:** You add an **e** to **ein**, making **eine** (*ayn*-e), for example, **eine Nacht** (*ayn*-e nâHt) (*a night*), **eine Adresse** (*ayn*-e ah-*drês*-e) (*an address*), and **eine Cousine** (*ayn*-e kooh-*zeen*-e) (*a female cousin*).

Not too difficult, right? But things can get a little more complicated. You know that the gender of a noun determines the articles that are used with it. But the endings of the articles also change depending on whether the noun they're attached to is in the nominative, genitive, dative, or accusative case. The endings specified in the preceding list are those of the nominative case. For more information about case and how it affects both definite and indefinite articles, head to the later section "Why all these cases matter."

Pronouns

Pronouns are the handy group of words that can punt for nouns so you don't sound redundant. In German, pronouns change form depending on their role in a sentence. For example, **ich** (iH) (*I*) can change into **mich** (miH) (*me*) or **mir** (mir) (*me*). For more on pronouns and case, see "Putting the Language in the Proper Case" later in this chapter.

Adjectives

Adjectives describe nouns. In German, adjectives have different endings depending on the gender, case (more about that later in this chapter), and number (singular or plural) of the noun they accompany. Adjective endings also depend on whether the adjective is accompanied by a definite article, an indefinite article, or no article at all.

The following list shows the endings for adjectives accompanied by a definite article in the nominative case (for more on case, see "Putting the Language in the Proper Case" later in this chapter). This list includes the adjectives **schön** (shern) (*beautiful*), **weiß** (vays) (*white*), **groß** (grohs) (*large*), and **klein** (klayn) (*small*). The adjective endings appear in italics:

▸ **der schön*e* Garten** (dêr *sher*-ne *gâr*-ten) (*the beautiful garden*)

▸ **die weiß*e* Tür** (dee *vays*-e tuer) (*the white door*)

▸ **das klein*e* Haus** (dâs *klayn*-e hous) (*the small house*)

▸ **die groß*en* Häuser** (dee *grohs*-en *hoy*-zer) (*the large houses*)

Following are the nominative case endings for adjectives used alone (that is, without an accompanying article) or adjectives accompanied by an indefinite article:

▸ **(ein) schön*er* Garten** ([ayn] *sher*-ner *gâr*-ten) ([*a*] *beautiful garden*)

▸ **(eine) weiß*e* Tür** ([ayn -e] *vays*-e tuer) ([*a*] *white door*)

▸ **(ein) klein*es* Haus** ([ayn] *klayn*-es hous) ([*a*] *small house*)

▸ **groß*e* Häus*er*** (*grohs*-e *hoy*-zer) (*large houses*)

All the adjectives (and their corresponding endings) in the preceding examples are in the subject case (that is, the nominative case). The endings for the other cases follow a little later in this chapter.

Verbs

Verbs express actions or states of being. The person doing the action is the verb's subject, and the verb always adjusts its ending to the subject. For example, you say *I open the door* and *the cat opens the door*. In the present tense in English, most verbs have two different forms, or spellings, for example, *open* and *opens*. Most German verbs, on the other hand, have four different forms. (For further information on tenses, check out the section later in this chapter, "The Tenses: Past, Present, and Future.")

The verb form in its basic, static state is called the *infinitive*. It's what you see in the mini-dictionary at the back of this book, or in any dictionary for that matter. In English, the infinitive verb form looks like the following examples: *to play, to think,* or *to ride,* and you can put it into a sentence like this: *I know how to ride a camel.* German infinitives, however, usually have the ending **-en**, as in **lachen** (*lāH*-en) (*to laugh*), stuck onto what's called the *stem.* For example, the stem of **lachen** is **lach-**. A small number of verbs have the infinitive ending **-n**.

The stems of most verbs don't change, and the endings of such verbs are always the same. The following table shows the endings of the verb **sagen** (*zah*-gen) (*to say*). You tack the appropriate ending onto the stem **sag-**, depending on how you're expressing the verb.

Conjugation	*Pronunciation*
ich sag-e	iH *zah*-ge
du sag-st	dooh *zâ*gst
Sie sag-en	zee *zah*-gen
er, sie, es sag-t	êr, zee, ês *zâ*gt
wir sag-en	veer *zah*-gen
ihr sag-t	eer *zâ*gt
Sie sag-en	zee *zah*-gen
sie sag-en	zee *zah*-gen

Seems easy, doesn't it? But — as usual — some exceptions to the rule do exist. When the stem of the verb ends in **-m**, **-n**, **-d**, or **-t**, you need to insert an **-e** before the ending in the **du**, **er/sie/es**, and **ihr** constructions, as shown in the following examples:

> **du atm-e-st** (*ât*-mêst) (*you* [singular, informal] *breathe*)
>
> **er arbeit-e-t** (*âr*-bay-têt) (*he works*)
>
> **ihr bad-e-t** (*ba*-dêt) (*you* [plural, informal] *bathe*)

Why the added **e**? Try to pronounce "atmst," and you'll know.

Adverbs

Adverbs accompany verbs or adjectives and their purpose is to describe them. In English, most adverbs end with -ly (as in: I *quickly* put my new black socks on.) In German, adverbs are generally spelled the same as their adjective counterparts in their barebones form, without special endings.

Take, for example, **vorsichtig** (*fohr*-ziH-tiH) (*careful/carefully*), which has the same spelling for both its adjective and its adverb meaning. When you use **vorsichtig** in a sentence as an adverb, it keeps the same spelling, for example, **Fahren Sie vorsichtig!** (*fahr*-en zee *fohr*-ziH-tiH!) (*Drive carefully!*) However, when you use **vorsichtig** in a sentence as an adjective, it changes its form (spelling) the way all German adjectives do; see the previous section about adjectives. The following sentence shows how **vorsichtig**, when used as an adjective, changes its spelling according to the noun it describes:

> **Sie ist eine vorsichtige Fahrerin** (zee ist *ayn*-e *fohr*-ziH-tig-e *fahr*-er-in) (She's a careful driver).

Constructing Simple Sentences

Nouns, pronouns, verbs, adjectives, and adverbs aren't just thrown together helter-skelter; instead, to create a logical sentence, you arrange words in a specific order. The correct order is determined by certain rules, which the next sections explain.

Arranging words in the right order

Standard word order in German is much like English word order. The subject comes first, then the verb, followed by the rest of the sentence. Look at the following example sentence.

Subject	Verb	Object
Meine Freundin	**hat**	**einen Hund.**
mayn-e *froyn*-din	hât	*ayn*-en hoont.
My girlfriend	*has*	*a dog.*

Putting the verb in second place

One of the most important things to remember is the place of the verb in a German sentence. In freestanding clauses (known as *independent clauses*), like the one in the preceding section, a one-word verb is always in second place, no matter what. The term "second place," however, doesn't necessarily mean the second *word* in the sentence. Rather, it refers to the second "placeholder," which may be comprised of more than one word. For example, **meine Freundin**, the subject of the earlier sentence, consists of two words but it's the first placeholder. In the following examples, the verb is **fahren** (*fahren*) (*to drive*), and it follows the second place rule.

> **Meine Freundin fährt nach Dänemark.** (*mayn*-e *froyn*-din fairt nâH *dê*-ne-mârk.) (*My girlfriend is driving to Denmark.*)

How about adding some more information?

> **Meine Freundin fährt morgen nach Dänemark.** (*mayn*-e *froyn*-din fairt *mor*-gen nâH *dê*-ne-mârk.) (*My girlfriend is driving to Denmark tomorrow.*)

Standard practice in German sentences is to place the reference to time, **morgen** (*mor*-gen) (*tomorrow*), before the reference to place, **nach Dänemark** (nâH *dê*-ne-mark) (*to Denmark*), as you can see in the previous sentence. What happens if you start the sentence with **morgen**?

> **Morgen fährt meine Freundin nach Dänemark.** (*mor*-gen fairt *mayn*-e *froyn*-din nâH *dê*-ne-mârk.) (*Tomorrow my girlfriend is driving to Denmark.*)

Morgen is in first place, and because the verb has to be in second place, the subject follows the verb. Technically, this arrangement is called *inversion of the verb*. All it means is that the verb and the subject switch places. Inversion of the verb occurs whenever anything other than the subject occupies first place in a sentence.

Having said that, what about the statement **Meine Freundin hat einen Hund** (from the preceding section)? Can you give that one a twirl and change the word order? Absolutely, as long as the verb stays in second place, like this: **Einen Hund hat meine Freundin.** But why would you want to rearrange word order? Generally, you do so to shift emphasis in the meaning. For example, you may hear something along the lines of the following conversation:

> **Hat deine Schwester einen Hund?** (hât *dayn*-e *shvês*-ter *ayn*-en hoont?) (*Does your sister have a dog?*)

> **Nein, sie hat eine Katze. Einen Hund hat meine Freundin Heike.** (nayn, zee hât *ayn*-e kâts-*e*. *ayn*-en hoont hât *mayn*-e *froyn*-din *hay*-ke.) (*No, she has a cat. It's my girlfriend Heike who has a dog.*)

Don't German speakers get all confused playing around with word order like that? That's where the (in)famous German case system comes into play. Adjectives and articles that appear alongside nouns and, in some instances, the nouns themselves, assume different endings depending on their function in a sentence. So no matter where a noun appears in a German sentence, you can figure out its role by checking the ending of the article, the noun itself, and/or the adjective. See "Putting the Language in the Right Case" later in this chapter for the details.

Pushing the verb to the end

The examples used so far in this section have all been independent, stand-alone sentences, but sometimes several thoughts combine to form a more complex structure:

> **Wir gehen nicht einkaufen, weil wir kein Geld haben.** (veer *gey*-en niHt *ayn*-kouf-en, vayl veer kayn gêlt *hah*-ben.) (*We're not going shopping because we have no money.*)

The verb **gehen** (*gey*-en) (*go*) is in second place as you would expect, but the verb in the second part of the sentence beginning with **weil** (vayl)) (*because*), gets kicked to the end. This arrangement of the verb happens in *dependent clauses.*

Dependent clauses typically start with *subordinating conjunctions* (words that link sentences) like **dass** (dâs) (*that*), **weil** (vayl) (*because*), **damit** (dâ-*mit*) (*so that*), **obwohl** (op-*vohl*) (*although*), **bevor** (be-*fohr*) (*before*), and **wenn** (vên) (*when*), and they always end with the verb.

Forming questions

The German word order for asking yes or no questions is straightforward. You begin with a verb, and the subject follows.

> **Tanzen Sie gern?** (*tan*-zen zee gêrn?) (*Do you like to dance?*)

> **Spricht er Spanisch?** (shpriHt êr *shpân*-ish?) (*Does he speak Spanish?*)

Note that you don't have the verb *do* in German when forming questions.

Another way to elicit information is to form a question using a question word like **wer** (vêr) (*who*), **was** (vâs) (*what*), **wo** (voh) (*where*), **wann** (vân) (*when*), **wie** (vee) (*how*), or **warum** (vah-*roohm*) (*why*). You can also form a question with words and phrases like **was für ein/e/en. . . ?** (vâs fuer ayn/e/ en. . . ?) (*what kind of. . . ?*) or **welche/r/s. . . ?** (*vêlH*-e/r/s. . . ?) (*which. . . ?*).

When forming questions with these words, the verb goes in its usual place —
second:

> **Was für ein Fahrrad kauft Helmut?** (vâs fuer ayn *fahr-r*âd kouft *hêl*-
> moot?) (*What kind of bicycle is Helmut buying?*)

> **Wer kauft ein Rennrad?** (vêr kouft ayn *rên*-râd?) (*Who's buying a racing
> bicycle?*)

> **Wo kauft er das Rad?** (voh kouft êr dâs râd) (*Where's he buying the
> bike?*)

> **Warum kauft er ein Rennrad?** (vah-*roohm* kouft êr ayn *rên*-râd?) (*Why's
> he buying a racing bicycle?*)

The Tenses: Past, Present, and Future

In grammar, the word "tense" is what the layperson calls "time." You pick
the appropriate tense to describe when the action you're talking about takes
place. The ways to look at the concept of time differ slightly from one culture
and language to the next, so the way tenses are used sometimes differs, too.

Looking at the present

The present tense is an incredibly useful tense in German. You can go a long
way using just this one tense. The German present tense corresponds to
three forms in English. For example, **ich denke** (iH *dên*-ke) can be used as the
equivalent of *I think, I do think,* or *I am thinking* in English. And it gets even
better: Depending on the context, the German present tense can correspond
to the past or future tense in English.

The present tense can be used to describe what's happening now:

> **Was machst du gerade?** (vâs mâHst dooh ge-*rah*-de?) (*What are you doing
> right now?*)

> **Ich lese die Zeitung.** (iH *ley*-ze dee *tsay*-toong.) (*I'm reading the newspaper.*)

Additionally, the present tense can describe what sometimes, usually,
always, or never happens:

> **Freitags gehe ich oft ins Kino.** (*fray*-tahks *gey*-e iH oft ins *kee*-noh.) (*I
> often go to the movies on Fridays.*)

The German present tense can also describe what's going to happen:

> **Wir fliegen im Dezember nach Portugal.** (veer *fleeg*-en im dey-*tsêm*-ber nâH *por*-tooh-gâl.) (*We're flying to Portugal in December.*)

> **Nächste Woche fahre ich nach Bremen.** (*naiH*-ste *voH*-e *fahr*-e iH nâH *brey*-men.) (*Next week I'm going to drive to Bremen.*)

Using the present tense is a very common way of talking about future events in German, particularly if the sentence includes a time expression that anchors the action clearly in the future — for example, **im Dezember** (im dey-*tsêm*-ber) (*in December*) or **nächste Woche** (*naiH*-ste *voH*-e) (*next week*).

And finally, Germans use the present tense to describe what's been happening up to now:

> **Ich lebe seit zehn Jahren in der selben Wohnung.** (iH *ley*-be zayt tseyn *yahr*-en in dêr *zêl*-ben *vohn*-oong.) (*I've been living in the same apartment for ten years.*)

> **Wie lange lernst du schon Deutsch?** (vee *lâng*-e lêrnst dooh shohn doych?) (*How long have you been learning German?*)

Note that English uses the present perfect tense to express the same thing.

Talking about the past: The perfect tense

The perfect tense, for example, **wir haben gegessen** (veer *hah*-ben ge-*gês*-en) (*we have eaten*) or **Jan hat gearbeitet** (yahn hât ge-*ahr*-bay-tet) (*Jan has worked*) is the main tense used to describe past events in spoken German. It's very versatile: You can use it to talk about most actions and situations in the past. Contrast this with the use of the English perfect tense (I have gone, I have eaten, and so on), which you can use only in specific contexts. For example, **Ich habe Anna letzte Woche gesehen** (iH *hah*-be *ân*-â *lêts*-te *voH*-e ge-*zey*-en) (*I have seen Anna last week*) is grammatically correct in German, even though it doesn't quite work in English.

In the preceding sentence, the verb has two parts, **habe** and **gesehen**. These two parts are described in grammatical terms as the *conjugated verb* (**habe** in this example) and the *past participle* (here, **gesehen**). German word order for using verbs that have two or more parts follows specific rules. When forming a sentence with multiple verb parts, the *conjugated verb* takes second position in the sentence, and the other part(s) of the verb — in this instance, it's the *past participle* — goes all the way to the end of the sentence. This rule holds true for all verbs that have two or more parts.

Most verbs form the perfect tense by combining the conjugated form of the verb **haben** (*hah*-ben) (*have*) and the past participle form of the verb. The following examples follow the German word order rule, meaning that the conjugated form of the verb **haben** is in second position in the sentence, and the past participle of the verb that is being expressed is kicked to the end of the sentence:

> **Luka hat mir geholfen.** (*looh*-kâ hât meer ge-*holf*-en.) (*Luka [has] helped me.*)
>
> **Gestern haben wir ein neues Auto gekauft.** (*gês*-tern *hah*-ben veer ayn *noy*-ês *ou*-toh ge-*kouft.*) (*Yesterday we bought a new car.*)
>
> **Hast du die Zeitung schon gelesen?** (hâst dooh dee *tsay*-toong shohn ge-*ley*-zen?) (*Have you read the newspaper yet?*)
>
> **Ich habe den Film vor einer Woche gesehen.** (iH *hah*-be deyn film fohr *ayn*-er *woH*-e ge-*zey*-en.) (*I saw the film a week ago.*)

Certain verbs require **sein** (zayn) (*to be*) instead of **haben** (*hah*-ben) (*to have*) to form the perfect tense. These verbs often describe some form of movement or a state. Here are a few examples:

> **Gestern bin ich ins Kino gegangen.** (*gês*-tern bin iH ins *kee*-noh ge-*gâng*-en.) (*I went to the movies yesterday.*)
>
> **Ich bin in Hamburg gewesen.** (iH bin in *hâm*-boorg ge-*vey*-zen.) (*I've been to Hamburg./I was in Hamburg.*)
>
> **Bist du mit dem Auto gekommen?** (bist dooh mit deym *ou*-toh ge-*kom*-en?) (*Did you come by car?*)
>
> **Sie ist nicht mit dem Zug gefahren.** (zee ist niHt mit deym tsoohk ge-*fahr*-en.) (*She didn't take the train.*)

You can find the verb forms for **haben** and **sein** in Appendix B.

German verbs fall into two categories: weak and strong verbs. Regular verbs, known as weak verbs, make up the largest group of German verbs.

Forming the past participle of a weak verb

Here's the formula for forming the past participle of a weak (regular) verb:

> **ge** + verb stem (the infinitive minus **-en**) + **(e)t** = past participle

For example, for the verb **fragen** (*frah*-gen) (*to ask*), the formula looks like this:

> **ge** + **frag** + **t** = **gefragt**

Some exceptions to this formula do exist. When the stem of the verb ends in **-m**, **-n**, **-d**, or **-t**, you need to insert an **-e** after the stem and before adding the **-t,** for example with the verbs **arbeiten** (*âr*-bay-ten) (*to work*) and **atmen** (*ât*-men) (*to breathe*) like this:

> **ge** + **arbeit** + **e** + **t** = **gearbeitet**
>
> **ge** + **atm** + **e** + **t** = **geatmet**

Forming the past participle of a strong verb

Here's the formula for constructing the past participle of a strong (irregular) verb:

> **ge** + verb stem (the infinitive minus **-en**) + **en** = past participle

For the verb **kommen** (*kom*-en) (*to come*), the past participle is

> **ge** + **komm** + **en** = **gekommen**

See Chapter 10 for more information on the perfect tense.

Writing about the past: Using the simple past tense of verbs

The simple past verb tense is used all the time in printed German, such as newspapers or books, but it's much less common in spoken German. For this reason, you don't come across it much in this book. One exception is the simple past tense of **sein** (zayn) (*to be*), which is often preferable to the perfect tense in both speech and writing. The following table shows you the various forms of the simple past tense of the verb **sein,**

Conjugation	*Pronunciation*
ich war	iH vahr
du warst	dooh vahrst
Sie waren	zee *vahr*-en
er, sie, es war	êr, zee, ês vahr
wir waren	veer *vahr*-en
ihr wart	eer vahrt
Sie waren	zee *vahr*-en
sie waren	zee *vahr*-en

The following example sentences use the simple past tense of the verb **sein**:

> **Ich war heute Nachmittag nicht zu Hause.** (iH vahr *hoy*-te *nāH*-mi-tâhk niHt tsooh *hou*-ze.) (*I wasn't home this afternoon.*)

> **Gestern waren wir sehr müde.** (*gês*-tern *vahr*-en veer zeyr *mue*-de.) (*We were very tired yesterday.*)

Talking about the future

The future tense isn't used as frequently in German as it is in English. In many situations, you can use the present tense instead (refer to "Looking at the present" earlier in this chapter). When talking about events that will take place in the future, you can, of course, also use the future tense. The way to form the future tense in German is pretty similar to English. You take the verb **werden** (*veyr*-den) (*will/to become*) and add an infinitive.

The following table shows you the forms of the verb **werden** in the present tense.

Conjugation	Pronunciation
ich werde	iH *veyr*-de
du wirst	dooh virst
Sie werden	zee *veyr*-den
er, sie, es wird	êr, zee, ês virt
wir werden	veer *veyr*-den
ihr werdet	eer *veyr*-det
Sie werden	zee *veyr*-den
sie werden	zee *veyr*-den

To incorporate the future tense of verbs into sentences, you follow the standard German word order for using verbs that have two parts: The *conjugated verb*, in this case it's **werden**, takes second position in the sentence. The other verb part, which, for the future tense, is the *infinitive* of the verb, goes all the way to the end of the sentence, as the following examples show:

> **Ich werde viel Geld verdienen.** (iH *veyr*-de feel gêlt fêr-*deen*-en.) (*I'm going to/I'll earn a lot of money.*)

> **Wir werden morgen skifahren.** (veer *veyr*-den *mor*-gen *shee*-fahr-en.) (*We'll go/We're going skiing tomorrow.*)

> **Es wird regnen.** (ês virt *reyg*-nen.) (*It's going to rain.*)

Putting the Language in the Proper Case

All languages have ways of showing what role each noun plays in a particular sentence, for example, who (or what) is doing what to whom. In English, you show a noun's role mainly by its position in a sentence. German speakers, on the other hand, indicate the function of a noun in a sentence mainly by adding endings to any articles or adjectives accompanying that noun (and sometimes to the noun itself).

A quick trip through the different cases

In a sentence, nouns appear in one of four cases, depending on their role: *nominative* for the subject, *accusative* for the direct object, *dative* for the indirect object, and *genitive* to show possession.

- ✔ **Nominative case:** The subject of a sentence is always in the nominative case. As a rule, the subject is the person or thing performing the action of the verb. For example, in the sentence **Der Junge stiehlt eine Wurst** (dêr *yoong*-e shteelt *ayn*-e voorst) (*The boy steals a sausage*), the boy is the subject of the sentence: He's the one stealing a sausage.

- ✔ **Accusative case:** The direct object of the sentence is always in the accusative case. The direct object is the person or thing directly affected by the action of the verb. So in the sentence **Der Junge stiehlt eine Wurst** (the example introduced in the preceding bullet), *sausage* is the direct object. It's the thing that's being stolen.

- ✔ **Dative case:** The indirect object of the sentence is always in the dative case. Think of the indirect object as the person or thing that receives the direct object. Look at the sentence **Der Junge gibt dem Hund die Wurst** (dêr *yoong*-e gipt deym hoont dee voorst) (*The boy gives the sausage to the dog*). Here, the dog is the indirect object because the boy gives the sausage to Fido. (The sausage is the direct object, the thing that's being given.)

   If a sentence has two objects, one of them is probably an indirect object. If in doubt, try translating the sentence into English: If you can put "to" before one of the nouns, that's the indirect object in the German sentence.

- ✔ **Genitive case:** The genitive case is used to indicate possession. The person or thing that possesses is in the genitive case. For example, in the phrase **der Hund des Jungen** (dêr hoont dês *yoong*-en) (*the boy's dog*), the boy possesses the dog, so *the boy* is in the genitive case.

In this book, you mainly encounter the nominative, accusative, and dative cases. The genitive case is used less frequently; we mention it here only for the sake of completeness.

Why all these cases matter

You may be wondering why we're making such a big deal about this case business. Understanding the various cases is a complex but necessary step when learning German. The different cases make pronouns change form. And the cases also make the endings of articles and adjectives change. Read on for the nitty-gritty.

How pronouns change

You use pronouns instead of nouns as a way to avoid clumsy repetition. Pronouns change form depending on how they're used in a sentence. Table 2-1 shows you the pronouns in the nominative, dative, and accusative cases. Notice how the pronouns change according to case.

Table 2-1			Personal Pronouns by Case
Nominative	*Dative*	*Accusative*	*English*
ich	mir	mich	*I, to me, me*
du	dir	dich	*you, to you, you* (singular, informal address)
Sie	Ihnen	Sie	*you, to you, you* (singular, formal address)
er	ihm	ihn	*he, to him, him*
sie	ihr	sie	*she, to her, her*
es	ihm	es	*it, to it, it*
wir	uns	uns	*we, to us, us*
ihr	euch	euch	*you, to you, you* (plural, informal address)
Sie	Ihnen	Sie	*you, to you, you* (plural, formal address)
sie	ihnen	sie	*they, to them, them*

Following are examples of the second person singular pronoun **du** appearing in the nominative, dative, and accusative cases depending on its function in a sentence:

> **Du bist sehr schön.** (dooh bist zeyr shern.) (*You're very beautiful.*) **du** = nominative.

> **Ich gebe dir einen Ring.** (iH *gey*-be deer *ayn*-en ring.) (*I'm giving you a ring.*) **dir** = dative.

> **Ich habe dich lieb.** (iH *hah*-be diH leep.) (I'm very fond of you). **dich** = accusative

How definite articles change

The definite articles (refer to the earlier section "The definite article") also morph depending on which case they're used in, as shown in Table 2-2.

Table 2-2	Definite Articles by Case			
Gender	*Nominative*	*Genitive*	*Dative*	*Accusative*
Masculine	der	des	dem	den
Feminine	die	der	der	die
Neuter	das	des	dem	das
Plural	die	der	den	die

The following examples show the masculine definite article **der** with its appropriate endings in the four different cases:

Der Fuchs läuft über die Straße. (dêr foox loyft *ue*-ber dee *shtrah*-se.) (*The fox is running across the road.*) **der** = nominative.

Sie lebt in der Wohnung des Freundes. (zee lêpt in dêr *vohn*-oong dês *froyn*-des.) (*She lives in the friend's apartment.*) **des** = genitive.

Ich leihe dem Freund mein Auto. (iH *lay*-he deym froynt mayn *ou*-toh.) (*I'm lending my car to the friend.*) **dem** = dative.

Kaufst du den Computer? (koufst dooh deyn computer [as in English]?) (*Are you buying the computer?*) **den** = accusative.

How indefinite articles change

The German indefinite article **ein** (ayn) (*a*) can assume different endings. Which ending **ein** takes depends on whether it accompanies the subject of a sentence (nominative), a possessive object (genitive), the direct object (accusative), or the indirect object (dative). Table 2-3 shows you the indefinite article **ein** being put through the paces of the various cases.

Table 2-3	Endings of Ein by Case			
Gender	*Nominative*	*Genitive*	*Dative*	*Accusative*
Masculine	ein	eines	einem	einen
Feminine	eine	einer	einer	eine
Neuter	ein	eines	einem	ein

The following examples show the indefinite article **ein** with its appropriate masculine endings in the four different cases:

> **Ein Fuchs läuft über die Straße.** (ayn foox loyft *ue*-ber dee *shtrah*-se.) (*A fox is running across the road.*) **ein** = nominative.

> **Sie lebt in der Wohnung eines Freundes.** (zee lêpt in dêr *vohn*-oong *ayn*-es *froyn*-des.) (*She lives in a friend's apartment.*) **eines** = genitive.

> **Ich leihe einem Freund mein Auto.** (iH *lay*-he *ayn*-em froynt mayn *ou*-toh.) (*I'm lending my car to a friend.*) **einem** = dative.

> **Kaufst du einen Computer?** (koufst dooh *ayn*-en computer [as in English]) (*Are you buying a computer?*) **einen** = accusative.

How possessives change

Possessive adjectives establish ownership. They mark the difference between what belongs to you ("your book") what belongs to me ("my book"), and so on. Here's a run-through of the forms for the different persons:

- ✔ **mein** (mayn) (*my*)
- ✔ **dein** (dayn) (*your*) (informal, singular address)
- ✔ **Ihr** (eer) (*your*) (formal, singular address)
- ✔ **sein**, **ihr**, **sein** (zayn, eer, zayn) (*his, her, its*)
- ✔ **unser** (*oon*-zer) (*our*)
- ✔ **euer** (*oy*-er) (*your*) (informal, plural address)
- ✔ **Ihr** (eer) (*your*) (formal, plural address)
- ✔ **ihr** (eer) (*their*)

Table 2-4 presents all the forms in the singular of a sample possessive, **mein** (mayn) (*my*). The other possessives take the same endings. These endings may look familiar; they're the same as those for the indefinite article **ein** (ayn) (*a, an*), as well as for the adjective that negates a noun, **kein** (kayn) (*no, not, not any*).

Table 2-4	Possessive Endings by Case			
Gender	*Nominative*	*Genitive*	*Dative*	*Accusative*
Masculine	**mein**	**meines**	**meinem**	**meinen**
Feminine	**meine**	**meiner**	**meiner**	**meine**
Neuter	**mein**	**meines**	**meinem**	**mein**
Plural	**meine**	**meiner**	**meinen**	**meine**

How adjective endings change

As we mention earlier in this chapter, adjectives and articles that accompany nouns change their endings according to the role of the noun in the sentence. To illustrate the endings for both adjectives and articles with nouns they're describing, Table 2-5 shows the endings in combination with an indefinite article, and Table 2-6 shows the definite article.

In Table 2-5 you see how the adjective endings change when an indefinite article precedes them. The so-called **ein-** words also follow the same pattern. **Ein-** words include **kein** (kayn) (*no, not, not any*) and the possessive adjectives, a list of which is in the previous section. This table includes the word **kein** for the plural forms because the indefinite article has no plural. For more information on using **kein**, see Chapter 5.

Table 2-5	Examples of Adjective Endings Preceded by Indefinite Articles or Ein- Words			
Gender	*Nominative*	*Genitive*	*Dative*	*Accusative*
Masculine	ein schöner Garten	eines schönen Gartens	einem schönen Garten	einen schönen Garten
Feminine	eine weiße Tür	einer weißen Tür	einer weißen Tür	eine weiße Tür
Neuter	ein kleines Haus	eines kleinen Hauses	einem kleinen Haus	ein kleines Haus
Plural	keine großen Häuser	keiner großen Häuser	keinen großen Häusern	keine großen Häuser

Table 2-6	Examples of Adjective Endings Preceded by Definite Articles			
Gender	*Nominative*	*Genitive*	*Dative*	*Accusative*
Masculine	der schöne Garten	des schönen Gartens	dem schönen Garten	den schönen Garten
Feminine	die weiße Tür	der weißen Tür	der weißen Tür	die weiße Tür
Neuter	das kleine Haus	des kleinen Hauses	dem kleinen Haus	das kleine Haus
Plural	die großen Häuser	der großen Häuser	den großen Häusern	die großen Häuser

Chapter 3

Hallo! Pronunciation and Basic Expressions

Greetings and introductions are your crucial first steps in establishing contact with other people and making a positive first impression. When handled correctly, that initial contact can open doors for you. To that end, this chapter helps you determine whether to use formal or informal language in various situations. Then it introduces the basic expressions of polite conversation: how to say hello and goodbye and how to ask and answer the universal question "How are you?" Finally, it shows you how to make introductions.

Of course, before you can speak German, you need to know how to pronounce German letters, many of which are *not* pronounced the same as they are in English. For that reason, this chapter begins with the information you need to be able to pronounce German words, if not exactly like a native speaker, at least close enough to be clearly understood. As with anything else, practice makes perfect. Read on for specifics.

Mouthing Off: Basic Pronunciation

Speaking a foreign language correctly is all about mastering the basics of pronunciation. And the key to decent pronunciation is to start small by knowing how the individual letters sound — then expand to syllables, words, and finally sentences. The rest is practice, practice, practice.

Dealing with stress in German

This type of stress doesn't have anything to do with meeting deadlines or having a BMW tailgate you at 110 miles per hour on the Autobahn. Instead, it's about stressed syllables in German words. In the pronunciation key that you see in parentheses following each word, the syllables you should stress are in *italics*.

Building the alphabet blocks

The German alphabet has all the letters that English does — 26 of 'em — plus four special letters: **ä**, **ö**, **ü**, and **ß**. The good news is that German words are generally pronounced just as they are spelled. This means there's no confusion, as we have in English with the likes of *bow* (*tie*), (*take a*) *bow*, and *tree bough*. The bad news is many of the normal-looking letters are pronounced differently from their English counterparts.

Table 3-1 shows you the sound of each letter of the alphabet when it's pronounced alone. Knowing how to say each individual letter may come in very handy, for example, if you need to spell your name when you make a table reservation at a German restaurant, tell a hotel receptionist how to spell your name, or compete in a German spelling bee with a grand prize of 500,000 euros.

Track 1 on the CD gives you the sounds of the letters in the German alphabet as shown in Table 3-1. Note that the German pronunciation of a single letter may be different from the way it's pronounced within a German word.

Table 3-1	Pronouncing the German Alphabet	
Letter	*German Pronunciation*	*German Word*
a	ah	**Ahnen** (*ahn*-en) (*ancestors*)
b	bey	**Bild** (bilt) (*image, picture*)
c	tsey	**Café** (kâ-*fey*) (*café*)
d	dey	**durstig** (*doohrs*-tiH) (*thirsty*)
e	ey	**Ehe** (*ey*-e) (*marriage*)
f	êf	**Feuer** (*foy*-er) (*fire*)
g	gey	**geben** (*gey*-ben) (*give*)
h	hah	**Haus** (house [as in English]) (*house*)
i	ee	**ihn** (een) (*him*)
j	yot	**Januar** (*yahn*-oo-âr) (*January*)

Letter	German Pronunciation	German Word
k	kah	**Kilometer** (ki-loh-*mey*-ter) (*kilometer*)
l	êl	**Liebe** (*lee*-be) (*love*)
m	êm	**Manager** (*as in English*) (*manager*)
n	ên	**Name** (*nah*-me) (*name*)
o	oh	**ohne** (*oh*-ne) (*without*)
p	pey	**Pause** (*pou*-ze) (*break, intermission*)
q	kooh	**Quatsch** (kvâch) (*nonsense*)
r	êr	**rot** (roht) (*red*)
s	ês	**S-Bahn** (*es*-bahn) (*suburban train*)
t	tey	**Taxi** (*tâx*-ee) (*taxi*)
u	ooh	**U-Boot** (*ooh*-boht) (*submarine*)
v	fou	**Vogel** (*foh*-gel) (*bird*)
w	veh	**Wald** (vâlt) (*forest*)
x	iks	**Fax** (fâx) (*fax*)
y	*uep*-si-lon	**System** (zers-*teym*) (*system*)
z	tset	**Zeit** (tsayt) (*time*)
ä	ah-*oom*-lout (Umlaut)	**Bäcker** (*bêk*-er) (*baker*)
ö	oh-*oom*-lout (Umlaut)	**hören** (*herr*-en) (*hear*)
ü	ooh-*oom*-lout (Umlaut)	**Tür** (tuer) (*system*)
ß	ês-*tsêt*	**Straße** (*strah*-se) (*street*)

Pronouncing vowels

In German, vowels (**a**, **e**, **i**, **o**, and **u**) can generally be pronounced in two ways — as short or long vowel sounds. The *short* vowel sounds are "clipped," and they're pronounced shorter than their English equivalents. *Long* vowel sounds are "steady-state" or "pure," meaning that the sound quality doesn't change even though it's a long sound. Here are the general rules:

- ✔ A vowel is long when it's followed by the letter *h,* as in **Stahl** (shtahl) (*steel*).

- ✔ A vowel is generally long when it's followed by a single consonant, as in **Tag** (tahk) (*day*).

- ✔ A vowel is long when it's doubled, as in **Teer** (teyr) (*tar*) or **Aal** (ahl) (*eel*).

- ✔ In general, a vowel is short when followed by two or more consonants, as in **Tanne** (*tân*-e) (*fir tree*).

Table 3-2 shows you how to pronounce German vowels by providing you with examples and a kind of phonetic script, the letter combinations that serve as the English equivalent of the German letter's pronunciation.

In this book's phonetic script, two short vowel sounds have a little "hat" over the letter, so they look like this: â and ê. Note that the phonetic spelling of ê in Table 3-2 is the same as that of the German short umlaut sound **ä** in Table 3-3. Go to Track 2 on the CD to hear how to pronounce these German vowels.

Table 3-2		Pronouncing German Vowels	
German Letter	*Symbol*	*As in English*	*German Word*
a (long)	ah	father	**Bahnhof** (*bahn*-hohf) (*station*)
a (short)	â	adore (clipped "a")	**Banner** (*bân*-er) (*banner*)
e (long)	ey	vein	**Leben** (*leh*-ben) (*life*)
e (short/ stressed)	ê	bet (clipped "e")	**Bett** (*bêt*) (*bed*)
e (short/ unstressed)	e	pocket	**Lachen** (*lâH*-en) (*laughter*)
i (long)	ee	see	**ihn** (*een*) (*him*)
i (short)	i	winter	**Mitte** (*mit*-e) (*middle*)
o (long)	oh	mope	**Lob** (*lohp*) (*praise*)
o (short)	o	gonna	**Sonne** (*zon*-e) (*sun*)
u (long)	ooh	moon	**Tube** (*tooh*-be) (*tube*)
u (short)	oo	push (clipped "u")	**muss** (*moos*) (*have to/must*)

Pronouncing ä, ö, and ü

German has three extra vowels: **ä**, **ö**, and **ü**. The German word for those curious double dots over the vowels is **Umlaut** (*oom*-lout) (umlaut). Umlauts slightly alter the sound of the vowels **a**, **o**, and **u**, as outlined in Table 3-3. These sounds have no equivalent in English, so try listening to them on Track 3, which demonstrates how to pronounce the German umlauts.

Table 3-3		Pronouncing Vowels with Umlauts	
German Letter	*Symbol*	*As in English*	*German Word*
ä (long)	ai	say ("ay" in "say" with spread lips)	**nächste** (*naiH*-ste) (*next*)
ä (short)	ê	bet (clipped "e")	**fällen** (*fêl*-en) (*to fell* [*a tree*])
ö	er	her (without the "r" sound)	**schön** (shern) (*pretty*) (remember: no "r" sound)
ü	ue	lure ("ooh" with pursed lips)	**Tür** (tuer) (*door*)

To make your German vowels **ä**, **ö**, and **ü** sound a bit more authentic, try progressing through the **ä**, **ö**, and **ü** sounds, pronouncing the vowels as though you're getting ready to kiss someone — in other words, round your lips and pucker up, baby! The **ü** sound is pronounced with very pursed lips.

Pronouncing diphthongs

Diphthongs, which you can hear on Track 4 of the CD, are combinations of two vowels in one syllable (as in the English "lie"), and German has a few of them, as shown in Table 3-4.

Table 3-4		Pronouncing German Diphthongs	
German Diphthong	*Symbol*	*As in English*	*German Word*
ai/ei/ay	ay	cry	**Mais** (mays) (*corn*)/**ein** (ayn) (*a*)/**Bayern** (*bay*-ern) (*Bavaria*)
au	ou	loud	**laut** (lout) (*noisy*)
au (in words of foreign origin)	uh	restaurant	**Restaurant** (res-tuh-*ron*) (*restaurant*)
äu/eu	oy	boy	**Häuser** (*hoy*-zer) (*houses*)/**Leute** (*loy*-te) (*people*)
ie	ee	see	**Miete** (*meet*-e) (*rent*)

Both the long German vowel **i** and the German vowel combination **ie** are pronounced like the English letter *e* in *see,* but the German **ei**, **ai**, and **ay** are pronounced like the English letter *y* in *cry.*

Pronouncing consonants

Ah, relief! The sounds of German consonants are easier to master than the German vowel sounds. In fact, they're pronounced either almost the same as their English equivalents or like other English consonants. Okay, you will find a couple of oddities and exceptions, which we show you later.

Pronouncing "f," "h," "k," "m," "n," "p," "t," "x," and "ß"

As part of a word, the letters **f**, **h**, **k**, **m**, **n**, **p**, **t**, and **x** are pronounced the same in German as they are in English. The letter **ß**, on the other hand, doesn't exist in English. It's kind of cool looking, though, don't you think? But even if you don't care about looks, you'll be glad to know that you pronounce it just like *ss* or *s.*

As far as the written language goes, whether a given German word is spelled with **ss** or **ß** depends on a couple of rules. Here's the scoop:

✔ After a long vowel or a diphthong, the *s* sound is spelled **ß** — for example, **Fuß** (foohs) (*foot*).

✔ After a short vowel, the *s* sound is spelled **ss** — for example, **Fass** (fâs) (*barrel*).

Note: In Switzerland, the **ß** is not used at all. Instead, the Swiss always spell words with the double **ss.**

Table 3-5 tells you how to pronounce the rest of the German consonants by providing you with examples and a phonetic script. To hear them all, listen to Track 5.

Table 3-5	Pronouncing Selected German Consonants		
German Letter	*Symbol*	*As in English*	*German Word*
b (see note)	p	*up*	**Abfahrt** (*âp*-fahrt) (*departure*)
b	b	*bright*	**Bild** (bilt) (*image, picture*)
c (beginning of word)	k	*cat*	**Café** (kâ-*fey*) (*café*)
c (mostly words of foreign origin)	ts	*tsar*	**Celsius** (*tsêl*-zee-oos) (*Celsius*)

German Letter	Symbol	As in English	German Word
c (mostly words of foreign origin)	ch	*cello*	**Cello** (*chêl*-oh) (*cello*)
d (see note)	t	*moot*	**blind** (blint) (*blind*)
d	d	*do*	**Dunst** (doonst) (*mist, haze*)
g	g	*go*	**geben** (*gey*-ben) (*give*)
g (see note)	k	*lag*	**Tag** (tahk) (*day*)
j	y	*yes*	**ja** (yah) (*yes*)
qu	kv	*kv* (pronounced together)	**Quatsch** (kvâch) (*nonsense*)
s (beginning of word)	z	*zoo*	**sieben** (*zee*-ben) (*seven*)
s (middle/end of word)	s	*sit*	**Haus** (house [as in English]) (*house*)
v	f	*f* as in *fire*	**Vogel** (*foh*-gel) (*bird*)
v (words of foreign origin)	v	*velvet*	**Vase** (*vah*-ze) (*vase*)
w	v	*vice*	**Wald** (vâlt) (*forest*)
y (mostly words of foreign origin)	y	*yes*	**Yoga** (*yoh*-gâ) (*yoga*)
y (mostly middle of word)	er	*her* (without the "r" sound)	**System** (zers-*teym*) (*system*)
z	ts	*ts* as in *tsar*	**Zahl** (tsahl) (*number*)
ß	s	*guess*	**Straße** (shtrah-se) (street)

Note: Table 3-5 shows you that when the letters *b, d,* and *g* are at the end of a word or syllable, or before voiceless consonants like *s* or *t,* they change sounds. The "b" changes to a "p" sound, "d" changes to "t," and "g" changes to "k."

Pronouncing the German "r" and "l"

The letters *r* and *l* are pronounced differently in German than they are in English. To replicate the "gargled" pronunciation of the German **r**, try making a gargling sound before saying *aahh,* so that you're saying *ra.* Also, don't roll the tip of your tongue or use it to pronounce the German **r**. To correctly pronounce the German letter **l**, you have to position your tongue differently than you do when you pronounce the English letter *l*. In English, you pronounce the *l* with your tongue in a spoon shape, hollowed out in the middle. To make the German **l**, you press the tip of your tongue against your gum ridge (just as you do in English), but you keep it flat instead of spoon-shaped. The German **l** sound is clipped, not drawled. On Track 6 of the CD, you can hear how to pronounce these letters. Here are some sample words:

    ✔ *l* as in **Bild** (bilt) (*picture*)

    ✔ *r* as in **richtig** (*riH*-tiH) (*correct*)

Pronouncing combinations of consonants

The German language has a few consonant sounds that are either different or don't occur in English. Most of them are easy to pronounce, except for the **ch**, which is unfamiliar to the English tongue.

Pronouncing "ch," "ck," "sch," "sp," "st," and "tsch"

The German letter combination **ch** is the trickiest one for English speakers to pronounce. There's absolutely no equivalent for it in English (that's why it's represented by a capital *H* in this book's phonetic script), and you actually have to learn a new sound — a kind of gentle "dry" gargling sound — in order to say it. The sound is a bit like trying to pronounce "hch," and not a "k" sound. The sound is similar to the guttural "ch" in Scottish, like in *Loch Ness*.

The good news is that in a few words, the **ch** is simply pronounced as an *x* sound, for example in **Wachs** (vâks) (*wax*) or **Fuchs** (fooks) (*fox*). And in a few other words, generally foreign words, the **ch** is pronounced like the sound "sh" in English, for example in **Champignon** (*shâm*-peen-yon) (*mushroom*) or **Champagner** (shâm-*pân*-yer) (*champagne*).

Table 3-6 shows you how to pronounce these common consonant combinations. Listen to Track 7 to hear how to pronounce these combinations.

Table 3-6		Pronouncing ch, ck, sch, sp, st, and tsch	
German Letter	*Symbol*	*As in English*	*German Word*
ch	H	*Loch(Ness)*	**mich** (miH) (*me*)
ck	k	*check*	**Dreck** (drêk) (*dirt*)
sch	sh	*shut*	**Tisch** (tish) (*table*)
sp	shp	*sh* as in *shut*, *p* as in *people*	**spät** (shpait) (*late*)
st (beginning of a word)	sht	*sh* as in *shut*, *t* as in *table*	**Stadt** (shtât) (*city*)
st (middle/end of a word)	st	*stable*	**fast** (fâst) (*almost, nearly*)
tsch	ch	*switch*	**Deutsch** (doych) (*German*)

The English "th" sound doesn't exist in the German language. The **th** combination is pronounced one of two ways in German:

- ✔ The **h** is silent, as in the words **Theorie** (tey-oh-*ree*) (*theory*) and **Theologie** (tey-oh-loh-*gee*) (*theology*).

- ✔ The **t** and **h** are pronounced separately, because they actually belong to different components of a compound noun, as in the words **Gasthaus** (*gâst*-hous) (*inn*), which is a combination of the German words for *guest* and *house,* or **Basthut** (*bâst*-hooht) (*straw hat*), a combo of the German for *raffia* and *hat.*

Getting Formal or Informal

German speakers generally place great value on showing respect toward each other and strangers. The language itself allows the speaker to make a clear distinction between formal and informal ways of saying *you.* (English used to do this too, but long ago the *thee* and *thou* forms were dropped.) In German, you use either the formal **Sie** (zee) (*you*) or one of the two informal forms: **du** (dooh) (*you*), if you're talking to one person, or **ihr** (eer) (*you*), if you're addressing two or more people.

Making the distinction between the informal and formal *you* forms is definitely important. Why? People are very likely to consider you impolite and disrespectful if you use the informal way of addressing them in a situation that calls for more formality.

In general, you use the formal **Sie** for everyday communication with people *outside* your circle of family and friends. Even among people who are in regular contact with one another, for example, neighbors or co-workers, **Sie** is often used as a means of showing respect. As you get to know somebody better, you may switch to **du**.

However, no hard and fast rules apply when it comes to using **du** or **Sie**. In fact, many exceptions exist. For example, suppose a German friend takes you to a party. Even though you and the other guests are complete strangers, the other guests may just address you with **du** — especially if they're easy-going — so you may address them with **du** as well.

If you're the least bit unsure of whether to use **du** or **Sie**, use **Sie** until the person you're addressing asks you to use **du** or addresses you with **du**.

Saying "Hello," "Goodbye," and "How Are You?"

The first part of your greeting is a basic hello. How you say hello depends on what time of day it is. Check out this list:

Guten Morgen! (*gooh*-ten *mor*-gen!) (*Good morning!*) This is the greeting you use in the morning (until about noon).

Guten Tag! (*gooh*-ten tahk!) (*Hello!*) This is the most common greeting you use, except early in the morning and late in the day.

Guten Abend! (*gooh*-ten *ah*-bent!) (*Good evening!*) Obviously, this is the greeting of choice in the evening.

Hallo! (*hâ*-loh!) (*Hello!*) You should be pretty comfortable with this informal greeting, because it's obviously very similar to English's *hello*.

When the time comes to part, you can say:

Auf Wiedersehen! (ouf *vee*-der-zey-en!) (*Goodbye!*) This is the standard, formal goodbye.

Gute Nacht! (*gooh*-te nâHt!) (*Good night!*) You use this farewell when you say goodbye late at night.

War nett, Sie kennenzulernen. (vahr nêt, zee *kên*-en-tsoo-lêrn-en.) (*It was nice meeting you.*) You use this phrase to tell people that you enjoyed meeting them for the first time.

Tschüs! (chues!) (*Bye!*) This is the informal way of saying goodbye.

You say "Grüß Gott," I say "Grüezi"

People in Southern Germany, Austria, and German-speaking Switzerland certainly understand you when you wish them **Guten Morgen/ Guten Tag/Guten Abend** (depending on the time of day). However, people in these regions also use some other greetings.

In Switzerland, you hear **Grüezi** (*grue*-e-tsee) (hello) most often. And people who know each other well use **salut** (sâ-*lue*) to say both *hi* and *bye*.)

In Southern Germany and Austria, you say *hello* with **Grüß Gott** (grues gôt) or its informal version, **Grüß dich**. Good friends express both *hi* and *bye* with the casual **Servus** (*sêr*-voohs).

Especially among younger German speakers, you hear the informal *goodbye,* **Ciao** (chou), which has made its way north across the Alps from Italy.

Mr., Mrs., and the slippery Miss

Herr (hêr) is the German word for *Mr.,* and **Frau** (frou) expresses *Mrs.* The same word, **die Frau** (dee frou), also means *woman,* as well as *wife,* as in **meine Frau** (*mayn*-e frou) (*my wife*). No German equivalent for the English **Ms.** exists, so you need to use **Frau**.

German also has the word **Fräulein** (*froy*-layn), which used to be the German version of *Miss* and was the proper way to address an unmarried woman. However, those days are long gone. So address a woman as **Frau,** regardless of her marital status. Or, when in doubt, leave it out. But what if you need to catch the attention of *any* person (for example, someone who has just dropped something)? Simply say **Entschuldigung!** (ênt-*shool*-dee-goong!) (*Excuse me!*)

Fräulein is also a bygone expression for a waitress, relegated to the days of yore. To get a German waitress's attention, simply apply the tried-and-true methods of making eye contact or raising your hand unobtrusively.

Asking "How are you?"

The next step after greeting someone in German is, of course, asking the question *How are you?* Whether you use the formal or the informal version of the question depends on whom you're talking to. Sound complicated? Well, figuring out which form to use is easier than you may think.

The following three versions of *How are you?* use three dative-case pronouns that represent *you.* **Ihnen** (*een*-en) is the dative equivalent of **Sie**, **dir** (deer) represents **du**, and **euch** (oyH) stands in for **ihr**. (See Chapter 2 for more information on personal pronouns in the dative case.) Here's a breakdown of what to use when:

> **Wie geht es Ihnen?** (vee geyt ês *een*-en?) (*How are you?*) This is the formal version.

> **Wie geht es dir?** (vee geyt ês deer?) (*How are you?*) This is the informal, singular version.

> **Wie geht's?** (vee geyts?) (*How's it going?*) When you know someone really well, you can use this casual question.

> **Wie geht es euch?** (vee geyt ês oyH?) (*How are you?*) Use this when talking to several people informally.

Meeting and greeting go hand in hand

Greetings and introductions are often accompanied by some form of bodily contact. In Germany, Austria, and Switzerland, hand-shaking is the most common form of bodily contact during greetings and introductions. Female friends may kiss each other on the cheek or give each other a hug. Men usually don't kiss or hug each other, although they may greet a woman friend with a hug (and a kiss). You may notice that people in Europe often stand closer to you than you're used to, for example, in stores, on the bus or subway, or when they're talking to you.

Replying to "How are you?"

In English, the question *How are you?* is often just a way of saying hello, and no one will raise an eyebrow if you don't answer. In German, however, a reply is customary. The following are acceptable answers to the question *How are you?*

> **Danke, gut.** (*dân*-ke, gooht.) (*Thanks, I'm fine.*) or **Gut, danke.** (gooht, *dân*-ke.) (*Fine, thanks.*)
>
> **Sehr gut.** (zeyr gooht.) (*Very good.*)
>
> **Ganz gut.** (gânts gooht.) (*Really good.*)
>
> **Es geht.** (ês geyt.) (*So, so.*) This German expression actually means *it goes.*
>
> **Nicht so gut.** (niHt zoh gooht.) (*Not so good.*)

As in English, the reply would usually be accompanied by the question *And (how are) you?*, which is easy: First the formal version:

> **Und Ihnen?** (oont *een*-en?) (*And you?*)

And here's how you pose the question informally:

> **Und dir?** (oont deer?) (*And you?*) (singular, informal *you*)
>
> **Und euch?** (oont oyH?*) (*And you?*) (plural, informal *you*)

Talkin' the Talk

In the following dialogue, you find some phrases that are commonly used for greetings in a more formal setting. (Track 8)

Herr Schulte: **Guten Tag, Frau Berger!**
gooh-ten tahk, frou *bêr*-ger!
Hello, Ms. Berger!

Frau Berger: **Herr Schulte, guten Tag! Wie geht es Ihnen?**
hêr *shool*-te, *gooh*-ten tahk! vee geyt ês *een*-en?
Mr. Schulte, hello! How are you?

Herr Schulte: **Danke, gut! Und Ihnen?**
dân-ke, gooht! oont *een*-en?
Thanks, I'm fine! And how are you?

Frau Berger: **Danke, gut.**
dân-ke, gooht.
Thanks, I'm fine.

Talkin' the Talk

Now check out this dialog between Mike and Christa, two old friends who run into each other on the street. (Track 9)

Mike: **Hallo Christa!**
hâ-loh christa [as in English]!
Hello Christa!

Christa: **Mike, hallo! Wie geht's?**
mike [as in English], *hâ*-loh! vee geyts?
Mike, hello! How's it going?

Mike: **Danke, mir geht's gut! Und selbst?**
dân-ke, meer geyts gooht! oont zêlpst?
Thanks, I'm fine! And yourself?

Christa: **Auch gut.**
ouH gooht.
I'm fine, too.

Introducing Yourself and Your Friends

Meeting and greeting often requires introductions. Your friends may want you to meet someone they know, or you may have to introduce your significant other to your colleague at a formal occasion. This section gives you the lowdown.

Introducing your friends

Commonplace, everyday introductions are easy to make. You start with

>   **Das ist . . .** (dâs ist . . .) (*This is . . .*)

Then you simply add the name of the person. Or if you're introducing a friend, begin with

>   **Das ist meine Freundin** (female)/**mein Freund** (male) . . . (dâs ist *mayn-e froyn*-din/mayn froynt . . .) (*This is my friend . . .*)

If you're introduced to someone, you may want to indicate that you're pleased to meet that person. In German, the casual, informal way of saying this is simply **Hallo** (*hâ*-loh) (*hello*) or **Guten Tag** (*gooh*-ten tahk) (*hello*).

If the introductions have been more formal, you express *Nice to meet you* by saying

>   **Freut mich.** (froyt miH) (*Nice to meet you.*)

The person you have been introduced to may then reply

>   **Mich auch.** (miH ouH) (*Pleased to meet you, too.*)

Introductions for special occasions

You may find yourself in a situation that calls for a very high level of formality. Here are some phrases you'd use then:

- ✔ **Darf ich Ihnen . . . vorstellen?** (dârf iH *een*-en . . . *fohr*-shtêl-len?) (*May I introduce you to. . . ?*)

- ✔ **Freut mich, Sie kennenzulernen.** (froyt miH, zee *kên*-en-tsoo-lêrn-en.) (*I'm pleased to meet you.*)

- ✔ **Meinerseits.** (*mayn*-er-zayts.)/**Ganz meinerseits.** (gânts *mayn*-er-zayts.) (*The pleasure is all mine.* Literally, *mine* or *all mine.*)

Talkin' the Talk

In this dialogue between the directors of two companies, listen to Herr Kramer and Herr Huber. They meet at an official function, and Herr Huber introduces his wife.

Herr Kramer: **Guten Abend, Herr Huber.**
gooh-ten *ah*-bent, hêr *hooh*-ber.
Good evening, Mr. Huber.

Herr Huber: **Guten Abend, Herr Kramer. Darf ich Ihnen meine Frau vorstellen?**
gooh-ten *ah*-bent, hêr *krah*-mer. dârf iH *een*-en *mayn*-e frou *fohr*-shtêl-len?
Good evening, Mr. Kramer. May I introduce my wife to you?

Herr Kramer: **Guten Abend, Frau Huber. Freut mich sehr, Sie kennenzulernen.**
gooh-ten *ah*-bent, frou *hooh*-ber. froyt miH zeyr, zee *kên*-en-tsoo-lêrn-en.
Good evening, Mrs. Huber. Very nice to meet you.

Frau Huber: **Ganz meinerseits, Herr Kramer.**
gânts *mayn*-er-zayts, hêr *krah*-mer.
And nice to meet you, Mr. Kramer.

Words to Know

auch	ouH	also
gut	gooht	good
sehr	zeyr	very
freuen	*froy*-en	to be glad/pleased
kennenlernen	*kên*-en-*lêrn*-en	to become acquainted with/to get to know
vorstellen	*fohr*-shtêl-len	to introduce
der Freund (m)	der froynt	friend
die Freundin (f)	dee *froyn*-din	friend

Introducing yourself

You can't always rely on someone else to introduce you. In those situations, you simply introduce yourself, which is easy. Often, you can introduce yourself simply by stating your name, even in a more formal setting. Simply say

> **Mein Name ist. . . .** (mayn *nah*-me ist. . . .) (*My name is. . . .*)

Or use the verb that expresses the same idea, **heißen** (*hay*-sen) (*to be called*):

> **Ich heiße. . . .** (iH *hay*-se. . . .) (*My name is. . . .*)

Talkin' the Talk

In the following conversation, Herr Hauser arrives at a meeting with several people he hasn't been introduced to yet. He's looking for a seat at the conference table.

Herr Hauser: **Guten Tag. Ist dieser Platz noch frei?**
gooh-ten tahk. îst *dee*-zer plâts noH fray?
Hello. Is this seat still free?

Frau Berger:	**Ja. Nehmen Sie doch bitte Platz.** yah. *ney*-men zee doH *bi*-te plâts. *Yes, it is. Do sit down.*
Herr Hauser:	**Vielen Dank. Mein Name ist Max Hauser.** *fee*-len dânk. mayn *nah*-me ist mâx *houz*-er. *Thank you very much. My name is Max Hauser.*
Frau Berger:	**Freut mich. Ich heiße Karin Berger.** froyt miH. iH *hay*-se *kah*-rin *bêr*-ger. *Pleased to meet you. I'm Karin Berger.*

The preceding conversation would sound very different among younger people meeting in an informal setting, like a party. They'd probably introduce each other like this:

Martin:	**Hallo, wie heißt du?** *hâ*-loh, vee hayst dooh? *Hello, what's your name?*
Susanne:	**Ich heiße Susanne. Und du?** iH *hay*-se zooh-*zân*-e. oont dooh? *My name is Susanne. And you?*
Martin:	**Ich bin der Martin. Und wer ist das?** iH bin dêr *mâr*-tin. oont vêr ist dâs? *I'm Martin. And who is that?*
Susanne:	**Das ist meine Freundin Anne.** dâs ist *mayn*-e *froyn*-din *ân*-e. *This is my friend Anne.*

Talkin' the Talk

In the next two conversations, people on a train are saying goodbye as the train comes into a station. Frau Egli is getting ready to exit the train. (Track 10)

Frau Egli:	**Das ist meine Station. War nett, Sie kennen-zulernen, Frau Myers.** dâs ist *mayn*-e shtâts-ee-*ohn*. vahr nêt, zee *kên*-en-tsoo-*lêrn*-en, frou myers [as in English]. *This is my stop. It was nice to meet you, Ms. Myers.*

Frau Myers: **Ganz meinerseits. Auf Wiedersehen, Frau Egli.**
gânts *mayn*-er-zayts. ouf *vee*-der-zey-en, frou *eyg*-lee.
And nice to meet you. Good bye, Ms. Egli.

Frau Egli: **Auf Wiedersehen.**
ouf *vee*-der-zey-en
Good bye.

Michelle and Claire are getting off the train as well.

Michelle und Claire: **Tschüs Mark.**
chues mark [as in English]
Bye, Mark.

Mark: **Tschüs Claire, tschüs Michelle. Schöne Ferien!**
chues Claire [as in English], chues michelle [as in English]. *shern*-e *fê*-ree-en!
Bye Claire, bye Michelle. Have a nice vacation!

Fun & Games

In each of the three conversations that follow, some words have gotten loose. See whether you can find a place for them.

1. Here's a dialog between Frau Lempert and the Hubers.

Ihnen   gut   geht   freut   ist   auch

Herr Huber: Guten Tag, Frau Lempert. Wie _____ es Ihnen?

Frau Lempert: Danke, gut. Und _____?

Herr Huber: Danke, auch _____ . Frau Lempert, das _____ meine Frau.

Frau Lempert: Guten Tag, Frau Huber! _____ mich sehr, Sie kennenzulernen.

Frau Huber: Mich _____.

2. In this conversation, Mike and Christa run into each other on the street.

mir   auch   selbst   geht's   hallo

Mike: Hallo Christa!

Christa: Mike, _____! Wie _____?

Mike: Danke, _____ geht's gut! Und _____?

Christa: _____ gut.

3. Susanne and Martin are making introductions at a party.

du   heiße   meine   wer   bin   heißt

Martin: Hallo, wie _____ du?

Susanne: Ich _____ Susanne. Und _____?

Martin: Ich _____ der Martin. Und _____ ist das?

Susanne: Das ist _____ Freundin Anne.

Chapter 4

Getting Numbers, Time, and Measurements Straight

In This Chapter

▶ Naming numbers and counting

▶ Tackling time and the days of the week

▶ Managing months and calendars

▶ Getting a handle on metric measurements

How much does that Mercedes cost? What time do you close? When did you move to Augsburg? How much cheese do I need to make fondue for four people? Knowing how to ask such questions in German is half the battle of communicating effectively. But understanding the answers makes you a major league player. In this chapter, you get up to speed with using numbers, dates, time, and measurements.

Juggling Numbers

Chances are you'll encounter German numbers in all kinds of situations: when you're trying to decipher prices, for example, or street numbers, departure times, exchange rates, and so on. Knowing the following numbers makes counting anything easy (for money matters, such as changing currency and accessing funds, see Chapter 14):

- ✔ **0 null** (nool)
- ✔ **1 eins** (ayns)
- ✔ **2 zwei** (tsvay)
- ✔ **3 drei** (dray)
- ✔ **4 vier** (feer)
- ✔ **5 fünf** (fuenf)

- ✔ **6 sechs** (zêks)
- ✔ **7 sieben** (*zee*-ben)
- ✔ **8 acht** (âHt)
- ✔ **9 neun** (noyn)
- ✔ **10 zehn** (tseyn)
- ✔ **11 elf** (êlf)
- ✔ **12 zwölf** (tsverlf)
- ✔ **13 dreizehn** (*dray*-tseyn)
- ✔ **14 vierzehn** (*feer*-tseyn)
- ✔ **15 fünfzehn** (*fuenf*-tseyn)
- ✔ **16 sechzehn** (*zêH*-tseyn)
- ✔ **17 siebzehn** (*zeep*-tseyn)
- ✔ **18 achtzehn** (*âHt*-tseyn)
- ✔ **19 neunzehn** (*noyn*-tseyn)
- ✔ **20 zwanzig** (*tsvân*-tsiH)
- ✔ **21 einundzwanzig** (*ayn*-oont-tsvân-tsiH)
- ✔ **22 zweiundzwanzig** (*tsvay*-oont-tsvân-tsiH)
- ✔ **23 dreiundzwanzig** (*dray*-oont-tsvân-tsiH)
- ✔ **24 vierundzwanzig** (*feer*-oont-tsvân-tsiH)
- ✔ **25 fünfundzwanzig** (*fuenf*-oont-tsvân-tsiH)
- ✔ **30 dreißig** (*dray*-siH)
- ✔ **40 vierzig** (*feer*-tsiH)
- ✔ **50 fünfzig** (*fuenf*-tsiH)
- ✔ **60 sechzig** (*zêH*-tsiH)
- ✔ **70 siebzig** (*zeep*-tsiH)
- ✔ **80 achtzig** (*âHt*-tsiH)
- ✔ **90 neunzig** (*noyn*-tsiH)
- ✔ **100 hundert** (*hoon*-dert)
- ✔ **200 zweihundert** (*tsvay*-hoon-dert)
- ✔ **300 dreihundert** (*dray*-hoon-dert)
- ✔ **400 vierhundert** (*feer*-hoon-dert)

> ↙ **500 fünfhundert** (*fuenf*-hoon-dert)
>
> ↙ **1000 tausend** (*tou*-zent)

Notice that, as words, the numbers between 21 and 25 in the preceding list appear to be backward. Take the number *21,* **einundzwanzig** (*ayn*-oont-tsvân-tsiH), for example. In German, you actually say, "One and twenty." Just remember to stick to this pattern for all the double-digit numbers, except for numbers in multiples of ten, like 30, 40, 50, and so on.

When describing one thing in a sentence, the number **eins** (ayns) (*one*) changes spelling. That's because, in these situations, **eins** is working as an adjective, and in German, adjectives can go through all kinds of spelling changes in a sentence. (See Chapter 2 for more info on adjectives.) Look at this example:

> **Er hat einen großen Hund.** (êr hât *ayn*-en *grohs*-en hoont.) (*He has a large dog.*)

Telling Time

Imagine you're sitting in a park under a tree on a hot sunny day, wondering what time it is. Suddenly, a white rabbit in a checkered jacket runs by, stops, pulls out a pocket watch, and mumbles about being late. My advice: Don't ask him what time it is. You're better off reading the following information on asking about and telling time, German style.

German speakers have two systems for telling time: one using the numbers 1–12 on a standard clock and one using a 24-hour format. They use the 12-hour system in casual conversation and the 24-hour system when they want to avoid any chance of misunderstanding. They don't use the a.m./p.m. system.

Asking for the time

Most people have at least one sort of device on them that tells the time. However, you should know the following two interchangeable phrases. With these, you can ask for the time just in case your devices fail you or you're looking for a safe way to start up a conversation:

> **Wie viel Uhr ist es?** (vee feel oohr ist ês?) (*What time is it?*)
>
> **Wie spät ist es?** (vee shpait ist ês?) (*What time is it?*)

When approaching somebody to ask the time, you can, as usual, make the request a little more polite by adding the phrase **Entschuldigen Sie, bitte** (ênt-*shool*-di-gen zee, *bi*-te) (*Excuse me, please*) to the beginning of your question.

Telling time with the 12-hour clock

Many German speakers choose the 12-hour format when talking casually. This system is one you're already familiar with: You use the numbers 1-12 on a standard clock. However, German doesn't have the expressions a.m. and p.m., so German speakers revert to the 24-hour format to avoid potential misunderstandings, for example, when discussing schedules. (For more about the 24-hour system, head to the upcoming section.)

On the hour

At the top of the hour, telling the time is very easy. You just say

> **Es ist . . . Uhr.** (ês ist . . . oohr.) (*It's . . . o'clock.*)

Of course, you include the number of the appropriate hour before the word **Uhr**.

Before and after the hour

Indicating times like quarter past three, ten to eight, or half past eleven is a little more complicated, but you only need to know three key expressions.

To use the German word for quarter, you include **Viertel** (*feer*-tel) (*quarter*) plus the word **nach** (nâH) (*past/after*) or **vor** (fohr) (*to/before*) followed by the appropriate hour, as shown in these examples:

> **Es ist Viertel nach. . . .** (ês ist *feer*-tel nâH. . . .) (*It's quarter past. . . .*)
>
> **Es ist Viertel vor. . . .** (ês ist *feer*-tel fohr. . . .) (*It's quarter to. . . .*)

Expressing the half hour isn't quite as straightforward. In German, the word **halb** (hâlp) (*half*) indicates half of the hour to come, rather than the past hour. You use the phrase **Es ist halb. . . .** (ês ist hâlp. . . .) (*It's half an hour before. . . .*) followed by the appropriate hour. For example, when it's 4:30, you say this:

> **Es ist halb fünf.** (ês ist hâlp fuenf.) (*It's half an hour before 5:00.*)

A few minutes before and after

When you need to break down the time in terms of minutes before or after the hour, you use **nach** (nâH) (*past/after*) and **vor** (fohr) (*to/before*), like this:

> **Es ist fünf Minuten vor zwölf.** (ês ist fuenf mi-*nooh*-ten fohr tsverlf.) (*It's five minutes to twelve.*)

> **Es ist zwanzig Minuten nach sechs.** (ês ist *tsvân*-tsiH mi-*nooh*-ten nâH zêks.) (*It's twenty minutes past six.*)

An alternative is to leave out the word **Minuten** in phrases such as those in the preceding list. For example, you can say **Es ist fünf vor zwölf** or **Es ist fünf Minuten vor zwölf.** Both phrases mean the same thing: *It's five [minutes] to twelve.*

Using the 24-hour system

Just as the a.m./p.m. system prevents misunderstanding, so does the 24-hour system. This is the key reason why all kinds of businesses — banks, stores, airlines, theaters, museums, cinemas, and so forth — use the 24-hour system.

Here's how this system works: After you reach 12, you keep on adding hours (13, 14, 15, and so on) until you get to 24 or **Mitternacht** (*mit*-er-nâHt) (*midnight*), which is also referred to as **null Uhr** (nool oohr) (literally: *zero hour*).

In this system of telling time, you don't use phrases like "half past" or "a quarter to" (the hour.) Everything is expressed in terms of minutes after the hour. Note in the following examples how the hour comes first and then the minutes:

> **Es ist 15 Uhr dreißig.** (ês ist *fuenf*-tseyn oohr *dray*-siH.) (*It's fifteen hours and thirty.*) This corresponds to 3:30 p.m.

> **Es ist 21 Uhr fünfzehn.** (ês ist *ayn*-oont-*tsvân*-tsiH oohr *fuenf*-tseyn.) (*It's twenty one hours and fifteen.*) That's 9:15 p.m.

> **Es ist 22 Uhr vierundvierzig.** (ês ist *tsvay*-oont-*ts*vân-tsiH oohr *feer*-oont-feer-tsiH.) (*It's twenty two hours and forty-four.*) You got it — 10:44 p.m.

> **Es ist null Uhr siebenundreißig.** (ês ist nool oohr *zee*-ben-oont-*dray*-siH.) (*It's zero hours and thirty-seven.*) That's the early, early morning — 12:37 a.m!

Times of the day

When you want to describe a slice of the day, such as morning or afternoon, you have several options in German. However, take the following time periods with a grain of salt; they're meant as guidelines. After all, night owls and early morning joggers have different ideas about when one part of the day starts and another ends.

- ✔ **der Morgen** (dêr *mor*-gen) (*morning;* 4:00 a.m. to noon)
- ✔ **der Vormittag** (dêr *fohr*-mi-tahk) (*morning;* 9:00 a.m. to noon)
- ✔ **der Mittag** (dêr *mi*-tahk) (*noon;* 12 noon to 2:00 p.m.)
- ✔ **der Nachmitag** (dêr *nāH*-mi-tahk) (*afternoon;* 2:00 p.m. to 6:00 p.m.)
- ✔ **der Abend** (dêr *ah*-bent) (*evening;* 6:00 p.m. to 12:00 a.m.)
- ✔ **die Nacht** (dee nāHt) (*tonight;* 12:00 a.m. to 4:00 a.m.)

Days of the week

Looking at a German calendar, you find that *the week,* **die Woche** (dee *woH*-e), starts on a Monday. In addition, the days of the week are all the same gender, masculine (**dêr**), but generally they're used without an article. For example, if you want to say that today is Monday, you say **Heute ist Montag** (*hoy*-te ist *mohn*-tahk).

Your basic days

Here are the days of the week followed by the abbreviations that you often see on schedules:

- ✔ **Montag** (*mohn*-tahk) (Mo) (*Monday*)
- ✔ **Dienstag** (*deens*-tahk) (Di) (*Tuesday*)
- ✔ **Mittwoch** (*mit*-voH) (Mi) (*Wednesday*)
- ✔ **Donnerstag** (*don*-ers-tahk) (Do) (*Thursday*)
- ✔ **Freitag** (*fray*-tâk) (Fr) (*Friday*)
- ✔ **Samstag/Sonnabend** (*zâms*-tahk/*zon*-ah-bênt) (Sa) (*Saturday*)
- ✔ **Sonntag** (*zon*-tahk) (So) (*Sunday*)

In northern Germany, *Saturday* is called **Sonnabend**. People living in southern Germany, Austria, and German-speaking Switzerland use the term **Samstag**.

To indicate that something always happens on a particular day of the week, an **s** is added to the word, and it's no longer capitalized. For example, you may get to a museum or a restaurant on a Monday and find it closed, in which case you're likely to see a sign on the door reading **montags geschlossen** (*mohn*-tahks ge-*shlos*-en*) (*closed on Mondays*).

Doing double duty

The word **morgen** (*mor*-gen) shows up in two different versions. Written with a lowercase *m,* **morgen** means *tomorrow.* The noun **der Morgen,** written with an uppercase *m,* means *morning.* Theoretically, **morgen Morgen** should mean *tomorrow morning,* but German speakers don't say that. Instead, they say **morgen früh** (*mor*-gen frue).

Morgen, morgen does, however, exist. It's the beginning of a German proverb, and sometimes only the auspicious beginning is invoked. The complete proverb is

Morgen, morgen, nur nicht heute, sagen alle faulen Leute. (*mor*-gen, *mor*-gen, noor niHt *hoy*-te, lzâ-gen *âl*-e *fou*-len *loy*-te.)

The more or less literal translation is *Tomorrow, tomorrow, just not today, is what all lazy folk say.* In essence, it's roughly equivalent to the English "Don't put off 'til tomorrow what you can do today."

Speaking of days . . .

Say it's Tuesday, and you want to confirm that you've planned to meet someone the next day. You can ask whether you're meeting on Wednesday, or you can ask whether the meeting is tomorrow. The following word list helps you refer to specific days:

✔ **heute** (*hoy*-te) (*today*)

✔ **gestern** (*gês*-tern) (*yesterday*)

✔ **vorgestern** (*fohr*-gês-tern) (*the day before yesterday*)

✔ **morgen** (*mor*-gen) (*tomorrow*)

✔ **übermorgen** (*ue*-ber-mor-gen) (*the day after tomorrow*)

To speak precisely about a particular time on a specific day, you can combine the preceding words with the times of day discussed in the section "Times of the day" earlier in this chapter. Try the following examples on for size:

heute Morgen (*hoy*-te *mor*-gen) (*this morning*)

heute Vormittag (*hoy*-te *fohr*-mi-tahk) (*this morning*)

gestern Abend (*gês*-tern *ah*-bent) (*yesterday evening/last night*)

Naming the Months

The following list shows you all the names of the months — notice how similar the German names are to the English! All the months' names are masculine, meaning that their article is **der**:

- **Januar** (*yā*-noo-ahr) (*January*)
- **Februar** (*fey*-broo-ahr) (*February*)
- **März** (mêrts) (*March*)
- **April** (ah-*pril*) (*April*)
- **Mai** (may) (*May*)
- **Juni** (*yooh*-nee) (*June*)
- **Juli** (*yooh*-lee) (*July*)
- **August** (ou-*goost*) (*August*)
- **September** (zêp-*têm*-ber) (*September*)
- **Oktober** (ok-*toh*-ber) (*October*)
- **November** (no-*vêm*-ber) (*November*)
- **Dezember** (dey-*tsêm*-ber) (*December*)

The following sentences show you how to build the *calendar*, **der Kalender** (der kâ-*lên*-der), in German:

Ein Jahr hat 12 Monate. (ayn yahr hât tsverlf *moh*-nâ-te.) (*A year has 12 months.*)

Ein Monat hat 30 oder 31 Tage. (ayn *moh*-nât hât *dray*-siH *oh*-der *ayn*-oont-dray-siH *tah*-ge.) (*A month has 30 or 31 days.*)

Der Februar hat 28 oder 29 Tage. (dêr *fey*-broo-ahr hât *āHt*-oont-tsvân-tsiH *oh*-der *noyn*-oont-tsvân-tsiH *tah*-ge.) (*February has 28 or 29 days.*)

Eine Woche hat 7 Tage. (*ayn*-e voH-e hât *zee*-ben *tah*-ge.) (*A week has seven days.*)

Measurements, Quantities, and Weights

You use the metric system in German-speaking countries, as well as most other countries around the globe. The various metric units crop up in all sorts of everyday situations, so coming to grips with the various equivalents for units of length, weight, and capacity is definitely worth your time. For example, you buy milk in a **Liter** (*lee*-ter) (*liter*) quantity rather than a quart, speed limits are indicated in **Kilometer** (ki-lo-*mey*-ter) (*kilometers*) per hour (1 kilometer = 0.6 mile), and a roughly 2.2-pound sack of potatoes sells as a unit of 1 **Kilo(gramm)** (*kee*-loh-[gram]) (*kilo[gram]*). ***Note:*** German speakers refer to 1,000 grams as either **Kilo or Kilogramm**, and neither one has an *s* in the plural form.

Here's what you need to know to buy something at a tantalizing open-air market. In fact, it's just the same as ordering in a restaurant, which you can read about in Chapter 8. You say

> **Ich hätte gern. . . .** (iH *hêt*-e gêrn. . . .) (*I would like to have. . . .*)

At the end of that phrase, simply say how much you want, which could include any of the following weights and measurements. Note that the plural forms for most of these measurements are the same as the singular form:

> **ein/zwei Kilo** (ayn/tsvay *kee*-loh) (*1 kilogram/2 kilograms*) (1 kilogram = 2.2 pounds)
>
> **ein/zwei Pfund** (ayn pfoont/tsvay pfoont) (*1 pound/2 pounds*) (1 metric pound = 500 grams) (In the U.S., a pound is 454 grams.)
>
> **ein/einhundert Gramm** (ayn/ayn-*hoon*-dêrt grâm) (*1/100 grams*)
>
> **ein/zwei Stück** (ayn/tsvay shtuek) (*one piece/two pieces*)
>
> **eine Scheibe/zwei Scheiben** (*ayn*-e *shay*-be/tsvay *shay*-ben) (*one slice/ two slices*)

To specify exactly what you want, simply add the appropriate word to the end of the whole phrase. For example, if you want one **Kilo** of apples, you say

> **Ich hätte gern ein Kilo Äpfel.** (iH *hêt*-e gêrn ayn *kee*-loh *êp*-fel.) (*I'd like to have one kilogram of apples.*)

Talkin' the Talk

 Frau Bauer buys all her produce at the open air market. Today she needs apples and tomatoes. Looking at the various stands, she approaches one where she's bought produce before and speaks to the saleswoman. (Track 11)

Verkäuferin: **Guten Tag. Was darf es sein?**
gooh-ten tahk. vâs dârf ês zayn?
Hello. What would you like?

Frau Bauer: **Zwei Kilo Äpfel und ein Pfund Tomaten, bitte.**
tsvay *kee*-loh *êp*-fel oont ayn pfoont toh-*mah*-ten, *bi*-te.
Two kilograms of apples and one pound of tomatoes, please.

Verkäuferin: **Sonst noch etwas?**
zonst noH *êt*-vâs?
Anything else?

Frau Bauer: **Danke, das ist alles.**
dân-ke, dâs ist *âl*-ês.
Thank you, that's all.

Next, Frau Bauer goes to a stand that sells dairy products.

Frau Bauer: **Ich hätte gern etwas von dem Gouda.**
iH *hêt*-e gêrn *êt*-vâs fon deym *gou*-dâ.
I'd like to have some Gouda.

Verkäuferin: **Wie viel hätten Sie denn gern?**
vee-feel *hêt*-en zee dên gêrn?
How much would you like?

Frau Bauer: **Zweihundert Gramm, bitte.**
tsvay-hoon-dert grâm, *bi*-te.
Two hundred grams, please.

Verkäuferin: **Sonst noch etwas?**
zonst noH *êt*-vâs?
Anything else?

Frau Bauer: **Nein, danke. Das wär's.**
nayn, *dân*-ke. dâs vêrs.
No thank you. That's it.

Words to Know

das Kilo	dâs <u>kee</u>-loh	kilogram
das Pfund	dâs pfoont	pound
das Gramm	dâs grâm	gram
wie viel	vee feel	how much
wie viele	vee <u>fee</u>-le	how many
Das wär's.	dâs vêrs	That's it.
Was darf es sein?	vâs dârf ês zayn?	What would you like?
Sonst noch etwas?	zonst noH <u>êt</u>-vâs?	Anything else?

Fun & Games

Alois Hailer needs to update his electronic calendar. Last week, the technology failed him, so to be on the safe side, he's writing out this week's appointments. Write each day, time, and appointment out as words. The activities are numbered in the calendar, and the first activity on Monday has already been done.

10 MO (1) 📱 Herr Hegele (2) Meeting 10.30-11.30	**14 FR** (6) 🍽️ 20.00
11 DI (3) 🏌️ 9.45	**15 SA** (7) 🖼️ 12.00 HAUS DER KUNST (8) 🎭 19.30 FAUST
12 MI (4) 🚂 14.21 Dortmund	**16 SO** (9) 🍸 18.00 MIT ANDREA!
13 DO (5) ✈️ 7.40 Innsbrück	Nächste Woche Urlaub!

1. Montag, acht Uhr, anrufen Herr Hegele

2. _____

3. _____

4. _____

5. _____

6. _____

7. _____

8. _____

9. _____

Chapter 5

Talking about Home and Family

* *

In This Chapter
▶ Describing home life
▶ Talking about family

* *

*T*alking about where you live and your family is a great way to open the lines of communication to a new acquaintance. In this chapter, I take you on a tour of the rooms in the home and provide useful information on German domestic lifestyles. You also find out about names of family members and how to talk about them.

Living in an Apartment or House

A far greater number of Germans live in apartments, either rented or owned, than do North Americans, and great value is placed on being able to own a single family dwelling. Land and construction materials are very costly, so living quarters tend to be smaller and more energy efficient.

Describing life within four walls

Here's some basic vocabulary you need to know to describe rooms in a home, along with a few other residence-related details:

✔ **das Bad/das Badezimmer** (dâs baht/dâs *bah*-de-tsi-mer) (*bathroom*)

✔ **der Balkon** (dêr bâl-*kon*) (*balcony*)

✔ **die Eigentumswohnung** (dee *ay*-gên-tooms-vohn-oong) (*condominium*)

✔ **das Einfamilienhaus** (dâs *ayn*-fâ-mi-lee-en-hous) (*single family home*)

✔ **das Esszimmer** (dâs *ês*-tsi-mer) (*dining room*)

- **der Garten** (dêr *gâr*-ten) (*yard/garden*)

- **der Keller** (dêr *kêl*-er) (*basement*)

- **die Küche** (dee *kueH*-e) (*kitchen*)

- **die Mietwohnung** (dee *meet*-vohn-oong) (*rented apartment*)

- **das Reihenhaus** (dâs *ray*-ên-hous) (*townhouse*)

- **das Schlafzimmer** (dâs *shlahf*-tsi-mer) (*bedroom*)

- **die Wohnung** (dee *vohn*-oong) (*apartment*)

- **das Wohnzimmer** (dâs *vohn*-tsi-mer) (*living room*)

- **das Zimmer** (dâs *tsi*-mer) (*room*)

Asking the right questions

Nothing is more embarrassing than being a guest in someone's home and making a blunder because you're not sure how to ask (and respond to) some simple questions.

The bathroom/toilet issue

You may find yourself in an uncomfortable situation if you ask to use the **Badezimmer** (*bad*-e-tsi-mer) (bathroom), when what you're probably looking for, believe it or not, is **die Toilette** (dee toy-*lêt*-e) (the toilet). So what's the story? Well, first, Germans have no hang-ups about using the T-word.

In addition, what constitutes a "bathroom" in German homes differs from the definition you're probably accustomed to. In Germany, the bathroom is a room where you can take a bath or shower, but it may or may not have a toilet. The toilet may be located in a separate room, euphemistically described in real-estate lingo as a half-bath. You, the guest, are probably not interested in taking a shower in the **Badezimmer**. So to avoid any confusion, whatever the plumbing situation may be, here's what you actually need to ask:

> **Darf ich ihre Toilette benutzen?** (dârf iH *eer*-e toy-*lêt*-e be-*noots*-en?) (*May I use the bathroom?* Literally: *May I use the toilet?*)

At the dinner table

Table etiquette in German-speaking countries involves a couple of polite phrases at the start of the meal, as well as appropriate eating customs. Before beginning a meal, it's customary to say **Guten Appetit** (*gooh*-ten âp-e-*teet*)

(*enjoy your meal*) or its more informal version, **Mahlzeit** (*māl*-tsayt) (*enjoy your meal*). You may also hear **Mahlzeit** used as a means of greeting colleagues at the workplace around the lunchtime. People gathered around a dinner table also use the phrase **zum Wohl** (tsoom vohl) (*cheers*) as they raise their glasses before taking the first sip of something like wine. **Prost** (prohst) (*cheers*) is an alternative expression more typically associated with drinking only.

Table manners in the German-speaking world deem it polite to have both hands on the table, but not the elbows. In fact, it would be considered strange to keep one hand hidden in one's lap. (No funny business, please, under the table!) By the same token, eating with your fork while still holding your knife in the other hand is acceptable.

During meal preparation, if you'd like to offer your help, by all means do so. You may use either the formal or informal version of "you." First, the formal "you" formulation:

> **Kann ich Ihnen helfen?** (kān iH *een*-en *hêlf*-en?) (*Can I help you?*)

The informal "you" version looks like this:

> **Kann ich dir helfen?** (kān iH deer *hêlf*-en?) (*Can I help you?*)

In another situation, you may be offered something (more) to eat or drink. Check out the question and some replies:

> **Darf/Kann ich Ihnen . . . anbieten?** (dārf/kān iH *een*-en . . . *ān*-beet-en?) (*May/Can I offer you. . . ?*)

> **Ja, bitte. Ich möchte . . . .** (yah, *bi*-te. iH *merH*-te . . . .) (*Yes, please. I'd like . . . .*)

> **Danke, nein.** (*dān*-ke, nayn.) (*No, thank you.*)

Living behind closed doors

Privacy plays a big role in German-speaking countries, so in general, people close doors between rooms in homes and office buildings. As an added benefit to maintaining privacy, closed doors keep noise levels down and may conserve energy. Germans are also great fans of fresh air, and even in winter, they like to sleep with the window open and the bedroom door closed. If this has you wondering how they stay warm in a cold bedroom, well, the secret is a **Federbett** (*fey*-der-bêt) (down-filled comforter) that keeps them toasty warm, even with snow blowing in the window.

Talking about Your Family

Discussing your family, **die Familie** (dee fâ-*mee*-lee-e) is a great way to get to know someone. Some people may even feel prompted to show their photos of family members. However, talking at great length about little Gretchen and Hansi, Jr. is a far less popular pastime in Germany than in America. It just may have to do with the value Germans place on privacy. At any rate, another reason you're not likely to fall asleep gazing at endless baby pictures is that the birth rate in Germany is very low.

You should find all the members of your family tree in the following list. Even if you don't have kids or in-laws, it's good to be familiar with these words so that you recognize them when discussing someone else's family (see Figure 5-1):

- **der Bruder** (dêr *brooh*-der) (*brother*)
- **der Cousin** (dêr *kooh*-zen) (*male cousin*)
- **die Cousine** (dee kooh-*zeen*-e) (*female cousin*)
- **die Eltern** (dee *êl*-tern) (*parents*)
- **die Frau** (dee frou) (*woman/wife*)
- **die Geschwister** (dee ge-*shvis*-ter) (*siblings*)
- **die Großeltern** (dee *grohs*-êl-tern) (*grandparents*)
- **die Großmutter** (dee *grohs*-moot-er) (*grandmother*)
- **der Großvater** (dêr *grohs*-fah-ter) (*grandfather*)
- **der Junge** (dêr *yoong*-e) (*boy*)
- **die Kinder** (dee *kin*-der) (*children, kids*)
- **das Mädchen** (dâs *maid*-Hên) (*girl*)
- **der Mann** (dêr mân) (*man/husband*)
- **die Mutter** (dee *moot*-er) (*mother*)
- **der Onkel** (dêr *on*-kel) (*uncle*)
- **die Schwester** (dee *shvês*-ter) (*sister*)
- **der Sohn** (dêr zohn) (*son*)
- **die Tante** (dee *tân*-te) (*aunt*)
- **die Tochter** (dee *toH*-ter) (*daughter*)
- **der Vater** (dêr *fah*-ter) (*father*)

Figure 5-1:
Who's who
in the family.

Use the following words for the in-laws:

- **der Schwager** (dêr *shvah*-ger) (*brother-in-law*)
- **die Schwägerin** (dee *shvai*-ger-in) (*sister-in-law*)
- **die Schwiegereltern** (dee *shvee*-ger-êl-tern) (*parents-in-law*)
- **die Schwiegermutter** (dee *shvee*-ger-moot-er) (*mother-in-law*)
- **der Schwiegersohn** (dêr *shvee*-ger-zohn) (*son-in-law*)
- **die Schwiegertochter** (dee *shvee*-ger-toH-ter) (*daughter-in-law*)
- **der Schwiegervater** (dêr *shvee*-ger-fah-ter) (*father-in-law*)

To express the term "step-," you use the prefix **Stief-** with the name of the relative, like this example: **Stiefbruder** (*steef*-brooh-der) (*step-brother*). The term for a "half" relative uses the prefix **Halb-**, so *half-sister* looks like this: **Halbschwester** (*hâlp*-shvês-ter).

Saying that you have a certain type of relative involves the following simple phrase:

Ich habe einen/eine/ein. . . . (īH *hah*-be *ayn*-en/*ayn*-e/ayn. . . .) (*I have a. . . .*)

The correct form of the indefinite article **einen** (masculine)/**eine** (feminine)/**ein** (neuter) (*ayn*-en/*ayn*-e/ayn) (*a*) depends on both gender and case. In the preceding phrase, you're using the accusative (direct object) case. The feminine and the neuter indefinite articles happen to be the same in the nominative (subject) case and the accusative (direct object) case, so their spelling doesn't change. The masculine indefinite article, however, takes a different form in the accusative. Here's how it works:

- **Masculine nouns:** Nouns like **der Mann, der Bruder, der Garten** (dêr *gâr*-ten) (*garden*), and **der Balkon** (dêr bâl-*kon*) (*balcony*) use the form **einen**.

- **Feminine nouns:** Nouns, like **die Frau, die Tochter, die Wohnung** (dee *vohn*-oong) (*apartment*), and **die Küche** (dee *kueH*-e) (*kitchen*) use **eine**.

- **Neuter nouns:** Nouns like **das Mädchen, das Haus** (dâs house [as in English]) (*house*), and **das Wohnzimmer** (dâs *vohn*-tsi-mer) (*living room*) use **ein**.

So what do you do if you want to express that you don't have siblings, a dog, a house, or whatever it may be? In English, you would say "I don't have any siblings/a dog/a house."

In German, you just use the negative, accusative form of the indefinite article **einen/eine/ein**, which you form by adding the letter **k** to the beginning of the word like this: **keinen/keine/kein** (*kayn*-en/*kayn*-e/kayn) (*no*). Look at the negative, accusative forms in the following sentences:

- **Masculine nouns:** Masculine nouns, such as **der Schwiegervater**, use **keinen**: **Ich habe keinen Schwiegervater.** (iH *hah*-be *kayn*-en shvee-ger-fah-ter.) (*I don't have a father-in-law.*)

- **Feminine nouns:** Feminine nouns, such as **die Familie**, use **keine**: **Ich habe keine große Familie.** (iH *hah*-be *kayn*-e *groh*-se fâ-*mi*-lee-e.) (*I don't have a large family.*)

- **Neuter nouns:** Neuter nouns, such as **das Haus**, use **kein**: **Ich habe kein Haus.** (iH *hah*-be kayn house.) (*I don't have a house.*)

- **Plural nouns:** Nouns in their plural form, or those that are always plural, like **die Geschwister**, use **keine**: **Ich habe keine Geschwister.** (iH *hah*-be *kayn*-e ge-*shvis*-ter.) (*I don't have any siblings.*)

Talkin' the Talk

 Herr Hanser and Frau Schneider have just met at a symposium in Frankfurt. They're talking about their families during a coffee break. (Track 12)

Herr Hanser:	**Wohnen Sie in Frankfurt?**
	vohn-en zee in frânk-foort?
	Do you live in Frankfurt?

Frau Schneider: **Nicht direkt. Mein Mann und ich haben ein Reihenhaus in Mühlheim. Und Sie?**

niHt dee-rêkt. mayn mahn oont iH hah-ben ayn ray-ên-hous in muel-haym. oont zee?

Not exactly. My husband and I have a townhouse in Mühlheim. And you?

Herr Hanser: **Wir haben eine Wohnung in der Innenstadt, aber unser Sohn wohnt in München. Haben Sie Kinder?**

veer hah-ben ayn-e vohn-oong in dêr in-en-shtât, ah-ber oon-zer zohn vohnt in muen-Hen. hah-ben zee kin-der?

We have an apartment in the center of the city, but our son lives in Munich. Do you have any kids?

Frau Schneider: **Ja, zwei Kinder. Mein Sohn Andreas arbeitet bei Siemens, und meine Tochter Claudia wohnt mit ihrem Mann in Italien.**

yah, tsvay kin-der. mayn zohn ân-drey-âs âr-bay-tet bay zee-mens, oont mayn-e toH-ter klou-dee-â wohnt mit eer-em mân in i-tah-lee-en.

Yes, two children. My son Andreas works at Siemens, and my daughter Claudia lives with her husband in Italy.

Herr Hanser: **Ach, meine Frau kommt aus Italien, aber ihre Eltern und ihre vier Geschwister wohnen alle in Deutschland.**

âH, mayn-e frou komt ous i-tah-lee-en, ah-ber eer-e êl-tern oont eer-e feer ge-shvis-ter vohn-en âl-e în doych-lânt.

Oh, my wife is from Italy, but her parents and her four siblings all live in Germany.

Fun & Games

Name the rooms of the house that are illustrated in the following drawing.

A. _____

B. _____

C. _____

D. _____

E. _____

Part II
German in Action

"Wait! Wait! I want to find out what gender 'eggplant' is so I know how to pick it up."

In this part . . .

In this part, we present German in the context of daily
life. We show you how to carry on a casual conversation
about such topics as the weather, where you live, or what
you do for a living. You find out how to talk about what
you do in your free time. You get the hang of how to order
food in a German restaurant, what to say when you're
shopping, how to communicate on the phone, and much,
much more. And we throw in some helpful grammar
lessons to boot. **Das klingt gut, oder?** (dâs klinkt gooht,
oh-der?) (*That sounds good, doesn't it?*)

Chapter 6

Getting to Know You: Making Small Talk

. . . .

In This Chapter

▶ Answering questions about yourself

▶ Exchanging stories about where you're from

▶ Chatting about the weather

. . . .

If you really want to get to know somebody, you have to engage in conversation. Small talk is an easy way to develop contacts and improve your German. Making small talk can be considered a social skill in itself, but luckily, starting up a light and casual conversation isn't too difficult. Whether you're meeting somebody at a party or want to talk to the person sitting next to you on the train, plane, or bus, you have several topics that always work as an opener: yourself, your job, where you're from, and, of course, the weather. We help you become familiar with discussing these topics throughout this chapter.

Talking about Yourself

When talking about yourself to a new acquaintance, you often answer many of the same key questions: What kind of job do you do? Where do you work? Are you self-employed? Are you a student? Where do you live? And later on in a conversation, your acquaintance may ask for your address and phone number. Because you'll encounter these topics often, you want to be prepared. The following sections provide you with the information you need.

Describing your work

If you start chatting with someone, that person may ask you what you do for a living. For example, he or she may ask any of the following:

Bei welcher Firma arbeiten Sie? (bay *vêlH*-er *fir*-mâ *âr*-bay-ten zee?) (*What company are you working for?*)

Was machen Sie beruflich? (vâs *mâH*-en zee be-*roohf*-liH?) (*What kind of work do you do?*)

Sind Sie berufstätig? (zint zee be-*roohfs*-tê-tiH?) (*Are you employed?*)

A few simple words and expressions help you describe your job and company. In most cases, you can describe what kind of work you do by connecting **Ich bin . . .** (iH bin . . .) (*I am . . .*) with the name of your occupation, without using any article. Most names for jobs exist in a female and male form. The male form frequently ends with **–er**; the female form usually ends with **–in**. Here are some examples:

Ich bin Handelsvertreter (m) / **Handelsvertreterin** (f). (iH bin *hân*-dels-fêr-trey-ter / *hân*-dels-fêr-trey-ter-in.) (*I am a sales representative.*)

Ich bin Student (m) / **Studentin** (f). (iH bin shtoo-*dênt* / shtoo-*dên*-tin.) (*I am a student.*)

If you're a student, you may want to say what you're studying. You do this with the phrase **Ich studiere . . .** (iH shtoo-*dee*-re . . .) (*I am studying . . .*). At the end of the sentence, you add the name of your field (without any article). Some fields you may use include the following:

- **Architektur** (âr-Hi-têk-*toohr*) (*architecture*)
- **Betriebswirtschaft** (be-*treeps*-virt-shâft) (*business administration*)
- **Softwaretechnik** (soft-wair-*têH*-nik) (*software engineering*)
- **Kunst** (koonst) (*art*)
- **Literaturwissenschaft** (li-te-rah-*toohr*-vis-en-shâft) (*literature*)
- **Biochemie** (bee-oh-Hey-*mee*) (*biochemistry*)

You also can describe what you do with the phrase **Ich bin . . .** (iH bin . . .) (*I am . . .*). You end the phrase with an appropriate adjective. For example, you may say any of the following:

Ich bin berufstätig / nicht berufstätig. (iH bin be-*roohfs*-tê-tiH / niHt be-*roohfs*-tê-tiH.) (*I am employed / not employed.*)

Ich bin pensioniert. (iH bin *pân*-zee-o-neert.) (*I am retired.*)

Ich bin öfteres geschäftlich unterwegs. (iH bin *erf*-ter-es ge-*shêft*-liH oon-ter-*veyks*.) (*I often travel on business.*)

Ich bin selbständig. (iH bin *zelpst*-shtênd-iH.) (*I am self-employed.*)

Your company name, place of work, or line of work may be almost as important as the actual work you do. The phrase **Ich arbeite bei . . . / in . . .** (iH *âr*-bay-te bay . . . / in . . .) (*I work at . . . / in . . .*) tells someone, in a nutshell, where you earn your money. Consider these examples:

> **Ich arbeite bei der Firma . . .** (iH *âr*-bay-te bay dêr *fir*-mâ . . .) (*I work at the company . . .*) After the word **Firma**, you simply insert the name of the company you work for.

> **Ich arbeite in einem Krankenhaus.** (iH *âr*-bay-te in ayn-em *krânk*-en-hous.) (*I work in a hospital.*)

> **Ich arbeite in der Gentechnik / in der Umweltforschung.** (iH *âr*-bay-te in dêr *geyn*-teH-nik / in dêr *oom*-velt-fohrsh-oong.) (*I work in genetic engineering / in environmental research.*)

> **Ich arbeite in einem Architekturbüro / in einem Forschungslabor.** (iH *âr*-bay-te in *ayn*-em âr-Hi-têk-*toohr*-bue-roh / in *ayn*-em *forsh*-oongs-lah-bor.) (*I work at an architecture office / in a research lab.*)

Providing your name and number (s)

Telling people where you live and how you can be reached is the key to continuing your social and business contacts. The following sections give you everything you need to offer your personal information to others.

A business card is worth 1,000 words, especially if your German is a little shaky. So if someone asks you about your personal info and you have your business card with you, why not save yourself the struggle of telling your vital statistics and present it with the following words: **Hier ist meine Visitenkarte.** (heer ist *mayn*-e vi-*zeet*-en-kâr-te.) (*Here is my business card.*). The later section "Looking at possessive pronouns" provides more information on how to use **mein** (mayn) and other possessive pronouns.

Telling someone where you live

When someone asks you **Wo wohnen Sie?** (voh *vohn*-en zee?) (*Where do you live?*), you can respond with any of the following:

> **Ich wohne in Berlin / in einem Vorort von Berlin.** (iH *vohn*-e in bêr-*leen* / in *ayn*-em *vohr*-ort von bêr-*leen*.) (*I live in Berlin / in a suburb of Berlin.*) Simply insert the name of your city into this expression.

> **Ich wohne in einer Kleinstadt / auf dem Land.** (iH *vohn*-e in *ayn*-er klayn-shtât / ouf deym lânt.) (*I live in a small town / in the country.*)

> **Ich habe ein Haus / eine Wohnung.** (iH *hah*-be ayn hous / *ayn*-e *vohn*-oong.) (*I have a house / an apartment.*)

CULTURAL WISDOM

Saying phone numbers

Germans often "spell" their phone numbers in pairs of numbers. If, for example, your number is 23 86 50, you say **dreiundzwanzig sechs undachtzig fünfzig** (*dray*-oont-tsvân-tsiH *zêks*-oont-âH-tsiH fuenf-tsiH). If the numbers are read one by one, you may hear the number 2, or **zwei** (tsvay), pronounced as **zwo** (tsvoh), making 23 86 50 sound like **zwo drei acht sechs fünf null** (tsvoh dray âHt zeks fuenf nool). Numbers in groups of three, such as area codes, are usually read one by one. For example, the area code for München is 089, so you would hear **null acht neun** (nool âHt noyn). (See Chapter 4 for more information on saying numbers in German.)

Depending on the circumstances, someone may ask you **Wie ist Ihre Adresse?** (vee ist *eer*-e â-*drês*-e?) (*What is your address?*). When you need to get down to specifics on where you live, you need to know the following words:

- **die Adresse** (dee â-*drês*-e) (*address*)
- **die Straße** (dee *shtrah*-se) (*street*)
- **die Hausnummer** (dee *hous*-noom-er) (*house / building number*)
- **die Postleitzahl** (dee *post*-layt-tsahl) (*zip code*)

When you tell someone your address, substitute the appropriate word into the following sentence: **Die Adresse / Straße / Hausnummer / Postleitzahl ist . . .** (dee â-*drês*-e / *shtrah*-se / *hous*-noom-er/ *post*-layt-tsahl ist . . .) (*The address / street / house number / zip code is . . .*)

Handing out your phone number and e-mail address

If your new acquaintance asks you for your phone number and e-mail address, don't worry. You can easily provide him or her with your contact information. Here's what you say:

Die Telefonnummer / die Handynummer / die Vorwahl / die Nebenstelle ist . . . (dee *tê*-le-fohn-noom-er / dee *hân*-dee-noom-er / dee *fohr*-vahl / dee *ney*-ben-shtêl-e ist . . .) (*The telephone number / the cell phone number / the area code / the extension is . . .*)

Meine E-mail Adresse ist . . . @ . . . dot com / net. (*mayn*-e e-mail [as in English] a-*drês*-e ist . . . at . . . dot com / net [as in English].) (*My e-mail address is . . . at . . . dot com / net*)

Talkin' the Talk

 Kurt Hanser is on the plane from München to Frankfurt. His seat is next to Frau Schneider, a businesswoman. After the two have introduced themselves, they talk about their jobs. (Track 13)

Herr Hanser: **Was machen Sie beruflich, wenn ich fragen darf?**
vâs *mâH*-en zee be-*roohf*-liH, vên iH *frah*-gen dârf?
What kind of work do you do, if I may ask?

Frau
Schneider: **Ich arbeite als Biochemikerin bei der Firma Agrolab.**
iH *âr*-bay-te âls bee-oh-*Hê*-mee-ker-in bay dêr *fir*-mâ
â-groh-lâb.
I work as a biochemist at a company called Agrolab.

Herr Hanser: **Das ist ja interessant. Haben Sie eine Visitenkarte?**
dâs ist yah in-te-re-*sânt*. *hah*-ben zee *ayn*-e
vi-*zeet*-en-kâr-te?
That's interesting. Do you have a business card?

Frau
Schneider: **Ja, hier bitte. Und was machen Sie beruflich?**
yah, heer *bi*-te. oont vâs *mâH*-en zee be-*roohf*-liH?
Yes, here it is. And what kind of work do you do?

Herr Hanser: **Ich arbeite in einem Architekturbüro. Leider habe ich
meine Visitenkarte nicht dabei.**
iH *âr*-bay-te in *ayn*-em âr-Hi-têk-*toohr*-bue-roh. lay-
der *hah*-be iH *mayn*-e vi-*zeet*-en-kâr-te niHt dâ-*bay*.
*I work at an architecture office. Unfortunately, I don't
have my business card with me.*

Frau
Schneider: **Ist Ihre Firma in Frankfurt?**
ist *eer*-e *fir*-mâ in *frânk*-foort?
Is your company in Frankfurt?

Herr Hanser: **Ja, unser Büro ist in der Bockenheimer Straße 27.**
yah, *oon*-zer *bue*-roh ist in deyr *bok*-en-haym-er
shtrah-se zee-ben-oont-tsvân-tsiH.
Yes, our office is at Bockenheimer Street 27.

Words to Know

fragen	<u>frah</u>-gen	to ask
geben	<u>gey</u>-ben	to give
dabei haben	dâ-<u>bay</u> <u>hah</u>-ben	to have on / with oneself
leider	<u>lay</u>-der	unfortunately

Looking at possessive pronouns

Take a moment to look at the German forms of "my," "our," and "your," which you can see in the previous dialogue: **mein** (mayn), **unser** (*oon*-zer), and **Ihr** (eer), respectively. These possessive pronouns are used to show that a noun belongs to somebody or something. The endings that these pronouns take depend on the gender, case, and number of the thing being possessed. Consider this example:

> **Hier ist meine Visitenkarte.** (heer ist *mayn*-e vi-*zeet*-en-kâr-te.) (*Here is my business card.*)

Visitenkarte (vi-*zeet*-en-kâr-te) is feminine, and the feminine possessive pronoun in the first person singular is **meine**.

The basic forms of the possessives (masculine and neuter) in the nominative case are

- ✔ **mein** (mayn) (*my*)
- ✔ **dein** (dayn) (*your;* singular, informal)
- ✔ **Ihr** (eer) (*your;* singular, formal)
- ✔ **sein, ihr, sein** (zayn, eer, zayn) (*his, her, its*)
- ✔ **unser** (*oon*-zer) (*our*)
- ✔ **euer** (*oy*-er) (*your;* plural, informal)
- ✔ **Ihr** (eer) (*your;* plural, formal)
- ✔ **ihr** (eer) (*their*)

Table 6-1 shows all the forms of **mein** (mayn) for all genders and all the different cases (the other possessives take the same endings).

Table 6-1		Forms of mein by Case		
Gender	*Nominative*	*Genitive*	*Dative*	*Accusative*
Masculine	**mein**	**meines**	**meinem**	**meinen**
Feminine	**meine**	**meiner**	**meiner**	**meine**
Neuter	**mein**	**meines**	**meinem**	**mein**

Conversing about Cities, Countries, and Nationalities

When you're getting to know someone, the conversation at some point will probably turn to familial origins. Most people enjoy exchanging such information about themselves. Using the handful of vocabulary words from this section, you can describe yourself with confidence. You'll be ready to step into situations where you tell people what city or country you're from and ask them where they come from, as well as what languages they speak.

Revealing where you come from

Saying where you're from in German in fairly easy. The magic words are

> **Ich komme aus . . .** (iH *kom*-e ous . . .) (*I come from . . .*)
>
> **Ich bin aus . . .** (iH bin ous . . .) (*I am from . . .*)

These few words go a long way. They work for countries, states, and cities. Take a look at these examples:

> **Ich komme aus Amerika.** (iH *kom*-e ous â-*mey*-ree-kâ.) (*I come from America.*)
>
> **Ich bin aus Pennsylvania.** (iH bin ous pennsylvania [as in English].) (*I am from Pennsylvania.*)
>
> **Ich komme aus Zürich.** (iH *kom*-e ous *tsue*-riH.) (*I come from Zurich.*)
>
> **Ich bin aus Wien.** (iH bin ous veen.) (*I am from Vienna.*)

The German language likes to be a bit challenging at times, so watch your step when discussing your origins. Here are a few specifics to be aware of:

✔ **Some countries' and regions' names are considered plural.** In this case, they use the plural definite article, **die** (dee) (*the*). The United States of America (USA) is one such country. In German, it's referred to as **die USA** (dee ooh-ês-*ah*) or **die Vereinigten Staaten** (dee fer-ay-nik-ten *shtah*-ten). It's quite easy to say **Ich bin aus Amerika.** (iH bin ous â-*mey*-ree-kâ.) (*I'm from America.*). However, technically, you could be referring to one of two American continents. So, to be a little more specific, you may say **Ich bin aus den USA.** (iH bin ous deyn ooh-ês-*ah*.) (*I'm from the USA.*). Or you may want to challenge yourself with **Ich bin aus den Vereinigten Staaten.** (iH bin ous deyn fer-ay-nik-ten *shtah*-ten.) (*I'm from the United States.*)

✔ **Some countries' names are considered female.** Switzerland, for example, is **die Schweiz** (dee shvayts) in German. Ms. Egli, whom you meet later in this chapter in a Talkin' the Talk dialogue, is Swiss. So to say where Ms. Egli is from, you say **Frau Egli ist aus der Schweiz.** (frou *ey*-glee ist ous dêr shvayts.) (*Ms. Egli is from Switzerland.*) The article **die** changes to the dative case — **der** — when it's combined with the preposition **aus** (ous) (*from*). (See Chapter 2 for more info on the dative case.)

Using the all-important verb "sein"

One of the most common and fundamental verbs in any language is "to be," or, in German, **sein** (zayn). You use this verb in the expressions **Das ist . . .** (dâs ist . .) (*This is . .*) and **Ich bin . . .** (iH bin . . .) (*I am . .*). As in English, the verb "to be" is used to describe everything from states of being (happy, sick, sad, and so on) to physical characteristics (such as being tall and dark-haired). And, unfortunately, **sein** is an irregular verb just as "to be" is in English. So the only way to figure this verb out is to dig in and memorize the different forms. The following table lays them out in German for you:

Conjugation	Pronunciation
ich bin	iH bin
du bist	dooh bist
Sie sind	zee zint
er, sie, es ist	êr, zee, ês ist
wir sind	veer zint
ihr seid	eer zayt
Sie sind	zee zint
sie sind	zee zint

Asking people where they come from

To ask people where they're from, you first need to decide whether to use the formal term of address **Sie**, or one of the two informal terms, **du** (for one person) or **ihr** (for several people). (Chapter 2 provides more information on when to use formal and informal pronouns.) Then you choose one of these three versions of the question:

Woher kommen Sie? (voh-*hêr kom*-en zee?) (*Where are you from?*)

Woher kommst du? (voh-*hêr* komst doo?) (*Where are you from?*)

Woher kommt ihr? (voh-*hêr* komt eer?) (*Where are you from?*)

The verb **kommen** (*kom*-en) (*to come*) is a verb that you hear often when speaking German. This regular verb is quite easy to remember; it even resembles its English cousin. Here's how it conjugates:

Conjugation	Pronunciation
ich komme	iH *kom*-e
du kommst	dooh komst
Sie kommen	zee *kom*-en
er, sie, es kommt	êr, zee, ês komt
wir kommen	veer *kom*-en
ihr kommt	eer komt
Sie kommen	zee *kom*-en
sie kommen	zee *kom*-en

Talkin' the Talk

Frau Egli and Frau Myers are on a train. During their trip, they strike up a conversation. They have just introduced themselves and are curious to learn a little more about each other.

Frau Egli: **Und woher kommen Sie, Frau Myers?**
oont voh-*hêr kom*-en zee, frou myers [as in English]?
And where do you come from, Ms. Myers?

Frau Myers: **Ich komme aus den USA, aus Pennsylvania.**
IH *kom*-e ous deyn ooh-ês-ah, ous pennsylvania [as in English].
I come from the USA, from Pennsylvania.

Frau Egli: **Aus den USA, wie interessant. Kommen Sie aus einer Großstadt?**
              ous deyn ooh-ês-*ah*, vee in-te-re-*sânt*. kom-en zee ous *ayn*-er *grohs*-shtât?
              From the U.S., how interesting. Do you come from a large city?

Frau Myers: **Nein, ich komme aus Doylestown, eine Kleinstadt, aber sie ist sehr schön. Und Sie, Frau Egli, woher kommen Sie?**
              nayn, iH *kom*-e ous Doylestown [as in English], *ayn*-e *klayn*-shtat, *ah*-ber zee ist zeyr shern. oont zee, frou ey-glee, voh-*hêr* kom-ên zee?
              No, I come from Doylestown, a small town, but it's very pretty. And you, Ms. Egli, where do you come from?

Frau Egli: **Ich bin aus der Schweiz, aus Zürich.**
              iH bin ous dêr shvayts, ous *tsue*-riH.
              I'm from Switzerland, from Zurich.

In the next compartment, Claire and Michelle, two young backpackers, are getting to know Mark, another backpacker. Being easygoing teenagers, they use the informal address **du** and **ihr** right from the start.

Claire: **Bist du aus Deutschland?**
              Bist dooh ous *doych*-lânt?
              Are you from Germany?

Mark: **Nein, ich bin aus Österreich, aus Wien. Und ihr, woher kommt ihr?**
              nayn, iH bin ous *er*-ste-rayH, ous veen. oont eer, voh-*hêr* komt eer?
              No, I'm from Austria, from Vienna. And you, where do you come from?

Michelle: **Wir sind aus Frankreich. Meine Freundin Claire kommt aus Lyon, und ich komme aus Avignon.**
              veer zint ous *frânk*-rayH. *mayn*-e *froyn*-din claire [as in English] komt ous lee-*on*, oont iH *kom*-e ous ah-vee-*nyon*.
              We're from France. My friend Claire comes from Lyon, and I come from Avignon.

Discovering nationalities

Unlike English, which describes nationality by using the adjective of a country's name (such as *She is French*), German indicates nationality with a noun. As you probably already know, genders are important in German. And these nationality nouns have genders, too. So an American man or boy is **ein Amerikaner** (ayn â-mey-ree-*kah*-ner), and a woman or girl is **eine Amerikanerin** (*ayn*-e â-mey-ree-*kah*-ner-in).

Table 6-2 lists the names of some selected countries along with the corresponding nationality (a noun) and adjective.

Table 6-2	Country Names, Nouns, and Adjectives		
Country in English	*Country in German*	*Nationality (noun)*	*Adjective*
Belgium	**Belgien** (*bêl*-gee-ên)	**Belgier(-in)** (*bêl*-gee-êr[-in])	**belgisch** (*bêl*-gish)
Germany	**Deutschland** (*doych*-lânt)	**Deutsche(r)** (*doych*-e[r])	**deutsch** (doych)
England	**England** (*êng*-lânt)	**Engländer(in)** (*êng*-lain-der[-in])	**englisch** (*êng*-lish)
France	**Frankreich** (*frânk*-rayH)	**Franzose/ Französin** (frân-*tsoh*-ze/frân-*tser*-zin)	**französisch** (frân-*tser*-zish)
Italy	**Italien** (i-*tah*-lee-ên)	**Italiener(in)** (i-tah-*lee-eyn*-er[-in])	**italienisch** (i-tah-lee-*eyn*-ish)
Austria	**Österreich** (*er*-ste-rayH)	**Österreicher(in)** (*er*-ste-rayH-er[-in])	**österreichisch** (*er*-ste-rayH-ish)
Switzerland	**die Schweiz** (dee shvayts)	**Schweizer(in)** (*shvayts*-er[-in])	**schweizerisch** (*shvayts*-er-ish)
USA	**die USA** (dee ooh-ês-*ah*)	**Amerikaner(in)** (â-mey-ree-*kah*-ner[-in])	**amerikanisch** (â-mey-ree-*kah*-nish)

Here are a few examples of how these words may be used in sentences:

> **Herr Marsh ist Engländer.** (hêr marsh [as in English] ist *êng*-lain-der.) (*Mr. Marsh is English.*)
>
> **Maria ist Italienerin.** (mah-*ree*-ah ist i-tah-lee-*eyn*-er-in.) (*Maria is Italian.*)
>
> **Ich bin Schweizerin.** (iH bin *shvayts*-er-in.) (*I am Swiss.*)
>
> **Ich bin Österreicher.** (iH bin *er*-ste-rayH-er.) (*I am Austrian.*)

Chatting about languages you speak

To tell people what language you speak, you use the verb **sprechen** (*shprêH*-en) (*to speak*) and combine it with the language's name (see Table 6-2 for a list of some common language names). If you want to ask somebody whether he speaks English, the question is (informally):

> **Sprichst du Englisch?** (shpriHst dooh *êng*-lish?) (*Do you speak English?*)

Or (formally)

> **Sprechen Sie Englisch?** (*shprêH*-en zee *êng*-lish?) (*Do you speak English?*)

Here's the conjugation of the verb **sprechen**:

Conjugation	Pronunciation
ich spreche	iH *shprêH*-e
du sprichst	dooh shpriHst
Sie sprechen	zee *shprêH*-en
er, sie, es spricht	êr, zee, ês shpriHt
wir sprechen	veer *shprêH*-en
ihr sprecht	eer shprêHt
Sie sprechen	zee *shprêH*-en
sie sprechen	zee *shprêH*-en

Talkin' the Talk

Claire, Michelle, and Mark are talking about languages they speak.

Claire:
Sprichst du Französisch?
shpriHst dooh frân-*tser*-zish?
Do you speak French?

Mark:
Nein, überhaupt nicht. Aber ich spreche Englisch. Und ihr?
nayn, ue-ber-*houpt* niHt. *ah*-ber iH *shprêH*-e êng-lish. oont eer?
No, not at all. But I speak English. How about you?

Michelle:
Ich spreche ein bisschen Englisch, und ich spreche auch Spanisch.
iH *shprêH*-e ayn *bis*-Hen êng-lish, oont iH *shprêH*-e ouH *shpah*-nish.
I speak a little English, and I speak Spanish, too.

Claire:
Spanisch spreche ich nicht, aber ich spreche Englisch sehr gut. Englisch finde ich leicht.
shpah-nish *shprêH*-e iH niHt, *ah*-ber iH *shprêH*-e êng-lish zeyr gooht. êng-lish *fin*-de iH layHt.
I don't speak Spanish, but I speak English very well. I think English is easy.

Mark:
Deutsch ist auch leicht, oder?
doych ist ouH layHt, *oh*-der?
German is easy, too, isn't it?

Claire:
Für mich nicht. Deutsch kann ich überhaupt nicht aussprechen!
fuer miH niHt. doych kân iH ue-ber-*houpt* niHt *ous*-sprê-Hen!
Not for me. I can't pronounce German at all!

Words to Know

leicht	layHt	easy / simple
groß	grohs	large / big
interessant	in-te-re-<u>sânt</u>	interesting
klein	klayn	small
schön	shern	pretty
aber	<u>ah</u>-ber	but
ein bisschen	ayn <u>bis</u>-Hen	a little (bit)
überhaupt nicht	ue-ber-<u>houpt</u> niHt	not at all
sein	zayn	to be
sprechen	<u>shprêH</u>-en	to speak

Making Small Talk about the Weather

People everywhere love to talk about **das Wetter** (dâs *vêt*-er) (*the weather*). After all, it affects major aspects of life — your commute to work, your plans for outdoor activities, and sometimes even your mood. Plus, it's always a safe topic of conversation that you can rant or rave about! In the following sections, we help you get comfortable making small talk about the goings-on outside.

Noting what it's like out there

The phrase **Es ist . . .** (ês ist . . .) (*It is . . .*) helps you describe the weather no matter what the forecast looks like. You simply supply the appropriate adjective at the end of the sentence. Check out these examples:

Es ist kalt. (ês ist kâlt.) (*It is cold.*)

Es ist heiß. (ês ist hays.) (*It is hot.*)

Es ist schön. (ês ist shern.) (*It is beautiful.*)

The following vocabulary allows you to describe almost any kind of weather:

- **bewölkt** (be-*verlkt*) (*cloudy*)
- **neblig** (*neyb*-liH) (*foggy*)
- **regnerisch** (*reyk*-ner-ish) (*rainy*)
- **feucht** (foyHt) (*humid*)
- **windig** (*vin*-diH) (*windy*)
- **kühl** (kuehl) (*cool*)
- **schwül** (shvuel) (*muggy*)
- **eiskalt** (*ays*-kâlt) (*freezing*)
- **warm** (vârm) (*warm*)
- **sonnig** (*son*-iH) (*sunny*)

You can also use the following phrases to give your personal weather report:

Die Sonne scheint. (dee *son*-e shaynt.) (*The sun is shining.*)

Es regnet / schneit. (ês *reyk*-nêt / shnayt.) (*It is raining / snowing.*)

Es gibt ein Unwetter. Es blitzt und donnert. (ês gipt ayn *oon*-vêt-er. ês blitst oont *don*-ert.) (*There's a storm. There's lightning and thunder.*)

Es wird hell / dunkel. (ês virt hêl / *doon*-kel.) (*It is getting light / dark.*)

Discussing the temperature

In the old country, 30-degree weather means you can break out your swimming gear, not your skis! In Europe (and most everywhere else in the world), the temperature isn't measured in degrees Fahrenheit but in degrees Celsius (*tsêl*-zee-oos) (also called Centigrade). If you want to convert Celsius to Fahrenheit and the other way around, you can use these formulas:

- **Celsius to Fahrenheit:** Multiply the Celsius temperature by 1.8 and then add 32.
- **Fahrenheit to Celsius:** Subtract 32 from the Fahrenheit temperature and multiply the result by .5.

It may help you to know that 0 degrees Celsius corresponds to 32 degrees Fahrenheit, 10 degrees Celsius to 50 degrees Fahrenheit, 20 Celsius to 68 Fahrenheit, and 30 Celsius to 86 Fahrenheit.

When the temperature is the topic of conversation, the following phrases are sure to come up:

Es ist zehn Grad. (ês ist tseyn graht.) (*It's ten degrees.*) Of course, you substitute the appropriate number before the word **Grad**. (See Chapter 4 for more information on numbers.)

Es ist minus zehn Grad. (ês ist *mee*-noos tseyn graht.) (*It is minus ten degrees.*) Again, substitute the proper number before **Grad**.

Es ist zehn Grad unter Null. (ês ist tseyn graht *oon*-ter nool.) (*It is ten degrees below zero.*)

Die Temperatur fällt / steigt. (dee *têm*-pê-rah-*toohr* fêlt / shtaykt.) (*The temperature is falling / is rising.*)

Describing the day's weather

Any of the following phrases can get the ball rolling on a discussion of the weather:

Was für ein herrliches / prächtiges Wetter! (vâs fuer ayn *hêr*-liH-ês / *praiH*-tig-es *vêt*-er!) (*What wonderful / glorious weather!*)

Was für ein schreckliches / schlechtes Wetter! (vâs fuer ayn *shrêk*-liH-ês / *shlêHt*-ês *vêt*-er!) (*What horrible / bad weather!*)

Was für ein schöner / herrlicher Tag! (vâs fuer ayn *shern*-er / *hêr*-liH-er tahk!) (*What a beautiful / lovely day!*)

Talkin' the Talk

 Anita and Rolf live across the hall from each other in the same apartment building. They have been planning to go to the park this Sunday afternoon. On Sunday morning, Rolf knocks on Anita's door to discuss their plans. (Track 14)

Rolf: **Was machen wir jetzt? Bei so einem Wetter können wir nicht in den Park gehen. Es ist regnerisch und windig.**
vâs *mâH*-en veer yêtst? bay zoh *ayn*-em *vêt*-er *kern*-nen veer niHt in deyn pârk *gey*-en. ês ist *reyk*-ner-ish oont *vin*-diH.
What do we do now? We can't go to the park in this weather. It's rainy and windy.

Anita:	**Ja, ja, ich weiß. Aber gegen Mittag soll es aufhören zu regnen.**
	yah, yah, iH vays. *ah*-ber *gey*-gen *mi*-tahk zoll ês *ouf*-herr-en tsooh *reyk*-nen.
	Yeah, yeah, I know. But around noon it's supposed to stop raining.

Rolf:	**Wirklich? Ich sehe nur Wolken am Himmel . . .**
	virk-liH? iH *zey*-he noohr *vol*-ken âm *him*-el . . .
	Really? I only see clouds in the sky. . . .

Anita:	**Keine Panik! Heute Mittag scheint bestimmt wieder die Sonne.**
	kayn-e *pah*-nik! *hoy*-te *mi*-tahk shaynt be-*stimmt* vee-der dee *zon*-e.
	Don't panic! Surely the sun will shine again around noon today.

Rolf:	**Na gut. Vielleicht hast du recht. Ich kann bis Mittag warten.**
	nâ gooht. vee-*layHt* hâst dooh rêHt. iH kân bis *mi*-tahk *vâr*-ten.
	Okay. Perhaps you're right. I can wait until noon.

Anita:	**Okay, bis später! Tschüs!**
	okay [as in English], bis *shpai*-ter! chues!
	Okay, see you later! Bye!

Words to Know

machen	<u>mâH</u>-en	to do
sehen	<u>zey</u>-hen	to see
wissen	<u>vis</u>-en	to know
Recht haben	rêHt <u>hah</u>-ben	to be right
vielleicht	vee-<u>layHt</u>	perhaps
wirklich	<u>virk</u>-liH	really
bis später	bis <u>shpai</u>-ter	til later

Fun & Games

· ·

It's Saturday, and you're planning some outdoor activities for the next few days. Read the following four-day weather forecast and fill in the missing weather words.

Regen   schneit   Temperatur   Unwetter

donnert   regnen   unter Null

1. Heute Nachmittag gibt es ein _____, und es blitzt und _____. (hoy-te nâH-mi-tahk gipt es ayn _____, oont ês blitst oont _____.) (_This afternoon there'll be a _____, and there'll be lightning and _____._)

2. Sonntag fällt die Temperatur _____, und es _____ ein bisschen. (zon-tahk fêlt dee têm-pê-rah-toohr _____, oont ês _____ ayn bis-Hen.) (_On Sunday, the temperature will drop _____, and it'll _____ a little bit._)

3. Montag steigt die _____, und es fängt an zu _____. (mohn-tahk shtaykt dee _____, oont ês fênkt ân tsooh _____.) (_On Monday the _____ will rise, and it will start to _____._)

4. In Berlin hört der _____ nicht vor Dienstag auf. (in bêr-_leen_ herrt deyr _____ niHt fohr _deens_-tahk ouf.) (_In Berlin, the _____ won't stop before Tuesday._)

Chapter 7

Asking for Directions

. . . .

In This Chapter

▶ Finding the places you want to go

▶ Discovering the German ordinal numbers

▶ Going by car or other vehicle

. . . .

The key to getting around is knowing how to get where you're going. Before you hop on that bus or train, or set out on your journey by car or on foot, you naturally want to plan your trip. Being able to ask about the location of a train station, open-air market, or museum is a good start.

And, of course, you also want to understand the directions someone gives you to your destination. For example, someone may say that the market is across from the subway station, behind the hotel, or next to the post office. Or they may tell you to take the second street on the left, turn right at the third traffic light, and so on. If you don't relish the thought of getting lost, read on. This chapter gets you on the right track.

"Wo?" — Asking Where Something Is

Where am I? Where do we go from here? Where would you be without the word "where"? Probably lost. Luckily, asking where something is in German is pretty easy. You start with the word **wo** (voh) (*where*) and frame your question like this:

> **Wo ist . . .?** (voh ist . . .?) (*Where is . . .?*)

Whenever you ask a stranger a question, you sound more polite (and therefore are more likely to get more or better assistance) if you preface the question with the following:

> **Entschuldigen Sie bitte** . . . (ênt-*shool*-di-gen zee *bi*-te . . .) (*Excuse me, please . . .*)

After you flag down a stranger and start your question with **Entschuldigen Sie bitte, wo ist . . .**, you can finish the question. You do so by supplying the name of the location you're looking for, which could include any of the following:

- ✔ **der Bahnhof** (dêr *bahn*-hohf) (*train station*)

- ✔ **der Taxistand** (dêr *tâx*-ee-shtânt) (*taxi stand*)

- ✔ **die U-Bahnstation** (dee *ooh*-bahn-shtât-see-ohn) (*subway station*)

- ✔ **die Bushaltestelle / die Straßenbahnhaltestelle** (dee *boos*-hâl-te-shtêl-e / dee *shtrah*-sen-bahn hâl-te-shtêl-e) (*bus stop / streetcar or tram stop*)

- ✔ **der Platz** (dêr plâtz) ([*town*] *square*)

- ✔ **der Hafen** (dêr *hah*-fen) (*harbor*)

- ✔ **die Bank** (dee bânk) (*bank*)

- ✔ **das Hotel** (dâs hotel [as in English]) (*hotel*)

- ✔ **die Kirche** (dee *kirH*-e) (*church*)

- ✔ **die Post** (dee post) (*post office*)

- ✔ **der Markt** (dêr mârkt) (*market*)

- ✔ **das Museum** (dâs moo-*zey*-oom) (*museum*)

- ✔ **der Park** (dêr pârk) (*park*)

- ✔ **das Theater** (dâs tey-*ah*-ter) (*theater*)

Of course, if you're in a town of any size at all, a general question like "Where is the bus stop?" or "Where is the bank" may be met with a quizzical look. After all, multiple bus stops or banks may be in close proximity. To make your questions as specific as possible, include the proper name of the bus stop, theater, church, or other location in your question. For example, you could ask any of the following:

> **Wo ist die Bushaltestelle Karlsplatz?** (voh ist dee *boos*-hâl-te-shtêl-e *kârlz*-plâts?) (*Where is the bus stop Karlsplatz?*)

> **Wo ist das Staatstheater?** (voh ist dâs *shtâts*-tey-ah-ter?) (*Where is the Staatstheater?*)

> **Wo ist der Viktualienmarkt?** (voh ist dêr vik-too-*ahl*-ee-en-mârkt?) (*Where is the Viktualien Market?*)

If you don't know the proper name of your destination, you can ask for directions to the nearest of whatever you're looking for. You simply insert the word **nächste** (*naiH*-ste) (*nearest*) after the article of the location in question. Check out the following questions that use **nächste**:

Wo ist der nächste Park? (voh ist dêr *naiH*-ste pârk?) (*Where is the nearest park?*)

Wo ist die nächste Bank? (voh ist dee *naiH*-ste bânk?) (*Where is the nearest bank?*)

Wo ist das nächste Hotel? (voh ist dâs *naiH*-ste hotel?) (*Where is the nearest hotel?*)

When it comes to getting around and asking for directions, you can use this helpful verb to indicate that you don't know your way around a place: **auskennen** (*ous*-kên-en) (*to know one's way around*). Here's an expression using this verb that you may want to memorize:

Ich kenne mich hier nicht aus. (iH *kên*-e miH heer niHt *ous.*) (*I don't know my way around here.*)

The verb **auskennen** belongs to a group of verbs called *separable verbs.* They all have a prefix that separates from the main part of the verb and gets shoved to the end of the sentence. The prefix of the verb **auskennen** is **aus-.** Notice how this prefix appears at the very end of the sentence. For more information on separable verbs, read the scoop in Chapter 15.

"Wie weit?" How Far Is It?

Before you decide whether you want to walk someplace or take public transportation, you probably want to find out how far away your destination is. You have a few options that help you discover how distant a location is, and the key word to know is **weit** (vayt) (*far*):

Ist . . . weit entfernt / weit von hier? (ist . . . vayt ênt-*fêrnt* / vayt fon heer?) (*Is . . . far away / far from here?*)

You just fill in the name of the location you're asking about. So, for example, if you're headed to the art museum, you may ask someone one of the following:

Ist das Kunstmuseum weit entfernt? (ist dâs *koonst* moo-*zey*-oom vayt ênt-*fêrnt?*) (*Is the art museum far away?*)

Ist das Kunstuseum weit von hier? (ist dâs *koonst* moo-*zey*-oom vayt fon heer?) (*Is the art museum far from here?*)

Hopefully, you'll get the answer

Nein, das Kunstmuseum ist nicht weit von hier. (nayn, dâs *koonst* moo-*zey*-oom ist niHt vayt fon heer.) (*No, the art museum isn't far from here.*)

If you want to know specifically how far away a location is, you can use this question:

> **Wie weit ist . . . von hier?** (vee vayt ist . . . fon heer?) (*How far is . . . from here?*)

You may also approach the issue the other way around and find out how close something is by using the word **nah** (nah) (*near*). You usually find the word **nah** in the following combination: **in der Nähe** (in dêr *nai*-he) (*nearby*). You can ask the question

> **Ist . . . in der Nähe?** (ist . . . in dêr *nai*-he?) (*Is . . . nearby?*)

Going Here and There

The words **hier** (heer) (*here*) and **dort** (dort) (*there*) may be small words, but they play an important part in communicating directions. How? Well, as their English equivalents do, they make directions just a little more concrete. Look at the following sample sentences to see how **hier** and **dort** work in explaining directions:

> **Das Museum ist nicht weit von hier.** (dâs moo-*zey*-oom ist niHt vayt fon heer.) (*The museum isn't far from here.*)

> **Das Hotel ist dort, neben dem Café.** (dâs hotel [as in English] ist dort, *ney*-ben deym café [as in English].) (*The hotel is there, next to the café.*)

Some key words that answer the question "where?" more specifically are easier to remember when you recognize them in commonly used word combinations. Try these combos on for size:

- ✔ **hier vorne** (heer *forn*-e) (*here in front*)
- ✔ **dort drüben** (dort *drue*-ben) (*over there*)
- ✔ **ziemlich weit / sehr weit** (*tseem*-leeH vayt / zeyr vayt) (*quite far / very far*)
- ✔ **gleich um die Ecke** (glayH oom dee *êk*-e) (*just around the corner*)
- ✔ **direkt gegenüber** (di-*rêkt* gey-gen-*ue*-ber) (*directly opposite*)

Check out the following sentences that use some of the preceding expressions:

> **Der Hauptbahnhof ist gleich um die Ecke.** (dêr *houpt*-bahn-hohf ist glayH oom dee *êk*-e.) (*The main train station is just around the corner.*)

> **Die U-Bahnstation ist dort drüben.** (dee *ooh*-bahn-shtât-see-ohn ist dort *drue*-ben.) (*The subway station is over there.*)

Asking "How Do I Get There?"

When you want to ask "How do I get there?" you use the verb **kommen** (*kom-en*), which means both "to come" and, when used with a preposition, "to get to." Refer to Chapter 6 for the conjugation of **kommen**.

The basic form of the question "How do I get there?" is

> **Wie komme ich . . .?** (vee *kom*-e iH . . .?) (*How do I get . . .?*)

To finish the rest of the sentence, you need to use a preposition to help you say "to the train station" or "to the city center." At this point, you need to shift into high gear — that is, high grammar gear.

In German, you don't just deal with one preposition as you do in English, in which you would simply use "to" (*How do I get to . . .?*). In fact, you may need to use any of a number of prepositions, all of which can mean "to." The most commonly used "to" prepositions in German are the following:

- ✔ **in** (in)
- ✔ **nach** (nahH)
- ✔ **zu** (tsooh)

The following sections discuss each of these prepositions and how to use them.

Using "in" to get into a location

You use the preposition **in** (in) when you want to get to, or into, a certain location, such as the city center, the zoo, or the mountains. For example:

> **Wie komme ich in die Innenstadt?** (vee *kom*-e iH in dee *in*-ên-shtât?)
> (*How do I get to the center of the city?*)

When you use the preposition **in** this way, the article that comes after it goes into the accusative case, meaning that some of the articles change form slightly. Chapter 2 has a complete explanation of the accusative case, but here's a quick reminder of how the articles change (or don't change):

- ✔ **der** becomes **den** (deyn) (masculine)
- ✔ **die** stays **die** (dee) (feminine)
- ✔ **das** stays **das** (dâs) (neuter)
- ✔ **die** stays **die** (dee) (plural)

For example, the article of a feminine noun like **die City** (dee *si*-tee) (*city center*) stays the same:

> **Wie komme ich in die City?** (vee *kom*-e iH in dee *si*-tee?) (*How do I get to the city center?*)

The article of a masculine noun like **der Zoo** (dêr tsoh) (*zoo*) changes like this:

> **Wie kommen wir in den Zoo?** (vee *kom*-en veer in deyn tsoh?) (*How do we get to the zoo?*)

The article of a plural noun like **die Berge** (dee *bêr*-ge) (*mountains*), stays the same:

> **Wie komme ich in die Berge?** (vee *kom*-e iH in dee *bêr*-ge?) (*How do I get to the mountains?*)

The article of a neuter noun like **das Zentrum** (dâs *tsên*-troom) (*center*) stays the same, but when the preposition **in** is used with neuter nouns in the accusative case, the preposition and article contract to form the word **ins**:

> **in** + **das** = **ins**

This contraction is almost always used, giving you phrases like

> **Wie komme ich ins Zentrum?** (vee *kom*-e iH ins *tsên*-troom?) (*How do I get to the city center?*)

Using "nach" to get to a city or country

The preposition **nach** (nahH), luckily, only comes into play in a specific context: when you want to get to a city or country:

> **Wie komme ich nach Köln?** (vee *kom*-e iH nahH kerln?) (*How do I get to Cologne?*)

You have no troublesome articles to bother with when using **nach** because city names and most country names don't need articles.

Using "zu" to get to institutions

If you're asking how to get to a place such as a train station or a museum, the preposition **zu** (tsooh) is a pretty safe bet. It may, however, go through a slight spelling change when used in a sentence. For example:

Wie kommen wir zum Flughafen? (vee *kom*-en veer tsoom *floohk-hä*-fen?) (*How do we get to the airport?*)

Wie komme ich zur Deutschen Bank? (vee *kom*-e iH tsoor *doych*-en bânk?) (*How do I get to the German bank?*)

The preposition **zu** requires the dative case. (See Chapter 2 for a complete explanation of the dative case.) As a result, the articles used right after **zu** change in the following ways:

- ✔ **der** becomes **dem** (deym) (masculine)
- ✔ **die** becomes **der** (dêr) (feminine)
- ✔ **das** becomes **dem** (deym) (neuter)
- ✔ **die** becomes **den** (deyn) (plural)

When **zu** is used with masculine nouns, like **der Bahnhof**, and neuter nouns, like **das Hotel**, the preposition and article contract to form the word **zum**. In other words, **zu + dem = zum**. The following two examples both use **zum**:

Wie komme ich zum Bahnhof? (vee *kom*-e iH tsoom *bahn*-hohf?) (*How do I get to the train station?*)

Wie komme ich zum Hotel Kempinski? (vee *kom*-e iH tsoom hotel kêm-*pin*-skee?) (*How do I get to Hotel Kempinski?*)

Similarly, take a look at how **zu** combines with a feminine noun like **die Post** (dee post) (*post office*) in its dative form, **der Post**: **zu + der = zur**. Look at this example:

Wie komme ich zur Post? (vee *kom*-e iH tsoor post?) (*How do I get to the post office?*)

Tracking down a taxi cab

The secret to getting a taxi cab in Germany is making a phone call or actually walking to the nearest taxi stand. You may be used to the idea that in big cities, you can just hail a cab on the street, but doing so isn't common practice in Germany — even in the larger cities. Why? Well, with the astronomical cost of gas in Europe, consider how much cab drivers would spend if they drove around until being hailed. So you have several choices: You can ask someone on the street where the nearest taxi stand is located and walk to it. Alternatively, you can find out the phone number of the taxi stand closest to you and call. And if you're at a restaurant or some other business, you can ask an employee to call a cab for you. Of course, you do find taxi stands in front of airports, train stations, and major hotels. Head to Chapter 15 for more on travelling by taxi.

To use plural nouns like **die Souvenirläden** (dee zoo-ven-*eer*-lê-den) (*souvenir shops*) together with **zu,** you simply change the article to **den,** like this:

> **Wie kommen wir zu den Souvenirläden?** (vee *kom*-en veer tsooh deyn zoo-ven-*eer*-lê-den?) (*How do we get to the souvenir shops?*)

Describing a Position or Location in Relation to Some Other Place

After you ask for directions, you must be ready to understand the answers you may receive. People commonly express the location of a place in relation to a well-known landmark or location. You can use quite a few prepositions to describe locations in this way. Luckily, all these prepositions used in this context use the dative case, so any articles after the preposition behave just like they do for the use of **zu,** as described in the preceding section. In addition, the preposition **bei** (bay) (*near / next to*) and the article **dem** almost always contract like this: **bei + dem = beim.**

Table 7-1 shows you some common prepositions that are used to express the location of one thing in relation to another.

Table 7-1	Prepositions that Express Locations		
Preposition	*Pronunciation*	*Meaning*	*Example*
an	ân	*at*	**an der Ecke** (ân dêr *êk*-e) (*at the corner*)
auf	ouf	*on*	**auf der Museumsinsel** (ouf dêr moo-*zey*-ooms-in-sel) (*on the Museum Island*)
bei	bay	*near / next to*	**beim Bahnhof** (baym *bahn*-hohf) (*near the train station*)
hinter	*hin*-ter	*behind*	**hinter der Kirche** (*hin*-ter dêr *kirH*-e) (*behind the church*)
neben	*ney*-ben	*next to*	**neben der Bank** (*ney*-ben dêr bânk) (*next to the bank*)
vor	fohr	*in front of*	**vor der Post** (fohr dêr post) (*in front of the post office*)
zwischen	*tsvi*-shen	*between*	**zwischen dem Theater und der Bank** (*tsvish*-en deym tey-*ah*-ter oont dêr bânk) (*between the theater and the bank*)

Talkin' the Talk

 Mike is on a business trip to **München** (*muen*-Hen) (*Munich*), a city he hasn't visited before. He wants to take a cab to get to a friend's house, but he needs some help finding the nearest taxi stand. So he approaches a woman on the street. (Track 15)

Mike: **Entschuldigen Sie bitte, wo ist der nächste Taxistand?**
ênt-*shool*-di-gen zee *bi*-te, voh ist dêr *naiH*-ste *tâx*-ee-shtant?
Excuse me, where is the nearest taxi stand?

Frau: **In der Sonnenstraße.**
in dêr *zon*-en-shtrah-se.
On Sonnen Street.

Mike: **Ich kenne mich in München leider nicht aus. Wie komme ich zur Sonnenstraße?**
iH *kên*-e miH in *muen*-Hen *lay*-der niHt ous. vee *kom*-e iH tsoor *zon*-en-shtrah-se?
Unfortunately, I don't know my way around Munich. How do I get to Sonnen Street?

Frau: **Sehen Sie die Kirche dort drüben? Hinter der Kirche ist der Sendlinger-Tor-Platz und direkt gegenüber ist der Taxistand.**
zey-en zee dee *kirH*-e dort *drue*-ben? *hin*-ter dêr *kirH*-e ist dêr zênd-leeng-er-*tohr*-plâts oont *d*i-rêkt gey-gen-*ue*-ber ist dêr *tâx*-ee-shtânt.
Do you see the church over there? Behind the church is Sendlinger-Tor Square and directly opposite is the taxi stand.

Mike: **Vielen Dank!**
fee-len dânk!
Thank you very much!

Words to Know

Wo ist...?	voh ist?	Where is...?
nächste	naiH-ste	nearest
sich auskennen	ziH ous-kên-en	to know one's way around
weit	vayt	far
in der Nähe	in dêr nai-he	nearby
hinter	hin-ter	behind
vor	fohr	in front of
neben	ney-ben	next to
an	ân	at

Getting Your Bearings Straight with Left, Right, North, and South

Unless you tackle the words for the various directions — such as left, right, straight ahead, and the compass points — you may find yourself trying to find the town hall by tugging at some stranger's sleeve and chanting **Rathaus** (*rât*-hous) over and over, hoping they'll lead you to the right building. With this section, you can put an end to your helplessness by mastering the few simple words you need to understand (and ask about) the various directions.

Left, right, straight ahead

When you ask for or give directions, you can't avoid using the key words for defining position: left, right, and straight ahead. Here are these key words in German:

- ✔ **links** (links) (*left*)
- ✔ **rechts** (rêHts) (*right*)
- ✔ **geradeaus** (ge-rah-de-*ous*) (*straight ahead*)

If you want to express that something is located to the left or right of something else, you add the preposition **von** (fon) (*of*), making the following:

- **links von** (links fon) (*to the left of*)
- **rechts von** (rêHts fon) (*to the right of*)

Check out these examples that use **von** and a defining position:

> **Der Markt ist links von der Kirche.** (dêr mârkt ist links fon dêr *kirH*-e.) (*The market is to the left of the church.*)

> **Die U-Bahnstation ist rechts vom Theater.** (dee *ooh*-bahn-shtât-see-ohn ist rêHts fom tey-*ah*-ter.) (*The subway station is to the right of the theater.*)

When the preposition **von** combines with **dem**, it usually contracts like this: **von + dem = vom**. (**Dem** is the dative form of the masculine definite article **der** and the neuter definite article **das**. Chapter 2 gives you more info on the dative case.)

You also may hear the word for side, **die Seite** (dee *zay*-te) in connection with directions. **Seite** can help directions be more specific. For example:

> **Das Museum ist auf der linken Seite.** (dâs moo-*zey*-oom ist ouf dêr *lin*-ken *zay*-te.) (*The museum is on the left side.*)

> **Die Bank ist auf der rechten Seite.** (dee bânk ist ouf dêr *rêHt*-en *zay*-te.) (*The bank is on the right side.*)

The cardinal points

Instead of using left, right, or straight ahead, some folks give directions using the points of the compass (also called the cardinal points). These points are

- **der Norden** (dêr *nor*-den) (*the north*)
- **der Süden** (dêr *zue*-den) (*the south*)
- **der Osten** (dêr *os*-ten) (*the east*)
- **der Westen** (dêr *wês*-ten) (*the west*)

If someone uses cardinal points to tell you the specific location of a place, you may hear something like

> **Der Hafen liegt im Norden** (dêr *hah*-fen leekt im *nor*-den) / **Süden** (*zue*-den) / **Osten** (*os*-ten) / **Westen** (*wês*-ten). (*The harbor lies [is] in the north / south / east / west.*

To describe a location, for example, in the north, you use the preposition **in** with a definite article in the dative case. When the definite article is masculine (**der**) or neuter (**das**), it changes to **dem**, and the preposition **in** usually contracts to **im** like this: **in** + **dem** = **im**.

Taking This or That Street

When you ask for directions, you may get the answer that you should take a specific street — the second street on the left or the first street on the right, for example. (The next section talks more about ordinals — first, second, and so on.)

The verbs you need to be familiar with in this context are **gehen** (*gey*-en) (*to go*) and **nehmen** (*ney*-men) (*to take*). In order to give directions, you use the imperative. (For the moment, just focus on the word order. You find out more about imperative sentences — those that give commands — in Chapter 14.) With the imperative, the verb goes at the beginning of the sentence. For example:

> **Nehmen Sie die zweite Straße links.** (*ney*-men zee dee *tsvay*-te *shtrah*-se links.) (*Take the second street on the left.*)

> **Gehen Sie die erste Straße rechts.** (*gey*-en zee dee *êrs*-te *shtrah*-se rêHts.) (*Go down the first street on the right.*)

And if you simply have to go straight ahead, the person may give you these instructions:

> **Gehen Sie geradeaus.** (*gey*-en zee ge-rah-de-*ous*.) (*Go straight ahead.*)

If you're looking for a specific building, you may hear something like:

> **Es ist das dritte Haus auf der linken Seite.** (ês ist dâs *drit*-e house [as in English] ouf dêr *lin*-ken *zay*-te.) (*It is the third house on the left side.*)

Using Ordinal Numbers: First, Second, Third, and More

One, two, and three are referred to as *cardinal numbers*. Numbers like first, second, third, fourth, and so on are called *ordinal numbers*. They indicate the specific order of something. For example, to answer the question "Which house?" you use an ordinal number to say, "The second house on the left."

In German, you form ordinal numbers by adding the suffix **-te** to the cardinal numbers for numbers between 1 and 19 — with the following exceptions:

- ✔ **eins** (ayns) (*one*) / **erste** (*êrs*-te) (*first*)
- ✔ **drei** (dray) (*three*) / **dritte** (*drit*-e) (*third*)
- ✔ **sieben** (*zee*-ben) (seven) / **siebte** (*zeep*-te) (*seventh*)
- ✔ **acht** (âHt) (*eight*) / **achte** (*âHt*-e) (*eighth*)

Ordinals 20 and above all add the suffix **-ste** to the cardinal number. Table 7-2 shows how to form the ordinal numbers 1 through 10, including one example of an ordinal number formed with a "-teen" number and another example for an ordinal above 20.

Table 7-2	Sample Cardinal and Ordinal Numbers
Cardinal Number	*Ordinal Number*
eins (ayns) (*one*)	**der / die / das erste** (*êrs*-te) (*first*)
zwei (tsvay) (*two*)	**zweite** (*tsvay*-te) (*second*)
drei (dray) (*three*)	**dritte** (*drit*-e) (*third*)
vier (feer) (*four*)	**vierte** (*feer*-te) (*fourth*)
fünf (fuenf) (*five*)	**fünfte** (*fuenf*-te) (*fifth*)
sechs (zêks) (*six*)	**sechste** (*zêks*-te) (*sixth*)
sieben (*zeeb*-en) (*seven*)	**siebte** (*zeep*-te) (*seventh*)
acht (âHt) (*eight*)	**achte** (*âHt*-e) (*eighth*)
neun (noyn) (*nine*)	**neunte** (*noyn*-te) (*ninth*)
zehn (tseyn) (*ten*)	**zehnte** (*tseyn*-te) (*tenth*)
siebzehn (*zeep*-tseyn) (*seventeen*)	**siebzehnte** (*zeep*-tseyn-te) (*seventeenth*)
vierzig (*fir*-tsiH) (*forty*)	**vierzigste** (*fir*-tsiH-ste) (*fortieth*)

See Chapter 4 for a list of the cardinal numbers.

Because they're used like adjectives, the ordinal numbers take the gender and case of the noun they refer to. Table 7-3 shows you how the adjective **erste** changes in each case along with the article that comes before it.

Table 7-3	Declining a Sample Ordinal Number: Erste (êrs-te) (first)			
Noun's Gender	*Nominative*	*Genitive*	*Dative*	*Accusative*
Masculine (**der**)	der erste	des ersten	dem ersten	den ersten
Feminine (**die**)	die erste	der ersten	der ersten	die erste
Neuter (**das**)	das erste	des ersten	dem ersten	das erste
Plural (**die**)	die ersten	der ersten	den ersten	die ersten

Talkin' the Talk

 Erika is in town on business and wants to meet an old friend who also happens to be in town on business. She has the address of the hotel her friend is staying at, but she isn't sure where the street is located, so she asks for help. (Track 16)

Erika: **Entschuldigung?**
ênt-*shool*-di-goong?
Excuse me?

Mann: **Ja, bitte?**
yah, *bi*-te?
Yes, please?

Erika : **Wie komme ich zur Beethovenstraße?**
vee *kom*-e iH tsoor *bey*-toh-fên-shtrah-se?
How do I get to Beethoven Street?

Mann: **Nehmen Sie die U-Bahn am Opernplatz.**
ney-men zee dee *ooh*-bahn âm *oh*-pêrn-plâts.
You have to take the subway at Opera Square.

Erika: **Und wo ist der Opernplatz?**
oont voh ist dêr *oh*-pêrn-plâts?
And where is Opera Square?

Mann: **Gehen Sie die Wodanstraße geradeaus. Dann gehen Sie links in die Reuterstraße. Rechts liegt die Post und direkt gegenüber ist der Opernplatz.**
gey-en zee dee *voh*-dahn-shtrah-se ge-rah-de-*ous*. dân *gey*-en zee links in dee *roy*-ter-shtrah-se. rêHts leekt dee post oont dee-*rêkt gey*-gen-*ue*-ber ist dêr *oh*-pêrn-plâts.
Go straight down Wodan Street. Then go left onto Reuter Street. On the right you see the post office and directly opposite is Opera Square.

Erika: **Und welche U-Bahn nehme ich?**
oont *vêlH*-e *ooh*-bahn *ney*-me iH?
And which subway do I take?

Mann: **Die U5 bis zur Station Beethovenstraße.**
dee ooh fuenf bis tsoor *shtat*-tsee-ohn *bey*-toh-fên-shtrah-se.
Take the subway 5 to the stop Beethoven Street.

Erika: **Vielen Dank!**
fee-len dânk!
Thank you very much!

Words to Know

links	links	left
rechts	rêHts	right
Wo ist . . . ?	voh ist . . . ?	Where is . . . ?
Nehmen Sie . . .	ney-men zee . . .	Take . . .
Gehen Sie . . .	gey-en zee . . .	Go . . .
die U-Bahn	dee ooh-bahn	subway

Traveling by Car or Other Vehicle

In English, it doesn't make a big difference whether you're going by car or on foot — distance aside, you're still going somewhere. However, the German verb **gehen** (*gey*-en) (*to go*) isn't that flexible. You may "go" on foot, which would require **zu Fuß gehen** (tsooh foohs *gey*-en). But if you take the car, the bus, or another form of transportation, you're "driving," which takes **fahren** (*fahr*-en) — not **gehen** — even if you aren't behind the wheel.

When using **fahren** in a sentence, you need three things: the word for the type of vehicle in which you're traveling, the preposition **mit** (mit) (*with*), and the dative version of the vehicle's article. Here's an example of how you use the verb **fahren** in a sentence to say that you're taking a specific kind of transportation:

> **Ich fahre mit dem Auto.** (iH *fahr*-e mit deym *ou*-toh.) (*I'm going by car. Literally: I'm driving with the car.*)

You don't need to be driving a car to use the following words and phrases about turning left and right. You can use them to describe turns you make on a bike, inline skates, a snowboard, and so on.

To tell somebody to make a left or right turn, you can use your old friend, the verb **fahren**. You say

> **Fahren Sie links / rechts.** (*fahr*-en zee links / rêHts.) (*Go left / right. Literally: Drive left / right.*)

If you get lost driving around, always remember to pull this expression from your memory:

> **Ich habe mich verfahren. Ich suche . . .** (iH *hah*-be miH fêr-*fahr*-en. iH *zoohH*-e . . .) (*I've lost my way. I'm looking for . . .*)

See Chapter 15 for more information on words you need for getting around in a car or other vehicle.

Talkin' the Talk

Paula has rented a car to go to Frankfurt for a day trip. She's on her way to Bockenheim, a district of Frankfurt, and she stops at a gas station to ask for directions.

Paula: **Entschuldigen Sie, wie komme ich nach Bockenheim?**
ênt-*shool*-di-gên zee, vee *kom*-e iH nahH
bok-en-haym?
Excuse me, how do I get to Bockenheim?

Tankwart: **Nehmen Sie die Ausfahrt Frankfurt-Messe. Das sind ungefähr vier Kilometer von hier.**
ney-men zee dee *ous*-fahrt *frânk*-foort *mês*-e. Dâs zint *oon*-ge-fair feer ki-lo-*mey*-ter fon heer.
Take the exit Frankfurt-Messe. That is approximately 4 kilometers from here.

Paula: **Alles klar! Danke.**
âl-es klahr! *dân*-ke.
Okay! Thank you.

Paula makes it to Bockenheim but then seems to have lost her way. She stops her car and asks a policeman for directions.

Paula: **Entschuldigen Sie, ich habe mich verfahren. Ich suche den Hessenplatz.**
ênt-*shool*-di-gên zee, iH *hah*-be miH fêr-*fahr*-en. iH *zoohH*-e deyn *hês*-ên-plâts.
Excuse me, I've lost my way. I'm looking for Hessen Square.

Polizei: **An der nächsten Kreuzung fahren Sie rechts. Dann fahren Sie geradeaus, ungefähr einen Kilometer. Der Hessenplatz liegt auf der linken Seite.**
ân dêr *naiH*-sten *kroy*-tsoong *fahr*-en zee rêHts. dân *fahr*-en zee ge-rah-de-*ous*, *oon*-ge-fair *ayn*-en ki-lo-*mey*-ter. dêr *hês*-en-plâts leekt ouf dêr *lin*-ken *zay*-te.
Go left at the next intersection. Then go straight on, approximately one kilometer. Hessen Square is on the left side.

Paula: **Vielen Dank!**
fee-len *dânk*!
Thank you very much!

Match the descriptions to the pictures.

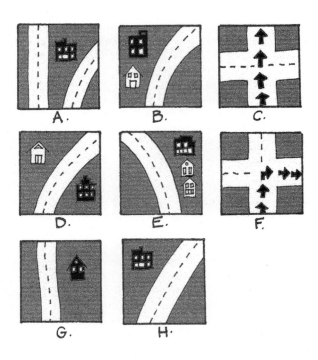

1._____Das Haus ist direkt gegenüber.

2._____Das Haus ist auf der rechten Seite.

3._____Es ist das dritte Haus auf der rechten Seite.

4._____Fahren Sie geradeaus.

5._____Das Haus ist auf der linken Seite.

6._____Es ist das zweite Haus auf der linken Seite.

7._____Das Haus ist zwischen den zwei Straßen.

8._____Biegen Sie rechts ab.

Chapter 8

Guten Appetit! Dining Out and Going to the Market

In This Chapter

▶ Talking about hunger, thirst, and meals
▶ Navigating a restaurant or other eatery
▶ Buying food at a grocery store or other shop

*F*inding out about the food and eating habits in another country is one of the most interesting — and tasty — ways of learning about its culture. Whether you're interested in having a business lunch, enjoying a casual dinner, or cooking for yourself, this chapter helps you find your way around food.

When eating out in German-speaking Europe, you'll likely notice that the food variety isn't much different from what you're used to. A typical German meal consists of meat, potatoes, and vegetables or a salad, and it isn't particularly fancy. However, local cuisines vary from region to region. We suggest you try them. In addition, you're also likely to find a surprisingly wide variety of authentic international cuisines, ranging from Spanish to Sicilian, Portuguese to Philippine, and Turkish to Tibetan.

Whatever your meal, remember to say **Guten Appetit** (*gooh*-ten âp-e-*teet*) (*enjoy your meal*) as the Germans do with each other before they start to eat!

Hast du Hunger? Hast du Durst?

When it comes to food, expressing your hunger and thirst are important! Otherwise, you have no cure for your grumbling stomach and parched throat. Here's how you talk about being hungry or thirsty in German:

Ich habe Hunger / Durst. (iH *hah*-be *hoong*-er / doorst.) (*I am hungry / thirsty.* Literally: *I have hunger/thirst.*)

Ich bin hungrig / durstig. (iH bin *hoong*-riH / *door*-stiH.) (*I am hungry / thirsty.*)

To satisfy your hunger or thirst, you have to eat — **essen** (*ês*-en) — and to drink — **trinken** (*trin*-ken). Here are the conjugations for **essen**, which is an irregular verb, and **trinken** (see Chapter 2 for more information on conjugating verbs):

Conjugation	*Pronunciation*
ich esse	iH *ês*-e
du isst (singular, informal)	dooh ist
Sie essen (singular, formal)	zee *ês*-en
er, sie, es isst	êr, zee, ês ist
wir essen	veer *ês*-en
ihr esst (plural, informal)	eer êst
Sie essen (plural, formal)	zee *ês*-en
sie essen	zee *ês*-en

Conjugation	*Pronunciation*
ich trinke	iH *trin*-ke
du trinkst (singular, informal)	dooh trinkst
Sie trinken (singular, formal)	zee *trin*-ken
er, sie, es trinkt	êr, zee, ês trinkt
wir trinken	veer *trin*-ken
ihr trinkt (plural, informal)	eer trinkt
Sie trinken (plural, formal)	zee *trin*-ken
sie trinken	zee *trin*-ken

Here are two examples using **essen** and **trinken**:

Wir essen gern Fisch. (veer *ês*-en gêrn fish.) (*We like to eat fish.*)

Trinkst du Bier? (trinkst dooh beer?) (*Do you drink beer?*)

All about Meals

German meals and meal times don't differ too much from their American counterparts. The three **Mahlzeiten** (*mahl*-tsayt-en) (*meals*) of the day are the following:

- ✔ **das Frühstück** (dâs *frue*-shtuek) (*breakfast*)

- ✔ **das Mittagessen** (dâs *mi*-tahk-ês-en) (*lunch*)

- ✔ **das Abendessen** (dâs *ah*-bent-ês-en) (*dinner*)

In most cafés and hotels, breakfast is served from 7 a.m. to 10 a.m., and it's often more substantial than the typical continental breakfast. Lunch is usually served between 11:30 a.m. and 2:00 p.m. For some Germans, lunch is the main meal of the day; for others the main meal comes at dinnertime. In restaurants, a full menu generally is available between 6:30 and 9:00 p.m. In larger cities and restaurants, a full menu may be served until 11 p.m. In addition, fast food places abound, including several well-known American hamburger restaurant chains, where, interestingly, you can order beer.

The traditional cold evening meal in German homes consists of bread with cold meats, cheeses, salad, and other cold dishes. This same fare is what families and friends in southern Germany have at the local **Biergarten** (dêr *beer*-gâr-ten) (*beer garden*), where they spread their food out on a picnic table and enjoy warm summer evenings with **eine Maß Bier** (*ayn*-e mahs beer [as in English]) (*a liter of beer*).

You may occasionally hear people say **Mahlzeit!** (*mahl*-tsayt) as a greeting at lunchtime. Roughly translated, the word means *mealtime* in English, and there is no equivalent greeting in English. This greeting is especially common among colleagues at the workplace. If someone says this to you, just say the same — **Mahlzeit!** — and smile.

Setting the Table for a Meal

The German table features all the same items that you find on your table at home, including the following:

- ✔ **das Glas** (dâs glahs) (*glass*)

- ✔ **die Tasse** (dee *tâs*-e) (*cup*)

- ✔ **der Teller** (dêr *têl*-er) (*plate*)

- **der Suppenteller** (dêr *zoop*-en-*têl*-er) (*soup bowl*)

- **die Serviette** (dee sêr-vee-êt-e) (*napkin*)

- **das Messer** (dâs *mês*-er) (*knife*)

- **die Gabel** (dee *gah*-bel) (*fork*)

- **der Löffel** (dêr *ler*-fel) (*spoon*)

- **das Besteck** (dâs be-*shtêk*) (*a set of a knife, fork, and spoon*)

If you're in a restaurant and need an item not found on the table (for example, a spoon, fork, or knife), call the waiter over by saying

Entschuldigen Sie bitte! (ênt-*shool*-di-gen zee *bi*-te!) (*Excuse me, please!*)

After you get the waiter's attention, ask for what you need:

Kann ich bitte einen Löffel / eine Gabel / ein Messer haben? (kân iH *bi*-te *ayn*-en *ler*-fel / *ayn*-e *gah*-bel / ayn mês-er *hah*-ben?) (*Can I please have a spoon / a fork / a knife?*)

Dining Out: Visiting a Restaurant

Eating out is quite popular in Germany, and you'll find little difference between going out to a restaurant in Germany and going to one in the U.S. Just a few minor differences exist. For instance, in many German restaurants, you don't have to wait to be seated as you do in the U.S. However, the waiter or waitress in more upscale places usually takes you to your table. Also, doggie bags aren't common practice in Germany. But, surprisingly, dogs are generally welcome in many restaurants if they sit under the table.

Europeans in general place great value on the dining experience. You can expect a more leisurely pace while enjoying your meal in Europe. In fact, don't expect to see the check after you've finished your meal — you have to ask for it.

In the following sections, we help you become acquainted with dining out so you get the most from your experience.

Deciding where to eat

Most German eateries post a menu (see Figure 8-1) at their entrances, making it easy to tell what kind of dining experience you can get there. This display is helpful when you're wandering around looking for a place to eat. However, if you want to ask someone about a particular kind of eatery, it helps to know what different kinds are available. Here are the most common ones:

- ✔ **das Restaurant** (dâs rês-tuh-*ron*) (*restaurant*): You can find a similar variety of restaurants in Germany that you can in the U.S., ranging from simple to fancy establishments with corresponding menus and prices.

- ✔ **die Gaststätte** (dee *gâst*-shtêt-e) (*local type of restaurant*): This restaurant is a simpler type where you're likely to find local specialties.

- ✔ **das Gasthaus** (dâs *gâst*-hous) / **der Gasthof** (dêr *gâst*-hohf) (*inn*): You usually find these inns in the country. They often offer home cooking, and the atmosphere may be rather folksy. In rural areas, some offer lodging.

- ✔ **die Raststätte** (dee *râst*-shtêt-e) (*roadside restaurant*): These restaurants usually are found on the Autobahn and have service station facilities and sometimes lodging. *Note:* In Austria, these restaurants are called **der Rasthof** (dêr *râst*-hohf).

- ✔ **der Ratskeller** (dêr *rahts*-kêl-er): This type of restaurant is named after an eatery in the **Keller** (*kêl*-er) (*cellar*) of the **Rathaus** (*raht*-hous) (*town hall*). You often find these in historic buildings.

- ✔ **die Bierhalle** (dee *beer*-hâl-e) / **die Bierstube** (dee *beer*-shtooh-be) (*beer hall*): Beer halls, of course, specialize in beer served from huge barrels. But, besides beer, you can also order hot dishes (usually deciding among a few dishes of the day), salads, and pretzels. The best-known beer halls are in Munich, Bavaria, where the **Oktoberfest** (ok-*toh*-ber-fêst) takes place for two weeks beginning in late September. At this event, each Munich brewery sets up a massive **Bierzelt** (*beer*-tsêlt) (*beer tent*).

- ✔ **die Weinstube** (dee *vayn*-shtooh-be) (*wine bar*): At this cozy restaurant, often found in wine-producing areas, you can sample wine with bar food and snacks.

- ✔ **die Kneipe** (dee *knayp*-e) (*bar-restaurant*): This type of bar-restaurant combination is similar to what you may find in the U.S. You usually find a casual atmosphere here where the locals hang out.

- ✔ **das Café** (dâs café [as in English]) (*café*): Cafés may range from places to have **Kaffee und Kuchen** (*kâf*-ey oont *koohH*-en) (*coffee and cake*) to upscale establishments with full menus. Vienna's café tradition is famous. In these cafés, you can sit down for a leisurely cup of fine coffee and read the newspaper.

- ✔ **der (Schnell)imbiss** (dêr (*shnêl*-)im-bis) (*snack bar, fast-food restaurant*): Here you can get food like **Wurst** (woorst) (*sausage*) and **Pommes frites** (pom frit) (*french fries*).

───────── Gasthaus zum Löwen ─────────

Speisekarte

Vorspeisen	(fohr-shpayz-en)	
Gemischter Salat	(ge-mish-ter zä-laht)	4,00 €
Grüner Salat	(gruen-er zä-laht)	3,50 €
Melone mit Schinken	(mê-loh-ne mit shin-ken)	5,20 €
Meeresfrüchtesalat mit Toast	(mey-res-frueH-te-zä-laht mit tohst)	6,50 €

Suppen	(zoop-en)	
Tomatensuppe	(toh-mah-ten-zoop-e)	3,00 €
Kartoffelcremesuppe	(kär-to-fel-kreym-zoop-e)	3,80 €
Gulaschsuppe	(gooh-lash-zoop-e)	6,20 €
Französische Zwiebelsuppe	(frän-tser-zi-she tsvee-bel-zoop-e)	5,50 €

Hauptspeisen	(houpt-shpayz-en)	
Gefüllte Hühnerbrust mit Kartoffelpüree	(ge-fuel-te huen-er-broost mit kär-to-fel-puer-ey)	9,50 €
Frischer Spargel mit Räucherschinken	(fri-sher shpär-gel mit royH-er-shin-ken)	12,90 €
Rumpsteak mit Pommes Frites und gemischtem Salat	(roomp-steak mit pom frit oont ge-mish-tem zä-laht)	14,50 €

───────── Gasthaus zum Löwen ─────────

Menu

Appetizers	
Mixed salad	4,00 €
Green salad	3,50 €
Melon with ham	5,20 €
Seafood salad with toast	6,50 €

Soups	
Tomato soup	3,00 €
Cream of potato soup	3,80 €
Hearty beef/pork soup	6,20 €
French onion soup	5,50 €

Main Dishes	
Stuffed chicken breast with mashed potatoes	9,50 €
Fresh asparagus with smoked ham	12,90 €
Rump steak with french fries and mixed salad	14,50 €

Figure 8-1:
German restaurants typically post a menu near the door.

Making reservations

Making reservations isn't always necessary in Germany. In fact, during the week you may be able to get a table without a reservation — unless you're going to a particularly trendy place or one with limited seating. You usually don't make reservations at a **Kneipe** or **Gaststätte** — you get a table on a first-come-first-served basis. However, when you want to be on the safe side, call ahead to make a reservation.

When making a reservation, consider using the following expressions:

> **Ich möchte gern einen Tisch reservieren / bestellen.** (iH *merH*-te gêrn *ayn*-en tish rê-zêr-*vee*-ren / be-*shtêl*-en.) (*I would like to reserve a table.*)

> **Haben Sie um . . . Uhr einen Tisch frei?** (*hah*-ben zee oom . . . oohr *ayn*-en tish fray?) (*Do you have a table free at . . . o'clock?*)

> **Ich möchte gern einen Tisch für . . . Personen um . . . Uhr.** (iH *merH*-te gêrn *ayn*-en tish fuer . . . pêr-*zohn*-en oom . . . oohr.) (*I would like a table for . . . people at . . . o'clock.*)

To get more specific about when you want the reservation, you can add the specific day of the week to your request, or one of the following appropriate phrases:

> ✔ **am Freitag Abend** (âm *fray*-tahk *ah*-bent) (*on Friday evening*)
>
> ✔ **heute Abend** (*hoy*-te *ah*-bent) (*this evening*)
>
> ✔ **morgen Abend** (*mor*-gen *ah*-bent) (*tomorrow evening*)
>
> ✔ **heute Mittag** (*hoy*-te *mi*-tahk) (*today at lunchtime*)
>
> ✔ **morgen Mittag** (*mor*-gen *mi*-tahk) (*tomorrow at lunchtime*)

So here's what you may say:

Ich möchte gern für heute Abend einen Tisch reservieren. (iH *merH*-te gêrn fuer *hoy*-te *ah*-bent *ayn*-en tish rê-zêr-*vee*-ren.) (*I would like to reserve a table for this evening.*)

Haben Sie am Sonntag Abend um . . . Uhr einen Tisch frei? (*hah*-ben zee âm *zon*-tahk *ah*-bent oom . . . oohr *ayn*-en tish fray?) (*Do you have a table free on Sunday evening at . . . o'clock?*)

Talkin' the Talk

Mike and his friend Ute want to check out the trendy new Restaurant Galleria. Mike calls the restaurant to make a reservation.

Restaurant: **Restaurant Galleria.**
rês-tuh-*ron* gâ-le-*ree*-â.
Restaurant Galleria.

Mike: **Guten Tag. Ich möchte gern einen Tisch für heute Abend bestellen.**
gooh-ten tahk. iH *merH*-te gêrn *ayn*-en tish fuer *hoy*-te *ah*-bent be-*shtêl*-en.
Hello. I would like to reserve a table for this evening.

Restaurant: **Für wie viele Personen?**
fuer vee *fee*-le pêr-*zohn*-en?
For how many people?

Mike: **Zwei Personen, bitte. Haben Sie um acht Uhr einen Tisch frei?**
tsvay pêr-*zohn*-en, *bi*-te. *hah*-ben zee oom âHt oohr *ayn*-en tish fray?
Two people, please. Do you have a table free at eight o'clock?

Restaurant: **Tut mir leid. Um acht Uhr ist alles ausgebucht. Sie können aber um acht Uhr dreißig einen Tisch haben.**
tooht meer layt. oom âHt oohr ist *âl*-ês *ous*-ge-boohHt. zee *kern*-en *ah*-bêr oom âHt oohr *dray*-siH *ayn*-en tish *hah*-ben.
I'm sorry. At 8:00 everything's booked. But you could have a table at 8:30.

Mike: **Acht Uhr dreißig wäre auch gut.**
âHt oohr *dray*-siH *vai*-re ouH gooht.
8:30 would be good, too.

Restaurant: **Und Ihr Name, bitte?**
oont eer *nah*-me, *bi*-te?
And your name, please?

Mike: **Evans.**
evans [as in English].
Evans.

Restaurant: **Geht in Ordnung, ich habe den Tisch für Sie reserviert.**
geyt in *ort*-noong, iH *hah*-be deyn tish fuer zee rê-zêr-*veert*.
That's all set. I have reserved the table for you.

Mike: **Vielen Dank. Bis heute Abend.**
fee-lên dânk. bis *hoy*-te *ah*-bent.
Thank you very much. Until this evening.

Occasionally, you'll call for a reservation and discover that no tables are available. In those instances, you may hear the following:

Es tut mir leid. Wir sind völlig ausgebucht. (ês tooht meer layt. veer zint *fer*-liH *ous*-ge-boohHt.) (*I'm sorry. We are totally booked.*)

If you show up at a busy restaurant without making a reservation, expect to hear one of the following:

In . . . Minuten wird ein Tisch frei. (in . . . mi-*nooh*-ten virt ayn tish fray.) (*In . . . minutes a table will be free.*)

Können Sie in . . . Minuten wiederkommen? (*kern*-en zee in . . . mi-*nooh*-ten *vee*-der-kom-en.) (*Could you come back in . . . minutes?*)

CULTURAL WISDOM

Sharing a table

With the exception of upscale restaurants, in German-speaking Europe, you're bound to notice that sharing a table with strangers is not unusual. Sharing is especially common in places that tend to be crowded and in places with large tables. If seats are still available at the table where you're sitting, someone may ask you **Ist hier noch frei?** (ist heer noH fray?)

(*Is this place still available?*) or **Können wir uns dazu setzen?** (*kern*-en veer oons dâ-*tsooh zêts*-en?) (*May we sit down with you?*). It's a very casual arrangement, and you're not obligated to start up a conversation with the party who's sharing the table with you. Some people may find the lack of privacy a little irritating, but it's also a good opportunity to meet the locals.

Arriving and being seated

When you arrive at a restaurant, you want to take your seat, **Platz nehmen** (plâts *neym*-en) and get your **Speisekarte** (shpayz-e-kâr-tê) (*menu*). In casual restaurants, you seat yourself. In upscale restaurants, a waiter, **der Kellner** (dêr *kêl*-ner), or a waitress, **die Kellnerin** (dee *kêl*-ner-in), directs you to your table.

Talkin' the Talk

Mike and Ute have been looking forward to eating at Restaurant Galleria since Mike made the reservation. They arrive at the restaurant and are seated. (Track 17)

Mike: **Guten Abend. Mein Name ist Evans. Wir haben einen Tisch für zwei Personen bestellt.**
gooh-ten *ah*-bent. mayn *nah*-me ist evans [as in English]. veer *hah*-ben *ayn*-en tish fuer tsvay pêr-*zohn*-en be-*shtêlt*.
Good evening. My name is Evans. We reserved a table for two people.

Kellner: **Guten Abend. Bitte, nehmen Sie hier vorne Platz.**
gooh-ten *ah*-bent. *bi*-te, *neym*-en zee heer *forn*-e plâts.
Good evening. Please take a seat over here.

Ute: **Könnten wir vielleicht den Tisch dort drüben am Fenster haben?**
kern-ten veer *fee*-layHt deyn tish dort *drue*-ben âm *fên*-ster *hah*-ben?
Could we perhaps have the table over there by the window?

Kellner:	**Aber sicher, kein Problem. Setzen Sie sich. Ich bringe Ihnen sofort die Speisekarte.**
	ah-ber *ziH*-er, kayn pro-*bleym*. *zêts*-en zee ziH. iH *bring*-e *een*-en zo-*fort* dee *shpayz*-e-kâr-te.
	But of course, no problem. Have a seat. I'll bring you the menu right away.

Words to Know

bringen	bring-en	to bring
vielleicht	fee-layHt	perhaps
hier vorne'	heer forn-e	over here
dort drüben	dort drue-ben	over there
Setzen Sie sich.	zêts-én zee ziH.	Have a seat.
Tut mir leid!	tooht meer layt!	I'm sorry!
Geht in Ordnung!	geyt in ort-noong!	That's all set.

Deciphering the menu

After you decide where to eat and how to get a reservation and table, you're ready for the fun part — deciding what you want to eat! Of course, what's on the menu depends entirely on what kind of place you go to. Unlike in the U.S., the prices shown on a German menu normally include taxes and service.

If you go to a French, Spanish, or Chinese restaurant, the menu may be in the language of the respective country, with a German translation below the original name of the dish. In popular tourist areas, you may even find an English translation.

The following sections tell you about foods you may find in European restaurants. Keep in mind, however, that these sections don't tell you about local cuisine, which differs substantially from region to region;

many areas have their local specialties. For example, there are certain regional dishes that you would commonly find on the menu in Bavaria or southern Germany but never in Hamburg or the northern parts of the country. Austria and Switzerland also have their own regional specialties.

Breakfast

The following items may be offered **zum Frühstück** (tsoom *frue*-shtuek) (*for breakfast*) in a German-speaking country:

- **das Brot** (dâs broht) (*bread*)
- **das Brötchen** (dâs *brert*-Hên) (*roll*)
- **der Toast** (dêr tohst) (*toast*)
- **der Aufschnitt** (dêr *ouf*-shnit) (*cold meats and cheese*)
- **die Butter** (dee *boot*-er) (*butter*)
- **die Marmelade** (dee mâr-me-*lah*-de) (*marmelade, jam*)
- **das Müsli** (dâs *mues*-lee) (*muesli*)
- **die Milch** (dee milH) (*milk*)
- **der Saft** (dêr zâft) (*juice*)
- **die Wurst** (dee voorst) (*sausage*)
- **das Ei** (dâs ay) (*egg*)
- **das Spiegelei** (dâs *shpee*-gêl-ay) (*fried egg, sunny side up*)
- **die Rühreier** (dee *ruehr*-ay-er) (*scrambled eggs*)

In Germany, **Brötchen** are popular for breakfast; however, you also may get all kinds of bread or croissants. It's also common to eat cold cuts for breakfast in Germany. And if you order an egg without specifying that you want it scrambled or sunny side up, you'll get it soft-boiled, served in an egg cup.

Appetizers

For **Vorspeisen** (*fohr*-shpayz-en) (*appetizers*), you may see the following German favorites:

- **Gemischter Salat** (ge-*mish*-ter zâ-*laht*) (*mixed salad*)
- **Grüner Salat** (*gruen*-er zâ-*laht*) (*green salad*)
- **Melone mit Schinken** (mê-*loh*-ne mit *shin*-ken) (*melon with ham*)
- **Meeresfrüchtesalat mit Toast** (*meyr*-es-frueH-te-zâ-laht mit tohst) (*seafood salad with toast*)

Soups

You may see the following **Suppen** (*zoop*-en) (*soups*) on a German menu:

- **Tomatensuppe** (to-*mah*-ten-zoop-e) (*tomato soup*)
- **Kartoffelcremesuppe** (kâr-*tof*-el-kreym-zoop-e) (*cream of potato soup*)
- **Gulaschsuppe** (*gooh*-lash-zoop-e) (*hearty beef and occasionally pork soup*)
- **Französische Zwiebelsuppe** (frân-*tser*-zi-she *tsvee*-bel-zoop-e) (*French onion soup*)

Main dishes

Hauptspeisen (*houpt*-shpayz-en) (*main dishes*) are as diverse in Germany as they are in any culture; here are some you may find on a German menu:

- **gefüllte Hühnerbrust mit Kartoffelpüree** (ge-*fuel*-te *huen*-er-broost mit kâr-*tof*-el-puer-ey) (*stuffed chicken breast with mashed potatoes*)
- **Frischer Spargel mit Räucherschinken** (*frish*-er *shpâr*-gel mit *royH*-er-shin-ken) (*fresh asparagus with smoked ham*)
- **Rumpsteak mit Pommes Frites und gemischtem Salat** (*roomp*-steak mit pom frit oont ge-*mish*-tem zâ-*laht*) (*rump steak with french fries and mixed salad*)
- **Kalbsschnitzel nach Art des Hauses** (*kâlps*-shnits-el nahH ârt dês *houz*-es) (*chef's style veal cutlet*)
- **Lammfrikassee mit Reis** (lâm-frik-â-sey mit rays) (*lamb fricassee with rice*)
- **Lachs an Safransoße mit Spinat und Salzkartoffeln** (lâks ân *zâf*-rahn-zohs-e mit shpi-*naht* oont *zâlts*-kâr-tof-eln) (*salmon in saffron sauce with spinach and boiled potatoes*)
- **Fisch des Tages** (fish dês *tah*-ges) (*fish of the day*)

Side dishes

You can sometimes order **Beilagen** (*bay*-lah-gen) (*side dishes*) separately from your main course. Consider the following popular items:

- **Butterbohnen** (*boot*-er-bohn-en) (*buttered beans*)
- **Gurkensalat** (*goork*-en-zâ-laht) (*cucumber salad*)
- **Kartoffelkroketten** (kâr-*tof*-el-kroh-ket-en) (*potato croquettes*)

Dessert

German restaurants commonly offer many fine dishes **zum Nachtisch** (tsoom *naH*-tish) (*for dessert*), including the following:

- **Frischer Obstsalat** (*frish*-er *ohpst*-zâ-laht) (*fresh fruit salad*)
- **Apfelstrudel** (*âp*-fel-shtrooh-del) (*apple strudel*)
- **Gemischtes Eis mit Sahne** (ge-*mish*-tes ays mit *zahn*-e) (*mixed ice cream with whipped cream*)
- **Rote Grütze mit Vanillesoße** (*roh*-te *grue*-tse mit vâ-*ni*-le-zohs-e) (*red berry compote with vanilla sauce*)

Beverages

When it comes to ordering **Wasser** (*vâs*-er) (*water*), you have the choice between the carbonated or noncarbonated one — **ein Wasser mit Kohlensäure** (ayn *vâs*-er mit *koh*-len-zoy-re) (*carbonated water*) or **ein Wasser ohne Kohlensäure** (ayn *vâs*-er *oh*-ne *koh*-len-zoy-re) (*noncarbonated water*). If you ask the waiter or waitress for **ein Mineralwasser** (ayn min-êr-*ahl*-vâs-êr) (*mineral water*), you usually get carbonated water. Germans usually don't drink **Leitungswasser** (*lay*-toongs-*vâs*-er) (*tap water*) in restaurants. However, if you'd like a glass of tap water, you can say this:

> **ein Glas Leitungswasser, bitte.** (ayn glahs *lay*-toongs-vâs-er, *bi*-te.) (*a glass of tap water, please.*)

You can order **Wein** (vayn) (*wine*) by the bottle — **die Flasche** (dee *flâsh*-e) — or by the glass — **das Glas** (dâs glahs). Occasionally, you also can get a carafe of wine, which is **die Karaffe** (dee kah-*râf*-e).

In the following list, you find some common beverages, **Getränke** (gê-*train*-ke), that you may see on a German menu:

- **Bier** (beer [as in English]) (*beer*)
- **das Export** (dâs export [as in English]) (*smooth lager beer*)
- **das Bier vom Fass** (dâs beer fom fâs) (*draft beer*)
- **das Pils / Pilsner** (dâs pils / pilsner [as in English]) (*pale lager beer*)
- **helles / dunkles Bier** (*hel*-es / *dunk*-les beer) (*light / dark beer*) (**Helles** refers to the beer's light color, not its alcoholic content.)
- **Wein** (vayn) (*wine*)
- **der Weißwein** (dêr *vays*-vayn) (*white wine*)
- **der Rotwein** (dêr *roht*-vayn) (*red wine*)

✔ **der Tafelwein** (dêr *tahf*-el-vayn) (*table wine, lowest quality*)

✔ **der Kaffee** (dêr *kâf*-ê) (*coffee*)

✔ **der Tee** (dêr tey) (*tea*)

Placing your order

As in English, in German you use a variety of common expressions to order your food. Luckily, they aren't too complicated, and you can use them both for ordering anything from food to drinks and for buying food at a store. Consider these expressions:

Ich hätte gern . . . (iH *hêt*-e gêrn . . .) (*I would like to have . . .*)

Für mich bitte . . . (fuer miH *bi*-te . . .) (*For me . . . please*)

Ich möchte gern . . . (iH *merH*-te gêrn . . .) (*I would like to have . . .*)

When ordering, you may decide to be adventurous and ask the waiter or waitress to suggest something for you. Here's how:

Könnten Sie etwas empfehlen? (kern-ten zee *êt*-vâs êm-*pfey*-len?) (*Could you recommend something?*)

Be prepared for your waiter or waitress to rattle off names of dishes you may be unfamiliar with. To avoid any confusion, try holding out your menu so he or she can point at it while responding.

Applying the subjunctive to express your wishes

Take a closer look at the verb forms **hätte**, **könnte**, and **möchte** in the previous section. These verbs require you to be able to use the subjunctive.

The *subjunctive* has a number of uses in German, such as describing a wish or condition or expressing your opinion. In the examples in this section, you use it for making polite requests. Basically, the subjunctive acts like the English "would."

Ich hätte . . . (iH *hêt*-e . . .) (*I would have . . .*) comes from **haben** (*hah*-ben) (*to have*). The big difference here between the German and the English usage is that in German you can combine "would" and "have" into one word: **hätte**.

Add **gern** to **hätte** and presto! You have the form for ordering: **Ich hätte gern . . .** (iH *hêt*-e gêrn) (*I would like to have . . .*)

You also have **Ich möchte . . .** (iH *merH*-te . . .) (*I would like . . .*), which comes from **mögen** (*mer*-gen) (*to like*). It's quite simple: **möchte** basically corresponds to the English "would like." You use it in a similar way when ordering. Consider the following example:

> **Ich möchte gern ein Glas Mineralwasser.** (iH *merH*-te gêrn ayn glahs min-êr-*ahl*-vâs-er.) (*I would like a glass of mineral water.*)

Both **hätte** and **möchte** are commonly used without the infinitive of a verb.

The phrase **Ich könnte . . .** (iH *kern*-te . . .) (*I could . . .*) comes from the verb **können** (*kern*-en) (*to be able to or can*). **Könnte** combines with the infinitive of a verb to make the following request:

> **Könnten Sie uns helfen?** (*kern*-ten zee oons *helf*-en?) (*Could you help us?*)

Talkin' the Talk

 Mike and Ute have had a chance to look at the menu. The waiter returns to take their orders. (Track 18)

Kellner:	**Darf ich Ihnen etwas zu trinken bringen?** dârf iH *een*-en êt-vâs tsooh *trin*-ken *bring*-en? *May I bring you something to drink?*
Mike:	**Ja, ich möchte gern ein Bier.** yah, iH *merH*-te gêrn ayn beer. *Yes, I'd like a beer.*
Kellner:	**Pils oder Export?** pils *oh*-der export? *A pils or an export?*
Mike:	**Export, bitte.** export, *bi*-te. *Export, please.*
Kellner:	**Ein Export. Und was darf es für Sie sein?** ayn export. oont vâs dârf ês fuer zee zayn? *One export. And what would you like?*

Ute:	**Mmm . . . Soll ich den Sylvaner oder den Riesling bestellen?**
	Mmm . . . zol iH deyn Sylvaner [as in English] *oh*-der deyn Riesling [as in English] be-*shtêl*-en?
	Mmm. Should I order the Sylvaner or the Riesling?
Kellner:	**Ich kann Ihnen beide Weißweine empfehlen.**
	iH kahn *een*-en *bay*-de *vays*-vayn-e êm-*pfey*-len.
	I can recommend both white wines.
Ute:	**Gut. Ich hätte gern ein Glas Sylvaner.**
	gooht. iH *hêt*-e gêrn ayn glahs Sylvaner.
	Good. I would like to have a glass of Sylvaner.

Using modals to modify what you say

You may want to know a little more about the verbs **darf**, **soll**, and **kann**. Here's the story: These verbs help you further determine or modify the action expressed by another verb (that's why they're called *modal auxiliaries*), and they work in a similar way as their English equivalents "may," "should" and "can." **Möchte**, which we discuss in the preceding section, does double duty as a modal auxiliary and as a subjunctive. You can find the conjugations for these verbs in Appendix B.

Ich darf . . . (iH dârf . . .) (*I may/I'm allowed to . . .*) comes from the verb **dürfen** (*duerf*-en) (*may/to be allowed to*). **Ich soll . . .** (iH zol . . .) (*I should . . .*) comes from the verb **sollen** (*zol*-en) (*should*). **Ich kann . . .** (iH kân . . .) (*I can . . .*) comes from the verb **können** (*kern*-en) (*can*). Here are some example sentences to familiarize you with **darf**, **soll**, and **kann**:

Darf ich die Speisekarte haben? (dârf iH dee *shpayz*-e-kâr-te *hah*-ben?) (*May I have the menu, please?*)

Dürfen wir dort drüben sitzen? (*duerf*-en veer dort *drueb*-en *zits*-en?) (*May we sit over there?*)

Sie sollten den Apfelstrudel bestellen. (zee *zol*-ten den *âp*-fel-shtrooh-del be-*shtêl*-en.) (*You should order the apple strudel.*)

Lighting up

You'll find only a few parts of Europe where smoking in restaurants is still permitted. In Germany, Austria, and Switzerland, you can generally expect public places to be smoke-free nowadays, and that includes restaurants and bars.

How would you like that prepared?

If you order meat — steak, for example — the waiter may ask you **Wie hätten Sie das Steak gern?** (vee *hêt*-en zee dâs steak gêrn?) (*How would you like your steak?*). You can respond with any of the following, depending on your tastes:

✔ **englisch** (*êng*-lish) (*rare*)

✔ **medium** (*mey*-dee-oom) (*medium*)

✔ **durchgebraten** (*doorH*-ge-braht-en) (*well-done*)

Soll ich Ihnen zwei Löffel bringen? (zol iH *een*-en tsvay *ler*-fel *bring*-en?) (*Shall I bring you two spoons?*)

Kann ich bitte eine Serviette haben? (*kân* iH *bi*-te *ayn*-e sêr-vee-*êt*-e *hah*-ben?) (*Can I have a napkin, please?*)

Können Sie uns bitte noch zwei Bier bringen? (*kern*-en zee oons *bi*-te noH tsvay beer *bring*-en?) (*Can you bring us two more beers, please?*)

Ordering something special

People all over the world are now more conscientious than ever about what they're eating, whether due to health or ethical concerns. So you may need the following phrases to order something a little out of the ordinary:

Haben Sie vegetarische Gerichte? (*hah*-ben zee vey-gê-*tahr*-ish-e ge-*riH*-te?) (*Do you have vegetarian dishes?*)

Ich kann nichts essen, was . . . enthält (iH *kân* niHts *ês*-en, vâs . . . *ênt*-hailt) (*I can't eat anything that contains . . .*)

Haben Sie Gerichte für Diabetiker? (*hah*-ben zee ge-*riH*-te fuer dee-â-*bey*-ti-ker?) (*Do you have dishes for diabetics?*)

Haben Sie Kinderportionen? (*hah*-ben zee *kin*-der-por-tsee-ohn-en?) (*Do you have children's portions?*)

Replying to "How did you like the food?"

After a meal, it's traditional for the server to inquire whether you liked the food by asking this question:

Hat es Ihnen geschmeckt? (hât ês *een*-en ge-*shmêkt?*) (*Did you enjoy the food?*)

Asking for your check and tipping your server

Wondering why the server is letting you sit at your table without ever bringing your check? In German-speaking regions, you have to ask for the check if you want to pay. It would be considered pushy and impolite to put the check on your table before you request it. In more casual establishments, such as a **Kneipe**, it's common to simply tell the waiter that you want to pay, and the payment is then made directly at the table, usually with cash. But don't feel like you have to tip as much as you do in North America. The servers receive a salary, and they don't live off their tips. If you're paying cash for the check at your table, just round up the sum of money you're paying by 8 to 10 percent. Consider using the phrase **Stimmt so.** (shtimt zoh.) (*Keep the change.*) It tells the server that the sum added on to the bill is their tip.

Hopefully, you enjoyed your meal and answer the question with one of the following:

- **danke, gut** (*dân*-ke, gooht) (*thanks, good*)
- **sehr gut** (zeyr gooht) (*very good*)
- **ausgezeichnet** (ous-ge-*tsayH*-net) (*excellent*)

Asking for the check

At the end of your meal, your server may ask you the following expression as a way to bring your meal to a close and find out whether you're ready for the check:

> **Sonst noch etwas?** (zonst noH *êt*-vâs?) (*Anything else?*)

Unless you'd like to order something else, it's time to pay **die Rechnung** (*rêH*-noong) (*bill*). You can ask for the bill in the following ways:

> **Ich möchte bezahlen.** (iH *merH*-te be-*tsahl*-en.) (*I would like to pay.*)

> **Die Rechnung, bitte.** (dee *rêH*-noong, *bi*-te.) (*The check, please.*)

If necessary, you can pay together with the other people you're dining with. In that case, use this phrase: **Alles zusammen, bitte.** (*âl*-es tsoo-*zâm*-en, *bi*-te.) (*Everything together, please.*). Or you can ask to pay separately with **Wir möchten getrennt bezahlen.** (veer *merH*-ten ge-*trênt* be-*tsahl*-en.) (*We would like to pay separately.*).

Many German restaurants, especially upscale establishments, allow you to pay with a credit card — **die Kreditkarte** (dee krê-*dit*-kâr-te). These restaurants have signs in the window or one at the door, indicating which cards they take (just as they do in American restaurants). If it's essential for you to pay with a credit card, simply look for these signs.

If you need a **Quittung** (*kvit*-oong) (*receipt*), ask the server for one after you've asked for the check:

> **Und eine Quittung, bitte.** (oont *ayn*-e *kvit*-oong, *bi*-te.) (*And a receipt, please.*)

Talkin' the Talk

Mike and Ute have enjoyed a great meal. They ask for the check, pay, and then tip the waiter. (Track 19)

Mike: **Die Rechnung, bitte.**
dee *rêH*-noong, *bi*-te.
The check, please.

Kellner: **Sofort. Das macht 45 Euro 80.**
zoh-*fort*. dâs mâHt fuenf-oont-*feer*-tsiH *oy*-roh *âHt*-tsiH.
Coming right up. That would be 45 euros 80 cents.

Mike puts 50 euros on the table.

Mike: **Stimmt so.**
shtimt zoh.
Keep the change.

Kellner: **Vielen Dank.**
fee-len dânk.
Thank you very much.

Mike: **Bitte.**
bi-te.
You're welcome.

Words to Know

bezahlen	be-<u>tsahl</u>-en	to pay
die Kreditkarte	dee krê-<u>dit</u>-kâr-te	credit card
die Quittung	dee <u>kvit</u>-oong	receipt
in bar bezahlen	in bâr be-<u>tsahl</u>-en	to pay cash
die Rechnung	dee rêH-noong	bill
Stimmt so!	shtimt zoh!	Keep the change!
Bitte.	<u>bi</u>-te.	You're welcome. / Please.

Shopping for Food

Sometimes you may not feel like eating out. You may prefer to buy food for a picnic or to do the cooking yourself. If you want to shop for food, you need to know where to go and what to buy. The following section provides you with words for types of stores and food. To find out about how to order specific quantities of food, check out the section in Chapter 4 on weights and measurements.

Knowing where to shop

As in the U.S., in Germany you can shop for food at a number of different stores and shops. The following is a list of stores you may visit:

- **das Lebensmittelgeschäft** (dâs *ley*-benz-mit-el-ge-shêft) (*grocery store*)
- **der Supermarkt** (dêr *zooh*-pêr-mârkt) (*supermarket*)
- **der Markt** (dêr mârkt) (*market*)
- **die Metzgerei** (dee mêts-ge-*ray*) (*butcher shop*)

✔ **die Bäckerei** (dee bêk-e-*ray*) (*bakery*)

✔ **die Konditorei** (dee kon-dee-to-*ray*) (*cake and pastry shop*)

✔ **die Weinhandlung** (dee *vayn*-hând-loong) (*wine store*)

You may purchase beer, wine, and other alcoholic beverages in German super-markets, grocery stores, discount stores, and even some gas stations. Large train stations may also have stores that sell food and alcoholic beverages, and some of the larger department stores have a full-fledged supermarket located in the basement.

Finding what you need

In the various shops listed in the preceding section, you may find the follow-ing types of foods:

✔ **die Backwaren** (dee *bâk*-vâr-en) (*bakery goods*)

✔ **das Gebäck** (dâs ge-*bêk*) (*cookies, pastries*)

✔ **das Gemüse** (dâs ge-*mue*-ze) (*vegetables*)

✔ **der Fisch** (dêr fish) (*fish*)

✔ **das Fleisch** (dâs flaysh) (*meat*)

✔ **das Obst** (dâs ohpst) (*fruit*)

Here are some specific food items you may be interested in purchasing:

✔ **das Brot** (dâs broht) (*bread*)

✔ **das Brötchen** (dâs *brert*-Hen) (*roll*)

✔ **das Roggenbrot** (dâs *rog*-en-broht) (*rye bread*)

✔ **das Schwarzbrot** (dâs *shvârts*-broht) (*brown bread*)

✔ **der Kuchen** (dêr *koohH*-en) (*cake*)

✔ **die Torte** (dee *tor*-te) (*cake, often multilayered*)

✔ **die Butter** (dee *boot*-er) (*butter*)

✔ **der Käse** (dêr *kai*-ze) (*cheese*)

✔ **die Milch** (dee milH) (*milk*)

✔ **die Sahne** (dee *zahn*-e) (*cream*)

✔ **die Flunder** (dee *floon*-der) (*flounder*)

✔ **die Forelle** (dee fohr-*e*-le) (*trout*)

✔ **der Kabeljau** (dêr *kah*-bel-you) (*cod*)

✔ **die Krabben** (dee *krâb*-en) (*shrimp*)

✔ **der Krebs** (dêr kreyps) (*crab*)

✔ **der Tunfisch** (dêr *toohn*-fish) (*tuna*)

✔ **die Bratwurst** (dee *braht*-voorst) (*fried sausage*)

✔ **das Hähnchen** (dâs *hain*-Hen) (*chicken*)

✔ **das Rindfleisch** (dâs *rint*-flaysh) (*beef*)

✔ **der Schinken** (dêr *shin*-ken) (*ham*)

✔ **das Schweinefleisch** (dâs *shvayn*-e-flaysh) (*pork*)

✔ **der Speck** (dêr shpêk) (*bacon*)

✔ **die Wurst** (dee voorst) (*sausage*)

✔ **der Apfel** (dêr *âp*-fel) (*apple*)

✔ **die Banane** (dee bâ-*nah*-ne) (*banana*)

✔ **die Birne** (dee *birn*-e) (*pear*)

✔ **die Bohne** (dee *bohn*-e) (*bean*)

✔ **der Brokkoli** (dêr *broh*-ko-lee) (*broccoli*)

✔ **die Erbse** (dee *êrp*-se) (*pea*)

✔ **die Erdbeere** (dee *eyrt*-beyr-e) (*strawberry*)

✔ **die Gurke** (dee goork-e) (*cucumber*)

✔ **die Karotte** (dee kâ-r*ot*-e) (*carrot*)

✔ **die Kartoffel** (dee kâr-*tof*-el) (*potato*)

✔ **der Knoblauch** (dêr *knoh*-blouH) (*garlic*)

✔ **der Kohl** (dêr kohl) (*cabbage*)

✔ **der Kopfsalat** (dêr *kopf*-zâ-laht) (*lettuce*)

✔ **die Orange** (dee oh-*ron*-ge [g as in the word *genre*]) (*orange*)

✔ **der Paprika** (dêr *pâp*-ree-kah) (*bell pepper*)

✔ **der Pilz** (dêr pilts) (*mushroom*)

✔ **der Reis** (dêr rays) (*rice*)

✔ **der Salat** (dêr zâ-*laht*) (*salad*)

✔ **das Sauerkraut** (dâs *zou*-er-krout) (*sauerkraut*)

- ✔ **der Spinat** (dêr shpi-*naht*) (*spinach*)
- ✔ **die Tomate** (dee to-*mah*-te) (*tomato*)
- ✔ **die Zucchini** (dee tsoo-*kee*-ni) (*zucchini*)
- ✔ **die Zwiebel** (dee *tsvee*-bel) (*onion*)

If you go shopping at a supermarket in Germany, you're bound to notice that plastic bags for your groceries aren't something you just get for free. You either have to bring your own bag or pay a small amount for a plastic bag at the cashier. So why not go with the flow and purchase a few cloth bags that you can reuse? Oh, and keep in mind that bagging your own groceries is customary.

Fun & Games

You have just ordered a glass of water, a cup of coffee, soup, salad, steak, and mashed potatoes for lunch at a café. Identify everything on the table to make sure that your waiter hasn't forgotten anything. Use the definite articles **der**, **die**, or **das** whenever you know which article to use.

A. _____

B. _____

C. _____

D. _____

E. _____

F. _____

G. _____

H. _____

I. _____

J. _____

Chapter 9

Shopping Made Easy

In This Chapter

▶ Deciding where and when to shop

▶ Finding items, browsing, and asking for help

▶ Looking for clothes while you shop

▶ Making purchases after finding what you need

▶ Comparing items before buying

S hopping in another country can be a fun way to dive into the culture and rub elbows with the locals. In European cities, you have a choice of hunting for unique items in enticing shops and boutiques, or if you're in the mood for one-stop shopping, you can head for the major department stores found in all the larger towns and cities.

City centers often have large pedestrian zones featuring all kinds of stores and restaurants, making them the ideal setting for a leisurely stroll or for some window shopping, which is called **Schaufensterbummel** (*shou*-fêns-ter-*boom*-el).

In this chapter, we help you become familiar with the terms and phrases you would use during a shopping trip — from asking for help and browsing to trying on and purchasing your finds.

Places to Shop around Town

If you need to purchase something, you can find plenty of shopping opportunities in all kinds of locales, including the following:

- **das Kaufhaus** (dâs *kouf*-hous) (*department store*)

- **das Fachgeschäft** (dâs *fâH*-ge-shêft) (*store specializing in a line of products*)

- **die Boutique** (dee booh-*teek*) (*a small, often high-end shop generally selling clothes or gifts*)

✔ **die Buchhandlung** (dee *boohH*-hând-loong) (*bookstore*)

✔ **die Fußgängerzone** (dee *foohs*-gêng-er-*tsoh*-ne) (*pedestrian zone*)

✔ **der Kiosk** (dêr *kee*-osk) (*newsstand*)

✔ **der Flohmarkt** (dêr *floh*-mârkt) (*flea market*)

Finding Out about Opening Hours

Shopping hours in Germany aren't quite what you're used to in the U.S. Opening hours are regulated by law. For the most part, stores may open at 6 a.m., and they close by 8 p.m. from Monday through Saturday. In small towns, some stores close between noon and 2 p.m. for lunch. Don't count on banks being open after 4 p.m. However, you may find some banks that stay open until about 6 p.m. on Thursdays. On Sundays, most businesses remain closed.

Bakeries, which sell fresh rolls, or **Brötchen** (*brert*-Hen), are an exception to the rule that businesses remain closed on Sundays. And some stores may be open in popular resort towns. Can't find any places to buy sandwich fixings? Look for 24/7 gas stations that sell a wide variety of grocery items. Also some shops at train stations in larger cities are open on Sundays.

To find out a store's open hours, ask the following questions:

✔ **Wann öffnen Sie?** (vân *erf*-nen zee?) (*When do you open?*)

✔ **Wann schließen Sie?** (vân *shlees*-en zee?) (*When do you close?*)

✔ **Haben Sie mittags geöffnet?** (*hah*-ben zee *mi*-tahks ge-erf-net?) (*Are you open during lunch?*)

Navigating Your Way around a Store

If you need help finding a certain item or section in a department store, you can consult the information desk — **die Auskunft** (dee *ous*-koonft) or **die Information** (dee in-for-mâ-tsee-*ohn*). The people there should have all the answers you need, and talking to the folks at the information desk provides you with a terrific opportunity to practice your questioning skills.

If you're searching for a certain item, you can ask for it by name with either of these phrases (at the end of the phrase, just fill in the plural form of the item you're looking for):

✔ **Wo bekomme ich . . .?** (voh be-*kom*-e iH . . .?) (*Where do I get . . .?*)

✔ **Wo finde ich . . .?** (voh *fin*-de iH . . .?) (*Where do I find . . .?*)

Whatever happened to the first floor?

Germans (and other Europeans) look at buildings differently than Americans do. They don't count the ground floor, **das Erdgeschoss** (dâs *êrt*-ge-shos), as the first floor. They start numbering with the floor above the ground floor. That system makes the American second floor the German first floor, and so on, all the way to the top.

When you question the people at the information desk, they may say . . . **führen wir nicht** (*fuer*-en veer niHt . . .) (*We don't carry . . .*). Or they may direct you to the appropriate section of the store, using one of the following phrases:

- **Im Erdgeschoss.** (im *êrt*-ge-shos.) (*On the ground floor.*)
- **Im Untergeschoss.** (im *oon*-ter-ge-shos.) (*In the basement.*)
- **In der . . . Etage.** (in dêr . . . ê-*tah*-zhe.) (*On the . . . floor.*)
- **Im . . . Stock.** (im . . . shtok.) (*On the . . . floor.*)
- **Eine Etage höher.** (*ayn*-e ê-*tah*-zhe *her*-her.) (*One floor above.*)
- **Eine Etage tiefer.** (*ayn*-e ê-*tah*-zhe *teef*-er.) (*One floor below.*)

If you'd like to browse through a section of the store or you're looking for a special feature of the store, you can use the phrase **Wo finde ich . . .?** (voh *fin*-de iH . . .?) (*Where do I find . . .?*), ending the phrase with one of the following expressions:

- **die Toiletten** (dee toy-*lêt*-en) (*restrooms*)
- **die Herrenabteilung** (dee *hêr*-en-âp-*tay*-loong) (*men's department*)
- **die Damenabteilung** (dee *dah*-mên-âp-*tay*-loong) (*ladies' department*)
- **die Kinderabteilung** (dee *kin*-der-âp-*tay*-loong) (*children's department*)
- **die Schuhabteilung** (dee *shooh*-âp-*tay*-loong) (*shoe department*)
- **die Schmuckabteilung** (dee *shmook*-âp-*tay*-loong) (*jewelry department*)
- **den Aufzug / den Fahrstuhl** (deyn *ouf*-tsook / deyn *fâr*-shtoohl) (*elevator*)
- **die Rolltreppe** (dee *rol*-trêp-e) (*escalator*)

When you want to sound particularly nice as you ask for help, you're always safe using the polite phrase **Entschuldigen Sie bitte** (ent-*shool*-di-gen zee *bi*-te) (*Excuse me, please*). Consider, for example, the following polite question:

> **Entschuldigen Sie bitte, wo ist die Rolltreppe?** (ent-*shool*-di-gen zee *bi*-te, voh ist dee *rol*-trêp-e?) (*Excuse me, please, where is the escalator?*)

See Chapter 3 for more details on polite expressions.

Just Browsing: Taking a Look at Merchandise

Sometimes you just want to check out the merchandise in the store on your own without anybody breathing down your neck. However, store assistants may offer their help by saying something like the following:

> **Suchen Sie etwas Bestimmtes?** (*zoohH*-en zee êt-*vâs* be-*shtim*-tes?) (*Are you looking for something in particular?*)

> **Kann ich Ihnen behilflich sein?** (kân iH *eehn*-en be-*hilf*-liH zayn?) (*Can I help you?*)

When all you want to do is browse, this phrase can help you politely turn down help:

> **Ich möchte mich nur umsehen.** (iH *merH*-te miH noohr *oom*-zey-en.) (*I just want to look around.*)

The store assistant will probably tell you it's okay to keep browsing by saying either of the following:

> **Aber natürlich. Sagen Sie Bescheid, wenn Sie eine Frage haben.** (*ah*-ber nâ-*tuer*-liH. *zah*-gen zee be-*shayt*, vên zee *ayn*-e *frah*-ge *hah*-ben.) (*Of course. Just let me know if you need help.*)

> **Rufen Sie mich, wenn Sie eine Frage haben.** (*rooh*-fen zee miH, vên zee *ayn*-e *frah*-ge *hah*-ben.) (*Call me if you have a question.*)

Getting Assistance as You Shop

In some situations, you may want or need assistance while you're shopping. Here are some useful phrases you may say or hear:

Würden Sie mir bitte helfen? Ich suche . . . (*vuer*-den zee meer *bi*-te *hêl*-fen. iH *zoohH*-e . . .) (*Would you help me, please? I'm looking for . . .*)

Aber gern, hier entlang bitte. (*ah*-ber gêrn, heer *ênt*-lâng *bi*-te.) (*Certainly. This way please.*)

Welche Größe suchen Sie? (*vêl*-He grer-se *zoohH*-en zee?) (*What size are you looking for?*)

Haben Sie so etwas in Größe . . .? (*hah*-ben zee zoh *êt*-vâs in grer-se . . .?) (*Do you have something like this in size . . .?*)

Wie gefällt Ihnen diese Farbe? (vee ge-*fêlt* een-en *deez*-e *fâr*-be?) (*How do you like this color?*)

Most sales people in Austrian, German, and Swiss stores are competent and knowledgeable. That's due in part to the education system. Salespeople, as is the case in most trades, generally complete a comprehensive three-year apprenticeship that combines on-the-job training with trade school instruction.

Words to Know

der Aufzug	dêr <u>ouf</u>-tsook	elevator
die Rolltreppe	dee <u>rol</u>-trêp-e	escalator
die Abteilung	dee âb-<u>tay</u>-loong	department
hier entlang	heer <u>ênt</u>-lâng	this way
gefallen	gê-<u>fâl</u>-en	to like; to please
die Größe	dee <u>grer</u>-se	size
die Farbe	dee <u>fâr</u>-be	color

Shopping for Clothes

When out shopping for clothes, you just have to decide what you want in terms of item, color, size, and, of course, price. Many terms for clothing are unisex, and others are typical for either men or women.

Some items that women wear include the following:

- **die Bluse** (dee *blooh*-ze) (*blouse*)
- **das Kleid** (dās klayt) (*dress*)
- **das Kostüm** (dās kos-*tuem*) (*suit*)
- **der Hosenanzug** (dēr *hoh*-zen-ân-tsook) (*pantsuit*)
- **der Rock** (dēr rok) (*skirt*)

The following words usually apply to clothing for men:

- **die Krawatte** (dee krâ-*vât*-e) (*tie*)
- **der Anzug** (dēr *ân*-tsook) (*suit*)

The following items are generally considered to be worn by both men and women:

- **der Pullover, der Pulli** (dēr poo-*loh*-ver, dēr *poo*-lee) (*sweater*)
- **die Strickjacke** (dee *shtrik*-yâ-ke) (*cardigan*)
- **das Jackett, die Jacke** (dās jhâ-*kêt,* dee *yâ*-ke) (*jacket*)
- **der Blazer** (dēr *bley*-zer) (*blazer*)
- **die Weste** (dee *vês*-te) (*vest*)
- **die Schuhe** (dee *shooh*-e) (*shoes*)
- **der Mantel** (dēr *mân*-tel) (*coat*)
- **die Hose** (dee *hoh*-ze) (*pants*)
- **das Hemd** (dās hêmt) (*shirt*)
- **das T-Shirt** (dās T-shirt [as in English]) (*T-shirt*)

Clothing items such as the ones in the preceding lists can come in any number of fabrics and styles, including the following:

- **die Seide** (dee *zay*-de) (*silk*)
- **die Wolle** (dee *vol*-e) (*wool*)
- **die Baumwolle** (dee *boum*-vol-e) (*cotton*)
- **das Leinen** (dās *layn*-en) (*linen*)
- **das Leder** (dās *ley*-der) (*leather*)
- **gestreift** (ge-*shtrayft*) (*striped*)
- **kariert** (kâr-*eert*) (*checkered*)

✔ **bunt** (boont) (*multicolored*)

✔ **gepunktet** (ge-*poonk*-tet) (*with dots*)

✔ **einfarbig** (*ayn*-fâr-biH) (*solid color*)

✔ **sportlich** (*shport*-liH) (*sporty, casual*)

✔ **elegant** (ê-le-*gânt*) (*elegant*)

Figure 9-1 shows a variety of clothing items with their German names.

Figure 9-1:
Common
clothing
items

Familiarizing yourself with the colors available

The basic **Farben** (*fâr*-ben) (*colors*) are

✔ **schwarz** (shvârts) (*black*)

✔ **weiß** (vays) (*white*)

✔ **rot** (roht) (*red*)

✔ **grün** (gruen) (*green*)

- **gelb** (gêlp) (*yellow*)
- **braun** (brown [as in English]) (*brown*)
- **lila** (*lee*-lâ) (*purple*)
- **orange** (o-*rânch*) (*orange*)
- **grau** (grou) (*gray*)
- **blau** (blou) (*blue*)

These color words are all adjectives. To find out more about how to fit them into phrases and sentences, check out Chapter 2.

Knowing your size

Finding the right size clothing can be a pain in the neck in any shopping situation. When shopping in German-speaking countries, though, you get a double whammy: Clothes sizes aren't the same as in the U.S. The following charts are a useful guideline to help you crack the code.

Here are the approximate equivalents for sizes of women's clothes:

American	4	6	8	10	12	14	16	18	20
German	34	36	38	40	42	44	46	48	50

For men's jacket and suit sizes, use the following approximate conversions:

American	38	40	42	44	46	48	50
German	48	50	52	54	56	58	60

Talkin' the Talk

 Frau Schulte is in the ladies' section of a department store. She wants to buy a blouse and is getting assistance from a saleswoman. (Track 20)

Verkäuferin: **Kann ich Ihnen behilflich sein?**
kân iH *een*-en be-*hilf*-liH zayn?
Can I help you?

Frau Schulte: **Ja bitte. Ich suche eine Bluse.**
yah *bi*-te. iH *zoohH*-e *ayn*-e *blooh*-ze.
Yes, please. I'm looking for a blouse.

Verkäuferin: **Hier entlang, bitte. Welche Farbe soll es denn sein?**
heer *ênt*-lang, *bi*-te. *vêlH*-e *fâr*-be zol ês dên zayn?
Please come this way. What color do you want?

Frau Schulte: **Weiß.**
Vays.
White.

Verkäuferin: **Suchen Sie etwas Lässiges?**
zoohH-en zee êt-vâs *lês*-ee-ges?
Are you looking for something casual?

Frau Schulte: **Nein, eher etwas Elegantes.**
nayn, ê-her êt-vâs ey-le-*gân*-tes.
No, rather something elegant.

Verkäuferin: **Gut. Welche Größe haben Sie?**
gooht. *vêlH*-e *grer*-se *hah*-ben zee?
Good. What is your size?

Frau Schulte: **Größe 38.**
grer-se *âHt*-oon-*dray*-siH.
Size 38.

Verkäuferin: **Wie gefällt Ihnen dieses Modell?**
vee ge-*fêlt* een-en *deez*-es mo-*dêl*?
How do you like this style?

Frau Schulte: **Sehr gut.**
zeyr gooht.
Very much.

Trying on the items you find

When you find something that looks promising, you probably want to try it on. In that case, you can ask the sales assistant the following question, supplying the name of the article that you want to try on:

> **Kann ich . . . anprobieren?** (kân iH . . . *ân*-pro-bee-ren?) (*Can I try . . . on?*)

Or a sales assistant may anticipate your question and ask this question:

> **Möchten Sie . . . anprobieren?** (*merH*-ten zee . . . *ân*-pro-bee-ren?) (*Would you like to try . . . on?*)

In either case, the next step is going to the dressing rooms, which you can ask about by saying:

> **Wo sind die Umkleidekabinen?** (voh zint dee *oom*-klay-de-kâ-*been*-en?) (*Where are the fitting rooms?*)

After you try your item on, the sales assistant may ask you one of the following questions to find out what you think of the article of clothing:

> **Passt . . . ?** (pâst . . . ?) (*Does . . . fit?*)
>
> **Wie passt Ihnen . . . ?** (wie pâst *een*-en . . . ?) (*How does . . . fit you?*)
>
> **Gefällt Ihnen . . . ?** (ge-*fêlt een*-en . . . ?) (*Do you like . . . ?*)

You can answer with any of the following, depending on how things went when you tried on your item:

> **Nein, . . . ist zu lang / kurz / eng / weit / groß / klein.** (nayn, . . . ist tsooh lâng / koorts / êng / vayt / grohs / klayn.) (*No, . . . is too long / short / tight / loose / big / small.*)
>
> **Können Sie mir eine andere Größe bringen?** (*kern*-en zee meer *ayn*-e *ân*-de-re *grer*-se *bring*-en?) (*Can you get me another size?*)
>
> **. . . passt sehr gut.** (. . . pâst zeyr gooht.) (*. . . fits very well.*)
>
> **. . . steht mir.** (. . . shteyt meer.) (*. . . suits me.*)
>
> **. . . gefällt mir.** (. . . ge-*fêlt* meer.) (*I like . . .*)
>
> **Ich nehme . . .** (IH *ney*-me . . .) (*I'll take . . .*)

Words to Know

(zu) eng	(tsooh) êng	(too) tight
weit	vayt	loose
lang	lâng	long
kurz	koorts	short
groß	grohs	big
klein	klayn	small
das Modell	dâs mo-dêl	style
anprobieren	ân-pro-bee-ren	to try on
bringen	bring-en	to bring
passen	pâs-en	to fit
stehen	stey-en	to suit
gefallen	ge-fâl-en	to like
gefällt mir	ge-fêlt meer	I like
die Umkleidekabine	dee oom-klay-de-kâ-been-e	fitting room
kaufen	kouf-en	to buy

Talkin' the Talk

 Frau Schulte likes the blouse the saleswoman has shown her and wants to try it on. Here's how their conversation may go. (Track 21)

Frau Schulte: **Ich möchte diese Bluse anprobieren. Wo sind die Umkleidekabinen, bitte?**
iH *merH*-te *deez*-e *blooh*-ze ân-pro-bee-ren.
voh zint dee *oom*-klay-de-kâ-*been*-en, *bi*-te?
I would like to try this blouse on. Where are the fitting rooms, please?

Verkäuferin: **Ja, natürlich. Da drüben sind die Umkleidekabinen.**
yah, nâ-*tuer*-liH. dâ *drue*-ben zint dee
oom-klay-de-kâ-*been*-en.
Of course. The fitting rooms are over there.

(A few minutes later Frau Schulte returns.)
Verkäuferin: **Passt die Bluse?**
pâst dee *blooh*-ze?
Does the blouse fit?

Frau Schulte: **Ja. Ich nehme die Bluse.**
yah. iH *ney*-me dee *blooh*-ze.
Yes. I'll take the blouse.

Paying for Your Shopping Items

Most of the time, when you go shopping, every piece of merchandise has a tag that tells you exactly how much it costs. The price you see on a price tag is what you pay for the item at the cash register, including sales tax, called the VAT (or value added tax). German word for VAT is **die Mehrwertsteuer (Mwst)** (dee *mêr*-vêrt-*shtoy*-er).

If you don't reside in a country of the European Union (EU), you usually can get a refund for the VAT tax when you leave the EU. The VAT refund is referred to as — take a deep breath — **die Mehrwertsteuerrückerstattung** (dee *mêr*-vêrt-shtoy-er-*ruek*-êr-shtât-oong). Although the German word for the VAT refund looks a bit daunting, the process for getting it back is usually simple. Just ask for a VAT refund form when you pay at the register. Collect all the receipts for merchandise you're taking out of the European Union, as well as the forms, and then you can have the lot approved by a customs agent at the airport before you leave the EU to return home. (Because you must show the items, don't pack them with your checked luggage!)

Occasionally, you may find yourself in a situation where you need to ask about the price (**der Preis**) (dêr prays) of an item. Price tags, being the devious little critters that they are, have a way of falling off or being indecipherable, especially when handwritten. Consider this case in point: The German number 1 can look a lot like the American number 7 when scrawled by hand. But not to worry. The following simple phrases take care of the price question should you need to ask it:

Was kostet . . .? (vâs *kos*-tet . . .?) (*What does . . . cost?*)

Wie viel kostet . . .? (vee *feel kos*-tet . . .?) (*How much does . . . cost?*)

Words to Know

kosten	<u>kos</u>-ten	to cost
der Preis	dêr prays	price
die Mehrwert- steuer (Mwst)	dee <u>mêr</u>-vêrt- shtoy-er	tax (VAT)
die Mehrwert- steuerrücker- stattung	dee <u>mêr</u>-vêrt- shtoy-er-<u>ruek</u>- êr-shtât-oong	VAT refund

Talkin' the Talk

Frau Schulte heads to the cash register to pay for her purchase.
Consider how her conversation with the cashier goes:

Kassiererin: **Das macht 49 Euro.**
dâs mâHt *noyn*-oont-*feer*-tsiH *oy*-roh.
That's 49 euros, please.

Frau Schulte: **Nehmen Sie Kreditkarten?**
ney-men see krey-*dit*-kâr-ten?
Can I pay by credit card?

Kassiererin: **Kein Problem.**
kayn pro-*bleym.*
No problem.

Frau Schulte: **Hier bitte.**
heer *bi*-te.
Here you are.

Kassiererin: **Danke. Würden Sie bitte unterschreiben? Und hier ist Ihre Quittung.**
dân-ke. *wuer*-den zee *bi*-te un-ter-*schray*-ben? oont heer ist *eer*-e *kvit*-oong.
Thanks. Would you please sign here? And here is your receipt.

Frau Schulte: **Danke!**
dân-ke!
Thanks!

Comparatively Speaking: Making Comparisons Among Objects

Comparisons are important when you're out shopping for gifts for yourself or others. In English, when you want to compare two things, you use the word "than" and an appropriate adjective or adverb. Comparisons in German are made in exactly the same way — all you need is the word **als** (âls) (*than*) plus the appropriate adverb or adjective. Consider these examples:

✔ **Die braunen Schuhe sind billiger als die schwarzen.** (dee *broun*-en *shooh*-e zint *bil*-ee-ger âls dee *shvârts*-en.) (*The brown shoes are cheaper than the black ones.*)

✔ **Das blaue Kleid gefällt mir besser als das Rote.** (dâs *blou*-e klayt ge-*fêlt* meer *bês*-er âls dâs *roh*-te.) (*I like the blue dress better than the red one.*)

✔ **Dieses Geschäft hat modischere Kleidung als das Andere gegenüber.** (*deez*-es ge-*shêft* hât *moh*-dish-er-e *klay*-doong âls dâs *ân*-dêre gey-gen-*ue*-ber.) (*This store has more fashionable clothes than the one across from it.*)

Fun & Games

Write the correct German word for the department beside the floor number where it is located. Read the following phrases to decide which department belongs on which floor. Notice that sentence A gives a clue for sentence B; sentence C has a clue for sentence D, and so on. (***Hint:*** **Erdgeschoss** is the North American first floor, **1. Etage** is the North American second floor, and so on. **Untergeschoss** is the German word for basement.)

A. Sie finden Schuhe im vierten Stock, und …

B. … die Kinderabteilung ist eine Etage tiefer.

C. Der Supermarkt ist im Untergeschoss, und …

D. … die Schmuckabteilung ist eine Etage höher.

E. Steve Jobs & Bill Gates sind im sechsten Stock, und …

F. …das Restaurant ist eine Etage höher.

G. Die Herrenabteilung ist im zweiten Stock, und …

H. … die Damenabteilung ist eine Etage tiefer.

I. TV/Telekommunikation sind im fünften Stock.

Kaufhaus Schlummer map

Etage/Stock (floor)	Abteilung (department)
7	_____
6	_____
5	_____
4	_____
3	_____
2	_____
1	_____
Erdgeschoss	_____
Untergeschoss	_____

Chapter 10

Going Out on the Town

You find a surprisingly large number of cultural venues in Germany, and that's mostly true all across Europe. Not only do the arts receive state and federal funds to support their efforts, but Europeans also have a long-standing appreciation of their cultural assets. To get a taste of German culture, check the media to find out what's going on. Along with local Web sites, the local newspapers and other media offer weekly guides of local events by publishing a **Veranstaltungskalender** (fêr-*ân*-shtâl-toongs-kâ-*len*-der) (*calendar of events*).

What Would You Like to Do?

Sometimes you may want to go out by yourself, and other times you may want company. If you're in the mood for companionship and want to toss around ideas with someone about what to do, you can ask

Was wollen wir unternehmen? (vâs *vol*-en veer oon-ter-*ney*-men?) (*What do we want to do?*)

Use the following phrases if you want to find out about somebody's plans. These phrases are also very useful when you want to know whether somebody is available:

Haben Sie (heute Abend) etwas vor? (*hah*-ben zee [*hoy*-te *ah*-bênt] *êt*-vâs fohr?) (*Do you have anything planned [for this evening]?*)

Haben Sie (heute Abend) Zeit? (*hah*-ben zee [*hoy*-te *ah*-bênt] tsayt) (*Do you have time this evening?*)

Hast du (morgen Vormittag) etwas vor? (hâst dooh [*mor*-gen *fohr*-mi-tahk] *êt*-vâs fohr?) (*Do you have anything planned [for tomorrow morning]?*)

Use the formal **Sie** (zee) (*you*) when you don't know the person you're speaking with very well, and use the informal **du** (dooh) (*you*) only when you're on mutually familiar terms.

Going to the Movies

When you want to tell someone that you're interested in going to the movies, you can use the following phrases:

> **Ich möchte ins Kino gehen.** (iH *merH*-te ins *kee*-noh *gey*-en.) (*I would like to go to the movies.*)

> **Ich möchte einen Film sehen.** (iH *merH*-te *ayn*-en film *zey*-en.) (*I would like to see a film.*)

Watching films in a language you want to learn is a terrific way of getting your ear accustomed to how the language sounds. At the same time, you can get used to understanding many different speakers. All around the world, in fact, people learn English by watching American movies.

Getting to the show

If you're searching for a movie to go to, your best bet is to check out local Web sites, weekly guides of local events, or newspaper listings. The listings usually tell you everything you need to know about **die Vorstellung** (dee *fohr*-stêl-oong) (*the show*): when and where the show is playing, who the actors are, and whether the movie is in its original language — **im Original** (im o-ri-gi-*nahl*) (*original*); **OmU**, which stands for **Original mit Untertiteln** (o-ri-gi-*nahl* mit *oon*-têr-ti-teln) (*original with subtitles*); or **synchronisiert** (zyn-kro-nee-*zeert*) (*dubbed*). (See the sidebar "What a strange voice you have" for more about language in movies.)

If you don't have access to the Internet or other sources of information, the following phrases can help you ask for information about a movie:

> **In welchem Kino läuft . . .?** (in *vêlH*-êm *kee*-noh loyft . . .?) (*In which movie theater is . . . showing?*)

> **Um wie viel Uhr beginnt die Vorstellung?** (oom *vee* feel oohr be-*gint* dee *fohr*-stêl-oong?) (*At what time does the show start?*)

> **Läuft der Film im Original oder ist er synchronisiert?** (loyft dêr film im o-ri-gi-*nahl* oh-der ist êr zyn-kro-nee-*zeert?*) (*Is the film shown in the original [language] or is it dubbed?*)

What a strange voice you have

Most foreign films shown in Germany are dubbed into German, although some movie theaters, especially the small independents, specialize in showing foreign films in the original language with German subtitles — **Originalfassung mit deutschen Untertiteln** (o-ri-gi-*nahl*-fâs-oong mit *doy*-chen *oon*-têr-ti-teln) (*original version with German subtitles*). So if you're not into the mind-altering experience of listening to Hollywood actors assume strange voices and speak in tongues, keep an eye open for the undubbed version of the film or go see movies filmed in German exclusively. And if you do go to the **Originalfassung mit Untertiteln** (o-ri-gi-*nahl*-*fâs*-oong mit *oon*-têr-ti-teln) (*original version with subtitles*) of an American movie, you have the advantage of reading the German as you listen to the English, and you may pick up some useful expressions.

Buying tickets

You can use the following phrase whenever you want to buy tickets, be it for the opera, the movies, or the museum:

> **Ich möchte (zwei) Karten / Eintrittskarten für . . .** (iH *merH*-te [tsvay] *kâr*-ten / *ayn*-trits-*kâr*-ten fuer . . .) (*I would like [two] tickets / entrance tickets for . . .*)

After buying your tickets, you may get some information from the ticket seller, including the following:

> **Die Vorstellung hat schon begonnen.** (dee *fohr*-shtêl-oong hât shon be-*gon*-en.) (*The show has already started.*)

> **Die . . .-Uhr-Vorstellung ist leider ausverkauft.** (dee . . .-oohr-*fohr*-stêl-oong ist *lay*-der *ous*-fêr-kouft.) (*The . . . o'clock show is unfortunately sold out.*)

> **Wir haben noch Karten für die Vorstellung um . . . Uhr.** (veer *hah*-ben noH *kâr*-ten fuer dee *fohr*-shtêl-oong oom . . . oohr.) (*There are tickets left for the show at . . . o'clock.*)

These phrases work for any type of show or performance, not just movies.

Talkin' the Talk

 Antje is talking to her friend Robert on the phone. Antje wants to go to the movies. After greeting her friend, Antje gets right to the point. (Track 22)

Antje: **Der neue Zeichentrickfilm von Pixar Studios soll super witzig sein.**
dêr *noy*-e *tsayH*-en-trik-film fon *pix*-ahr *shtooh*-dee-ohs sol *sooh*-per *vits*-eeH zayn.
The new animated film from Pixar Studios is supposed to be incredibly funny.

Robert: **Wann willst du gehen?**
vân vilst dooh *gey*-en?
When do you want to go?

Antje: **Morgen Abend habe ich Zeit.**
mor-gen *ah*-bênt *hah*-be iH tsayt.
I have time tomorrow evening.

Robert: **Morgen passt mir auch. In welchem Kino läuft der Film?**
mor-gen pâst meer ouH. in *vêlH*-êm *kee*-noh loyft dêr film?
Tomorrow works for me as well. In which movie theater is the film showing?

Antje: **Im Hansatheater. Die Vorstellung beginnt um 20 Uhr.**
im *hân*-sâ-tey-*ah*-ter. dee *fohr*-shtêl-oong be-*gint* oom *tsvân*-tsiH oohr.
In the Hansa Theater. The show starts at 8 p.m.

Robert: **Gut, treffen wir uns um Viertel vor acht vor dem Kino.**
gooht, *trêf*-en veer oons oom *fir*-tel fohr âHt fohr deym *kee*-noh.
Okay. Let's meet at a quarter to eight in front of the movie theater.

Antje: **Prima. Bis morgen dann.**
pree-mâ. bis *mor*-gen dân.
Great. Until tomorrow then.

Words to Know

das Kino	dâs <u>kee</u>-no	movie theater
der Spielfilm	dêr <u>shpeel</u>-film	feature film
die Vorstellung	dee <u>fohr</u>-shtêl-oong	show
die Karte	dee <u>kâr</u>-te	ticket
die Eintrittskarte	dee <u>ayn</u>-trits-<u>kâr</u>-te	entrance ticket
witzig	<u>vits</u>-eeH	funny
sehen	<u>zey</u>-en	to see
laufen	<u>louf</u>-en	to show

There are two German words that mean ticket (for a show), **Karte** and **Eintrittskarte**. The difference is simply the fact that **Eintrittskarte** is a compound word that translates roughly as *entrance ticket*. You come across many such compound words in German, and they're frequently a combination of two words, in this case, **Eintritt(s)** and **Karte**.

What Was That? The Simple Past Tense of "Sein"

Chapter 2 discusses the present tense of **sein** (zayn) (*to be*): **Ich bin . . . / du bist . . .** (iH bin . . . / dooh bist . . .) (*I am . . . / you are . . .*) and so on. When talking about things that happened in the past — with phrases such as "I was . . .", "You were . . .," and "They were . . ." — you put the verb **sein** into the simple past tense. The simple past tense of the verb **sein** looks like this:

Conjugation	*Pronunciation*
ich war	iH vahr
du warst	dooh vârst
Sie waren	zee *vah*-ren
er, sie, es war	êr, zee, es vahr
wir waren	veer *vah*-ren
ihr wart	eer vârt
Sie waren	zee *vah*-ren
sie waren	zee *vah*-ren

You can use the simple past tense of **sein** to express many different ideas and questions. Take a look at the past tense of **sein** in action:

Ich war gestern im Kino. (iH vahr *gês*-tern im *kee*-noh.) (*I was at the movies yesterday.*)

Wie war der Film? (vee vahr dêr film?) (*How was the film?*)

Wir waren heute Morgen im Kunstmuseum. (veer *vah*-ren *hoy*-te mor-gen im *koonst*-moo-*sey*-oom.) (*We were at the art museum this morning.*)

Warst du letzte Woche in Wien? (vârst dooh *lêts*-te *voH*-e in veen?) (*Were you in Vienna last week?*)

Wo waren Sie am Freitag? (vo *vah*-ren zee âm *fray*-tahk?) (*Where were you on Friday?*)

Going to the Museum

Germany has a long and rich museum tradition, with many world-renowned museums sprinkled liberally across the country. Most German museums receive state or federal funds and, as a consequence, often charge surprisingly low entrance fees.

If you're into art, keep an eye open for the **Kunstmuseum** (koonst-moo-*sey*-oom) (*art museum*). If you want to find out more about the traditional lifestyle of a certain area, go to the **Freilichtmuseum** (*fray*-leeHt-moo-*sey*–oom) (*open-air museum*). You can find museums for virtually everything a human being might fancy, including a **Biermuseum** (beer-moo-*sey*-um) (*beer museum*) in Munich and several other locations!

Closed on Mondays

Museum mavens beware: German museums, like many European museums and other cultural centers, are closed on Mondays — **montags geschlossen** (*mohn*-tahks ge-*shlos-en*).

Others are closed on **dienstags** (*deens-tahks*) (*Tuesdays*). Make sure to check **die Öffnungszeiten** (dee *erf*-noongs-*tsayt*-en) (*the opening hours*) before heading out.

When you want to catch an exhibition — **Ausstellung** (*ous*-shtêl-oong) — the following phrases come in handy:

Ich möchte ins Museum gehen. (iH *merH*-te ins moo-*sey*-oom *gey*-en.) (*I would like to go to the museum.*)

Ich möchte die . . . Ausstellung sehen. (iH *merH*-te dee . . . *ous*-shtêl-oong *zey*-en.) (*I would like to see the . . . exhibition.*)

In welchem Museum läuft die . . . Ausstellung? (in *vêlH*-em moo-*sey*-oom loyft dee . . . *ous*-shtêl-oong?) (*At which museum is the . . . exhibit running?*)

Ist das Museum montags geöffnet? (ist dâs moo-*sey*-oom *mohn*-tahks ge-*erf*-net?) (*Is the museum open on Mondays?*)

Um wie viel Uhr öffnet das Museum? (oom *vee*-feel oohr *erf*-net dâs moo-*sey*-oom?) (*At what time does the museum open?*)

Gibt es eine Sonderausstellung? (gipt ês *ayn*-e *zon*-der-*ous*-shtêl-oong?) (*Is there a special exhibit?*)

Talkin' the Talk

Jan and Mona are planning a trip to a museum. They invite their friend Ingo to join them.

Jan: **Hallo, Ingo. Wir wollen morgen ins Städtische Museum.**
hâ-lo, *in*-go. veer *vol*-en *mor*-gen ins *shtê*-ti-she moo-*sey*-oom.
Hi, Ingo. We want to go to the city museum tomorrow.

Mona:	**Wir wollen uns die Ausstellung über die Bronzezeit ansehen. Kommst du mit?**
	veer *vol*-en oons dee *ous*-shtêl-oong *ue*-ber dee *bron*-tse-tsayt *ân*-zey-en. komst dooh mit?
	We want to see the exhibit about the Bronze Age. Do you want to come along?

Ingo:	**Hmm, ich weiß nicht. Die Ausstellung habe ich schon letzte Woche gesehen.**
	hmm, iH vays niHt. dee *ous*-shtêl-oong *hah*-be iH shohn *lets*-te *voH*-e ge-*zey*-en.
	Hmm, I don't know. I already saw the exhibit last week.

Mona:	**Hat sie dir gefallen?**
	hât zee deer ge-*fâl*-en?
	Did you like it?

Ingo:	**Ja. Vielleicht komme ich noch einmal mit.**
	yah. fee-*layHt kom*-e iH noH *ayn*-mahl mit.
	Yes. Maybe I'll come along for a second time.

Jan:	**Wir wollen morgen um 10.00 Uhr in die Ausstellung.**
	veer *vol*-en *mor*-gen oom tseyn oohr in dee *ous*-shtêl-oong.
	We want to go to the exhibit tomorrow at ten o'clock.

Ingo:	**Gut. Ich treffe euch dort.**
	gooht. iH *trêf*-e oyH dohrt.
	Good. I'll meet you there.

Talking about Action in the Past

Earlier in this chapter, you discover how to use the simple past tense of the verb **sein** (zayn) (*to be*) in order to say things like "I was at the museum yesterday" or "It was cold yesterday." To communicate a full range of actions that happened in the past, you need to use a different form of the verb.

To refer to actions that took place in the past, the perfect tense is the name of the beast you need to use. To form the perfect tense, you need two verb parts, and you need to know where to put them in a sentence:

✔ You need the appropriate present tense form of either **haben** (*hah*-ben) (*have*) or **sein**. If you're asking a yes/no type of question, this present tense form appears as the first word of the question. If your sentence is a straightforward statement, it appears in the second position of the sentence.

✔ You need the past participle of the verb, which goes at the end of the sentence (or phrase). Whether you use **haben** or **sein** with the past participle of the verb depends on which verb you're working with. Simply put, most verbs require **haben**, and some use **sein**. You simply have to memorize which verbs use **haben** and which ones use **sein**. (We tell you more about how to form the past participle of a verb in the next section.)

You should consider the perfect tense a real lifesaver. This tense is very versatile in German, and you can use it to refer to most actions and situations that took place in the past. In fact, you won't have much use for the other past tenses until you're writing a novel in German or are preparing to address the German Parliament. Hey, stranger things have happened!

Forming the past participle

Try to get to know the past participle form of each new verb. A few rules make grasping the past participles easier. To apply the rules, you need to know which category the verb in question falls into.

Weak (regular) verbs

Weak verbs, also known as regular verbs, form the largest group of German verbs. When forming the past participle of a weak verb, use this formula:

ge + verb stem (the infinitive minus **-en**) + **(e)t = past participle**

Honest, this isn't really as hard as algebra! Look at how the formula plays out on the common verb **fragen** (*frah*-gen) (*to ask*):

ge + frag + t = gefragt

Now check out a verb that has the ending **-et** instead of **-t**, like **reden** (*rey-den*) (*to talk*):

ge + red + et = geredet

In this case, you add **-et**, and consequently another syllable. The **-et** ending is added to verbs that have a stem ending in **-d**, **-t**, **-fn** or **-gn**, and the reason for doing this is so you can actually pronounce (and hear) the word ending.

Another verb that follows this pattern is **öffnen** (*erf-*nen) (*to open*):

ge + öffn + et = geöffnet

Strong (irregular) verbs

Some verbs, the so-called strong verbs (also known as irregular verbs) follow a different pattern. They add **ge-** in the beginning and **-en** at the end. Forming the past participle of a strong verb entails the following:

ge + verb stem (the infinitive minus **-en**) + **en** = **past participle**

The verb **kommen** (*kom-*en) (*to come*) is a good example of this:

ge + komm + en = gekommen

Pesky critters that they are, some strong verbs change the spelling of their verb stem when forming a past participle. For example, a stem vowel, and sometimes even a stem consonant, can change.

The verb **helfen** (*hêlf-*en) (*to help*) changes its stem vowel from **e** to **o**:

ge + holf + en = geholfen

The verb **gehen** (*gey-*en) (to go) undergoes a bigger change, from **geh** to **gang**:

ge + gang + en = gegangen

Using "haben" in the perfect tense

Because the present tense forms of **haben** are so important to forming the perfect tense with many verbs, here's a quick reminder of the conjugation of **haben** in the present tense:

Conjugation	*Pronunciation*
ich habe	iH *hah*-be
du hast	dooh hâst
Sie haben	zee *hah*-ben
er, sie, es hat	êr, zee, ês hât
wir haben	veer *hah*-ben
ihr habt	eer hâpt
Sie haben	zee *hah*-ben
sie haben	zee *hah*-ben

Table 10-1 shows you some common German verbs that use **haben** in the perfect tense.

Table 10-1	Verbs That Use Haben in the Perfect Tense
Verb	*Past Participle*
arbeiten (*âr*-bay-ten) (*to work*)	**gearbeitet**
essen (*ês*-en) (*to eat*)	**gegessen**
hören (*her*-en) (*to hear*)	**gehört**
kaufen (*kouf*-en) (*to buy*)	**gekauft**
lachen (*lâH*-en) (*to laugh*)	**gelacht**
lesen (*ley*-zen) (*to read*)	**gelesen**
machen (*mâH*-en) (*to make, do*)	**gemacht**
nehmen (*ney*-men) (*to take*)	**genommen**
schlafen (*shlâf*-en) (*to sleep*)	**geschlafen**
sehen (*zey*-en) (*to see*)	**gesehen**
spielen (*shpee*-len) (*to play*)	**gespielt**
trinken (*trin*-ken) (*to drink*)	**getrunken**

Take a look at some examples of how the verb **haben** combines with a past participle to make the perfect tense:

Ich habe den Film gesehen. (iH *hah*-be deyn film ge-*zey*-en.) (*I have seen the film.*)

Hast du eine Theaterkarte bekommen? (hâst dooh *ayn*-e tey-*ah*-ter-*kâr*-te be-*kom*-en?) (*Did you get a theater ticket?*)

Wir haben das Kino verlassen. (veer *hah*-ben dâs *kee*-noh vêr-*lâs*-en.) (*We left the movie theater.*)

Habt ihr Karten für die Matinee gekauft? (hâpt eer *kâr*-ten fuer dee mâ-tee-*ney* ge-*kouft?*) (*Did you buy tickets for the matinee?*)

Ich habe viel gelacht. (iH *hah*-be feel ge-*lâHt.*) (*I laughed a lot.*)

Using "sein" in the perfect tense

Some verbs don't use the present tense of **haben** to form the perfect tense; instead they use **sein**. As a reminder, here are the present tense forms of **sein**:

Conjugation	*Pronunciation*
ich bin	iH bin
du bist	dooh bist
Sie sind	zee zînt
er, sie, es ist	êr, zee, ês ist
wir sind	veer zint
ihr seid	eer zayt
Sie sind	zee zint
sie sind	zee zint

Verbs in that category include the verb **sein** itself as well as many verbs that indicate a change of place or a change of state. Sound a bit theoretical? Table 10-2 shows you some common verbs that take **sein** in the perfect tense.

All verbs conjugated with **sein** are strong verbs: Their past participles are irregular. Try to memorize the past participle whenever you pick up a new verb that's used with **sein**.

Table 10-2	Verbs That Use "sein" in the Perfect Tense
Verb	*Past Participle*
fahren (*fahr*-en) (*to drive/ride*)	**gefahren**
fliegen (*flee*-gen) (*to fly*)	**geflogen**
gebären (gê-*bê*-ren) (*to give birth*)	**geboren**
gehen (*gey*-en) (*to go*)	**gegangen**

Verb	*Past Participle*
kommen (*kom*-en) (*to come*)	**gekommen**
laufen (*louf*-en) (*to run*)	**gelaufen**
sein (zayn) (*to be*)	**gewesen**
sterben (*shtêr*-ben) (*to die*)	**gestorben**

Take a look at these examples of verbs forming the present perfect tense with the present tense of **sein** and the past participle:

> **Ich bin ins Theater gegangen.** (iH bin ins tey-*ah*-ter ge-*gâng*-en.) (*I went to the theater.*)

> **Bist du mit dem Auto gekommen?** (bist dooh mit deym *ou*-to ge-*kom*-en?) (*Did you come by car?*)

> **Sie ist mit dem Zug gefahren.** (zee ist mit deym tsoohk ge-*fahr*-en.) (*She went by train.*)

> **Wir sind letzte Woche ins Kino gegangen.** (veer zint *lêts*-te *woH*-e ins *kee*-noh ge-*gâng*-en.) (*We went to the movies last week.*)

Going Out for Entertainment

Wherever you may be staying in Europe, you're probably just a short trip away from cultural centers presenting **Oper** (*oh*-per) (*opera*), **Konzert** (kon-*tsêrt*) (*concert*), **Sinfonie** (sin-foh-*nee*) (*symphony*), and **Theater** (tey-*ah*-ter) (*theater*). Performing arts centers abound in Europe.

If you're up for going out on the town, say

> **Ich möchte heute Abend ausgehen.** (iH *merH*-te *hoy*-te *ah*-bênt *ous-gey*-en.) (*I would like to go out this evening.*)

Worried about the dress code? It's relatively liberal, although Europeans do enjoy getting decked out for opera and symphony performances, especially for **Premiere** (prêm-*yee*-re) (*opening night*) or a **Galavorstellung** (*gâ*-lâ-fohr-shtêl-oong) (*gala performance*). Other than that, as long as you stay away from the T-shirt, jeans, and sneakers look, you won't stick out like a sore thumb.

The following words and phrases may be helpful during a night out:

> **Ich möchte ins Theater/Konzert gehen.** (iH *merH*-te ins tey-*ah*-ter/kon-*tsert* *gey*-en.) (*I would like to go to the theater/a concert.*)

> **Ich möchte in die Oper gehen.** (iH *merH*-te in dee *oh*-per *gey*-en.) (*I would like to go to the opera.*)

Gehen wir ins Theater/Konzert. (*gey*-en veer ins tey-*ah*-ter/kon-*tsert*.) (*Let's go to the theater/a concert.*)

Gehen wir ins Ballet. (*gey*-en veer ins bâ-*lêt*.) (*Let's go to the ballet.*)

Wann ist die Premiere von. . . ? (vân ist dee prêm-*yee*-re fon. . . ?) (*When is the opening night of. . . ?*)

In welchem Theater spielt. . . ? (in *vêlH*-em tey-*ah*-ter shpeelt. . . ?) (*In which theater is . . . showing?*)

Words to Know

das Theater	dâs tey-<u>ah</u>-ter	theater
die Oper	dee <u>oh</u>-per	opera/opera house
die Sinfonie	dee sin-foh-<u>nee</u>	symphony
das Ballett	dâs bâ-<u>lêt</u>	ballet
die Pause	dee <u>pou</u>-ze	intermission
der Sänger/die Sängerin	dêr <u>zên</u>-ger/ dee <u>zên</u>-ge-rin	singer
der Schauspieler/ die Schauspielerin	dêr <u>shou</u>-shpee-ler/ dee <u>shou</u>-spee-le-rin	actor/ actress
der Tänzer/die Tänzerin	dêr <u>tên</u>-tser/ dee <u>tên</u>-tse-rin	dancer
singen	<u>zing</u>-en	to sing
tanzen	<u>tân</u>-tsen	to dance
klatschen	<u>klâch</u>-en	to clap
der Beifall	dêr <u>bay</u>-fâl	applause
die Zugabe	dee <u>tsooh</u>-gah-be	encore
die Kinokasse / Theaterkasse	dee <u>kee</u>-noh-kâs-e / tey-<u>ah</u>-ter-kâs-e	movie/theater box office
der Platz	dêr plâts	seat

How Was It? Talking about Entertainment

When it comes to entertainment, everybody seems to have an opinion. So why miss out on the fun?

Asking for an opinion

Somebody may ask you one of the following questions — or you may pose one of them to someone else — in order to start a conversation about an exhibition, film, or performance (the first version is for speaking with someone formally; the second is for informal speaking):

> **Hat Ihnen die Ausstellung/der Film/die Oper gefallen?** (hât *een*-en dee *ous*-shtêl-oong/dêr film/dee *oh*-per ge-*fâl*-en?) (*Did you like the exhibition/ the movie/the opera?*)

> **Hat dir die Ausstellung/der Film/die Oper gefallen?** (hât deer dee *ous*-shtêl-oong/dêr film/dee *oh*-per ge-*fâl*-en?) (*Did you like the exhibition/the movie/the opera?*)

Telling people what you think

Now comes the fun part — telling someone what you think about a film or performance you've just seen. For starters, you can say whether you liked the entertainment. Try one of the following on for size:

> **Die Ausstellung/der Film/die Oper hat mir (sehr) gut gefallen.** (dee *ous*-shtêl-oong/dêr film/dee *oh*-per hât meer [zeyr] gooht ge-*fâl*-en.) (*I liked the exhibition/the movie/the opera [a lot].*)

> **Die Ausstellung/der Film/die Oper hat mir (gar) nicht gefallen.** (dee *ous*-shtêl-oong/dêr film/dee *oh*-per hât meer [gâr] niHt ge-*fâl*-en.) (*I didn't like the exhibition/the movie/the opera [at all].*)

You may want to follow up a statement with a reason. Start out by saying

> **Die Ausstellung/der Film/die Oper war wirklich. . . .** (dee *ous*-shtêl-oong/dêr film/dee *oh*-per vahr *virk*-liH. . . .) (*The exhibition/the movie/the opera was really. . . .*)

Then you can finish the thought with any of the following adjectives that apply. You can always string a few of them together with the conjunction **und** (oont) (*and*) if you like:

- **aufregend** (*ouf*-rey-gent) (*exciting*)

- **ausgezeichnet** (ous-ge-*tsayH*-net) (*excellent*)

- **enttäuschend** (ênt-*toy*-shênt) (*disappointing*)

- **fantastisch** (fân-*tâs*-tish) (*fantastic*)

- **langweilig** (*lâng*-vay-liH) (*boring*)

- **sehenswert** (*zey*-êns-veyrt) (*worth seeing*)

- **spannend** (*shpân*-ênt) (*thrilling, suspenseful*)

- **unterhaltsam** (oon-ter-*hâlt*-tsahm) (*entertaining*)

- **wunderschön** (*voon*-der-shern) (*beautiful*)

Talkin' the Talk

Frau Peters went to the theater last night. Today, at the office, she's telling her colleague Herr Krüger about the show. (Track 23)

Herr Krüger: **Sind Sie nicht gestern im Theater gewesen?**
zint zee niHt *gês*-tern im teh-*ah*-ter ge-*vey*-zen?
Weren't you at the theater last night?

Frau Peters: **Doch. Ich habe das neue Ballet gesehen.**
doH. iH *hah*-be dâs *noy*-e bâ-*lêt* ge-*zey*-en.
Indeed. I saw the new ballet.

Herr Krüger: **Wie hat es Ihnen gefallen?**
vee hât ês *een*-en ge-*fâl*-en?
How did you like it?

Frau Peters: **Die Tänzer waren fantastisch. Die Vorstellung hat mir ausgezeichnet gefallen.**
dee *tên*-tser *vahr*-ren fân-*tâs*-tish. dee *fohr*-shtêl-oong hât meer ous-ge-*tsayH*-net ge-*fâl*-en.
The dancers were fantastic. I liked the performance very much.

Herr Krüger: **War es einfach, Karten zu bekommen?**
vahr ês *ayn*-fâH, *kâr*-ten tsooh be-*kom*-en?
Was it easy to get tickets?

Frau Peters: **Ja. Ich habe die Karte gestern Morgen an der Theaterkasse gekauft.**
yah. iH *hah*-be dee *kâr*-te *gês*-tern *mor*-gen ân dêr tey-ah-ter-*kâs*-e ge-*kouft*.
Yes. I bought the ticket at the box office yesterday morning.

Going to a Party

Just as Americans do, German speakers have different ideas about what makes a good party. They enjoy organizing all kinds of gatherings, ranging from formal sit-down dinners to Sunday afternoon barbecues. If you're invited to a rather formal gathering at somebody's home, it's considered polite to bring a small gift, such as a bottle of wine or a bouquet of flowers.

And if you're invited to an informal get-together, your host or hostess may ask you to bring along something to eat or drink. You can also take the initiative and ask whether you should bring anything by asking

> **Soll ich etwas mitbringen?** (zol iH *êt*-vâs *mit*-bring-en?) (*Do you want me to bring anything?*)

If you're invited to **Kaffee und Kuchen** (*kâ*-fey oont *koohH*-en) (*coffee and cake*) in the afternoon, a German institution, do arrive on time. In fact, some Germans like to arrive ten minutes early just to be on the safe side, and they wait out on the street until the exact hour to ring the doorbell. Don't expect to stay for dinner. You may be asked, but don't count on it.

Getting an invitation

You may hear any of the following common phrases when receiving an invitation — **die Einladung** (dee *ayn*-lah-doong) — to a party:

> **Ich würde Sie gern zu einer Party einladen.** (iH *vuer*-de zee gêrn tsooh *ayn*-er *pâr*-tee *ayn*-lah-den.) (*I would like to invite you to a party.*)

> **Wir wollen ein Fest feiern. Hast du Lust zu kommen?** (veer *vol*-en ayn fêst *fay*-ern. hâst dooh loost tsooh *kom*-en?) (*We want to have a party. Do you feel like coming?*)

Declining

If you can't make it (or don't want to go for some reason), you can politely turn down the invitation by saying the following:

Nein, tut mir leid, ich kann leider nicht kommen. (nayn, toot meer layt, iH kân *lay*-der niHt *kom*-en.) (*No, sorry, unfortunately I won't be able to make it.*)

Nein, da kann ich leider nicht. Ich habe schon etwas anderes vor. (nayn, dâ kân iH *lay*-der niHt. iH *hah*-be shohn êt-vâs *ân*-de-res fohr.) (*No, unfortunately I won't be able to make it. I have other plans.*)

Accepting

If you'd like to go, you can accept an invitation with the following phrases:

Vielen Dank. Ich nehme die Einladung gern an. (*fee*-len dânk. iH *neh*-me dee *ayn*-lah-doong gêrn ân.) (*Thank you very much. I'll gladly accept the invitation.*)

Gut, ich komme gern. (gooht, iH *kom*-en gêrn) (*Good, I'd like to come.*)

Talking about a party

When someone asks you **Wie war die Party am Samstag?** (vee vahr dee *pâr*-tee âm *zâms*-tahk?) (*How was the party on Saturday?*), here are some possible responses:

Toll, wir haben bis . . . Uhr gefeiert. (tol, veer *hah*-ben bis . . . oohr ge-*fay*-êrt.) (*Great. We partied until . . . o'clock.*)

Wir haben uns ausgezeichnet unterhalten. (veer *hah*-ben oons ous-ge-*tsayH*-net oon-ter-*hâl*-ten.) (*We had a great time.*)

Das Essen war. . . . (dâs *ês*-en vahr. . . .) (*The food was. . . .*)

Wir haben sogar getanzt. (veer *hah*-ben zoh-*gahr* ge-*tântst*.) (*We even danced.*)

Die Musik war. . . . (dee mooh-*zeek* vahr. . . .) (*The music was. . . .*)

Das Fest war. . . . (dâs fêst vahr. . . .) (*The party was . . . .*)

Check out the list of adjectives in the earlier section "Telling people what you think" for appropriate descriptions to fill in the preceding phrases.

Fun & Games

Many words in German have cognates (words similar in meaning and spelling) in English. In the following statements, some people are describing what they thought of an event. You decide which form of entertainment they're speaking of and then write that word at the end of the statement. Choose from the list of cognates shown below.

Museum   Ballet   Film

Oper   Party   Sinfonie

1. Die Ausstellung hat uns sehr gut gefallen. _____

2. Die Zugabe war auch ausgezeichnet. _____

3. Ich habe die Originalfassung gesehen. _____

4. Die Tänzer haben mir gut gefallen. _____

5. Die Sänger sind fantastisch gewesen. _____

6. Wir haben viel gegessen und getrunken. _____

Chapter 11

Taking Care of Business and Telecommunications

. . . .

In This Chapter

▶ Placing phone calls

▶ Sending letters, faxes, and e-mails

▶ Becoming familiar with basic business terminology

. . . .

Telecommunications increasingly drive daily interaction with others, from ordering pizza to conducting business between continents. The first step involves deciding which interface you want to use in order to convey your message — phone, e-mail, fax, or a good old-fashioned letter. This chapter delves into each of these mediums. We wrap things up with a brief primer in office terminology and some tips on conducting business.

Phoning Made Simple

When German speakers pick up **das Telefon** (dâs *tê*-le-fohn) (*the telephone*), they usually answer the call by stating their last name — particularly when they're at the office. If you call somebody at home, you sometimes may hear a simple **Hallo?** (hâ-*loh?*) (*Hello?*).

If you want to express that you're going to call somebody or that you want somebody to call you, you use the verb **anrufen** (*ân*-roohf-en) (*to call*). It's a separable verb, so the prefix **an** (ân) (*to*) gets separated from the stem **rufen** (*roohf*-en) (*call*), when you conjugate it:

Conjugation	Pronunciation
ich rufe an	îH *roohf*-e ân
du rufst an	dooh roohfst ân
Sie rufen an	zee *roohf*-en ân
er, sie, es ruft an	êr, zee, ês roohft ân
wir rufen an	veer *roohf*-en ân
ihr ruft an	eer roohft ân
Sie rufen an	zee *roohf*-en ân
sie rufen an	zee *roohf*-en ân

For more info on separable verbs, see Chapter 15.

Asking for your party

If the person you want to speak to doesn't pick up the phone, you need to ask for your party. As in English, you have some options when it comes to expressing that you want to speak with somebody:

Ich möchte gern Herrn/Frau . . . sprechen. (îH *merH*-te gêrn hêrn/ frou . . . *shprêH*-en.) (*I would like to talk to Mr./Mrs. . . .*)

Ist Herr/Frau . . . zu sprechen? (ist hêr/frou . . . tsooh *shprêH*-en?) (*Is Mr./ Mrs. . . . available?*)

Kann ich bitte mit Herrn/Frau . . . , sprechen? (kân îH *bi*-te mit hêrn/ frou . . . , *shprêH*-en?) (*Can I speak to Mr./Mrs. . . . , please?*)

Herrn/Frau . . . , bitte. (hêrn/frou . . . , *bi*-te.) (*Mr./Mrs. . . . , please.*)

If you find that somebody talks too fast for you to understand, try these solutions:

Können Sie bitte langsamer sprechen? (*kern*-en zee *bi*-te *lâng*-zahm-er *sprêH*-en?) (*Could you please talk more slowly?*)

Können Sie das bitte wiederholen? (*kern*-en zee dâs *bi*-te vee-der-*hoh*-len?) (*Could you repeat that, please?*)

And if the person on the other end starts speaking English in response to your question, don't consider it a failure on your part. The other person probably just wants to practice his or her English!

Saying goodbye on the phone

Does **auf Wiederhören!** (ouf *vee*-der-herr-en!) sound somewhat familiar? It's the phone equivalent to **auf Wiedersehen** (ouf *vee*-der-zey-en), the expression you use if you say good-bye to somebody you've just seen in person.

Auf Wiedersehen combines **wieder** (*vee*-der) (*again*) with the verb **sehen** (*zey*-en) (*to see*), whereas **auf Wiederhören** uses the verb **hören** (*herr*-en) (*to hear*), so it literally means "hear you again." Makes sense, doesn't it?

Making the connection

After you ask to speak to a specific person, you may hear any number of responses depending on whom you're calling and where they are:

> **Am Apparat.** (âm â-pa-*raht*.) (*Speaking.* [literally, *on the phone*])

> **Einen Moment bitte, ich verbinde.** (*ayn*-en moh-*mênt bi*-te, îH fêr-*bin*-de.) (*One moment please, I'll put you through.*)

> **Er/sie telefoniert gerade.** (êr/zee tê-le-foh-*neert* ge-rah-de.) (*He/she is on the telephone right now.*)

> **Die Leitung ist besetzt.** (dee *lay*-toong ist *be*-zêtst.) (*The line is busy.*)

> **Können Sie später noch einmal anrufen?** (*kern*-en zee *shpai*-ter noH *ayn*-mahl *ân*-roohf-en?) (*Could you call again later?*)

> **Kann er/sie Sie zurückrufen?** (kân êr/zee zee tsoo-*ruek*-roohf-en?) (*Can he/she call you back?*)

> **Hat er/sie Ihre Telefonnummer?** (hât êr/zee *eer*-e tê-le-*fohn*-noom-er?) (*Does he/she have your phone number?*)

Here are some expressions that may be helpful if something goes wrong with your connection:

> **Es tut mir leid. Ich habe mich verwählt.** (ês tooht meer layt. iH *hah*-be miH fer-*vailt*.) (*I'm sorry. I have dialed the wrong number.*)

> **Die Verbindung ist schlecht.** (dee fêr-*bin*-doong ist shlêHt.) (*It's a bad connection.*)

> **Er/sie meldet sich nicht.** (êr/zee *mêl*-det ziH niHt.) (*He/she doesn't answer the phone.*)

Talkin' the Talk

 The following is a conversation between Frau Bauer, the personal assistant of Herr Huber, and Herr Meißner, a client of the company. (Track 24)

Frau Bauer:	**Firma TransEuropa, Bauer. Guten Morgen!** fir-mâ *trâns-oy-roh*-pâ, *bou*-er. gooh-ten *mor*-gen! *TransEuropa company, (Mrs.) Bauer speaking. Good morning!*
Herr Meißner:	**Guten Morgen! Herrn Huber, bitte.** gooh-ten *mor*-gen! hêrn *hooh*-ber, *bi*-te. *Good morning! Mr. Huber, please.*
Frau Bauer:	**Wie ist ihr Name, bitte?** vee ist eer *nah*-me, *bi*-te? *What is your name, please?*
Herr Meißner:	**Meißner. Ich bin von der Firma Schlecker.** *mays*-ner. iH bin fon dêr *fir*-mâ *shlêk*-er. *(This is Mr.) Meißner. I'm from the Schlecker company.*
Frau Bauer:	**Ich verbinde . . .Tut mir leid. Herr Huber ist in einer Besprechung. Kann er Sie zurückrufen?** iH fêr-*bin*-de . . . tooht meer layt. hêr *hooh*-ber ist in *ayn*-er be-*shprêH*-oong. kân êr zee tsoo-*ruek*-roohf-en? *I'll connect you . . . I'm sorry. Mr. Huber is in a meeting. Can he call you back?*
Herr Meißner:	**Selbstverständlich. Er hat meine Telefonnummer.** zêlpst-fêr-*shtant*-liH. êr hât *mayn*-e tê-le-*fohn*-noom-er. *Of course. He has my telephone number.*
Frau Bauer:	**Gut, Herr Meißner. Auf Wiederhören!** gooht, hêr *mays*-ner. ouf *vee*-der-herr-en! *Good, Mr. Meißner. Good bye!*
Herr Meißner:	**Vielen Dank. Auf Wiederhören!** *fee*-len dânk. ouf *vee*-der-herr-en! *Thanks a lot. Good bye!*

Using the phone

If you'd like the convenience of using a cellphone while you're in Germany, or almost anywhere in Europe for that matter, shop around before you leave for Europe. You may want a prepaid SIM card for your cellphone, but you need to ask your provider beforehand whether it works in Europe. Your other options are to get a prepaid cellphone or a rental cellphone. If you want to make a call from a public phone — **die** **Telefonzelle** (dee tê-le-*fohn*-tsêl-e) (*the phone booth*) — in Germany, be prepared to do some sleuthing to find one. When you do, you'll need to figure out how it works (and you'll probably need to purchase a telephone card — **Telefonkarte** (tê-le-*fohn*-kâr-te) — elsewhere beforehand). It may be easier to get your own cellphone — **das Handy** (dâs *hên*-dee) — at a telephone shop in Germany.

Words to Know

das Telefon	dâs <u>tê</u>-le-fohn	phone
das Handy	dâs <u>hên</u>-dee	cellphone
anrufen	<u>ân</u>-roohf-en	to call
zurückrufen	tsoo-<u>ruek</u>-roohf-en	to call back
auf Wiederhören!	ouf <u>vee</u>-der-herr-en	Good-bye! (on the phone)
das Telefonbuch	dâs tê-le-<u>fohn</u>-boohH	phone book
das Telefonge-spräch	dâs tê-le-<u>fohn</u>-ge-shpraiH	phone call
die Telefon-nummer	dee tê-le-<u>fohn</u>-noom-er	phone number
der Anrufbeant-worter	dêr <u>ân</u>-roohf-be-ânt-for-ter	answering machine

Making Appointments

You may need to make an appointment to see someone. Here's some of the vocabulary that can help you get past the gatekeepers:

Ich möchte gern einen Termin machen. (iH *merH*-te gêrn *ayn*-en têr-meen *mâH*-en.) (*I would like to make an appointment.*)

Kann ich meinen Termin verschieben? (kân iH *mayn*-en têr-*meen* fêr-*shee*-ben?) (*Can I change my appointment?*)

And here are some of the answers you may hear:

Wann passt es Ihnen? (vân pâst ês *een*-en?) (*What time suits you?*)

Wie wäre es mit . . . ? (vee *vai*-re ês mit . . . ?) (*How about . . . ?*)

Heute ist leider kein Termin mehr frei. (*hoy*-te ist *lay*-der kayn têr-*meen* meyr fray.) (*Unfortunately, there is no appointment available today.*)

Talkin' the Talk

Frau Bauer has to make an appointment at the doctor's office. She is talking to the doctor's assistant, Liza.

Liza: **Praxis Dr. Eggert.**
prâx-is *dok*-tor *êg*-ert.
Dr. Eggert's office.

Frau Bauer: **Guten Tag, Anita Bauer. Ich möchte einen Termin für nächste Woche machen.**
gooh-ten tahk, â-*nee*-tâ *bou*-er. iH *merH*-te *ayn*-en têr-*meen* fuer *naiH*-ste *voH*-e *mâH*-en.
Hello. (This is) Anita Bauer. I would like to make an appointment for next week.

Liza: **Wann passt es Ihnen?**
vân pâst ês *een*-en?
What time suits you?

Frau Bauer: **Mittwoch wäre gut.**
mit-vôH *vai*-re gooht.
Wednesday would be good.

Liza:	**Mittwoch ist leider kein Termin mehr frei. Wie wäre es mit Donnerstag?** *mit*-voH îst *lay*-der kayn têr-*meen* meyr fray. vee *vai*-re ês mit *don-ers*-tahk? *Unfortunately, there is no appointment available on Wednesday. How about Thursday?*
Frau Bauer:	**Donnerstag ist auch gut. Geht fünfzehn Uhr?** *don-ers*-tahk ist ouH gooht. geyt *fuenf*-tseyn oohr? *Thursday is good, too. Does 3:00 p.m. work?*
Liza:	**Kein Problem. Dann bis Donnerstag.** kayn proh-*bleym*. dân bis *don-ers*-tahk. *No problem. Until Thursday.*
Frau Bauer:	**Danke schön. Auf Wiederhören.** *dân*-ke shern. ouf *vee-der-herr*-en. *Thank you very much. Good-bye.*

Leaving Messages

Unfortunately, you often don't get through to the person you're trying to reach, and you have to leave a message. In that case, some of the following expressions may come in handy (some of these phrases use dative pronouns, which you can read about in the next section):

Kann ich ihm/ihr eine Nachricht hinterlassen? (kân îH eem/eer *ayn*-e *nahH*-riHt hin-ter-*lâs*-en?) (*Can I leave him/her a message?*)

Kann ich ihm/ihr etwas ausrichten? (kân iH eem/eer *êt*-vâs *ous*-rîH-ten?) (*Can I give him/her a message?*)

Möchten Sie eine Nachricht hinterlassen? (*merH*-ten zee *ayn*-e *naH*-riHt hin-ter-*lâs*-en?) (*Would you like to leave a message?*)

Ich bin unter der Nummer . . . zu erreichen. (iH bin *oon*-ter dêr *noom*-er . . . tsooh êr-*ayH*-en.) (*I can be reached at the number . . . .*)

A Few Words about Dative Pronouns

Ihm (eem) (*him*) and **ihr** (eer) (*her*) are personal pronouns in the dative case. In German, you need the dative case of these pronouns when they are combined with the dative preposition **mit** (mit) (*with*). So when you want to express that you'd like to talk to or speak with a person (him or her), you can say

> **Ich möchte gern mit ihm/ihr sprechen.** (iH *merH*-te gêrn mit eem/eer *shprêH*-en.) (*I would like to speak with him/her.*)

And if you can't get through to the person you want to speak to, here's how to indicate that you're leaving that person a message:

> **Ich hinterlasse ihm/ihr eine Nachricht.** (iH hin-ter-*lâs*-e eem/eer *ayn*-e *nahH*-riHt.) (*I'm leaving him/her a message.*)

Talkin' the Talk

Frau Bauer, an assistant at the company TransEuropa, answers a phone call from Hans Seibold, who is an old friend of her boss, Herr Huber.

Frau Bauer: **Firma TransEuropa, guten Tag!**
fir-mâ *trâns*-oy-roh-pâ, *gooh*-ten tahk!
TransEuropa company, hello!

Herr Seibold: **Guten Tag, Seibold hier. Kann ich bitte mit Herrn Huber, sprechen?**
gooh-ten tahk *zay*-bolt heer. kân iH *bi*-te mit hêrn hooh-ber, *shprêH*-en?
Hello,(this is Mr.) Seibold. Can I speak to Mr. Huber, please?

Frau Bauer: **Guten Tag, Herr Seibold. Einen Moment bitte, ich verbinde.**
gooh-ten tahk hêr zay-bolt. *ayn*-en moh-*mênt bi*-te, iH fêr-*bin*-de.
Hello, Mr. Seibold. One moment, please. I'll connect you.

(After a short moment)

Frau Bauer:	**Herr Seibold? Herr Huber spricht gerade auf der anderen Leitung. Möchten Sie ihm eine Nachricht hinterlassen?**
	hêr *zay*-bolt? hêr *hooh*-ber shpriHt ge-*rah*-de ouf dêr *ân*-de-ren *lay*-toong. *merH*-ten zee eem *ayn*-e *nahH*-riHt hin-ter-*lâs*-en?
	Mr. Seibold? Mr. Huber is on the other line. Would you like to leave him a message?
Herr Seibold:	**Ja bitte. Ich bin unter der Nummer 089 57 36 488 zu erreichen.**
	yah, *bi*-te. iH bin *oon*-têr dêr *noom*-er nool âHt noyn fuenf *zee*-ben dray zeks feer âHt âHt tsooh ê-*rayH*-en.
	Yes, please. I can be reached at the number 089 57 36 488.
Frau Bauer:	**Ich werde es ausrichten!**
	iH *vêr*-de ês *ous*-riH-ten!
	I'll forward the message!
Herr Seibold:	**Vielen Dank! Auf Wiederhören!**
	vee-len dânk! ouf *vee*-der-*herr*-en!
	Thanks a lot! Good-bye!

Sending Written Correspondence

Considering all the tasks you can accomplish with a (cell)phone, you may ask yourself why anyone would bother with the hassle of putting pen to paper. Yet people still like, and need, to send written correspondence from time to time. Entire books have been written about the art of writing letters in German; this section just gives you enough information to begin and end a letter appropriately.

You use certain conventions in German, just as you do in English, to write letters. In German, the phrase you begin with is **Sehr geehrte Frau . . ./ Sehr geehrter Herr . . .** (zeyr ge-*eyr*-te frou/zeyr ge-*eyr*-ter hêr) (*Dear Mrs . . ./ Dear Mr . . .*). And the phrase most often used to sign off a letter is **Mit freundlichen Grüßen** (mit *froynt*-liH-en *grues*-en) (*Sincerely*).

Contrary to English convention, the first letter of the first word in the opening sentence of a German letter is not capitalized, unless it's a noun.

Assuming you don't have a carrier pigeon at your disposal, the following sections explain how to send your correspondence where it needs to go.

Sending a letter or postcard

With people standing in line behind you, it pays to be prepared with some simple phrases that get you in and out of **das Postamt** (dâs *post*-âmt) (*post office*) as quickly and hassle-free as possible and send **der Brief** (dêr breef) (*letter*), **die Postkarte** (dee *post*-kâr-te) (*postcard*), **die Ansichtskarte** (dee *ahn*-zîHts-kâr-te) (*picture postcard*) or **das Paket** (dâs pâ-*keyt*) (*package*) on its merry way.

Buying stamps

In Germany, you usually buy **Briefmarken** (*breef*-mâr-ken) (*stamps*) — or, if you need only one, **die Briefmarke** (dee *breef*-mâr-ke) (*stamp*) — at the post office. To get your stamps, say the following to the postal worker:

> **Ich möchte gern Briefmarken kaufen.** (iH *merH*-te gern *breef*-mâr-ken *kouf*-en.) (*I would like to buy stamps.*)

To specify how many stamps and what values you want, state your request like this:

> **5-mal 50 Cent und 10-mal 20 Cent.** (*fuenf*-mahl *fuenf*-tsiH sent oont *tseyn*-mahl *tsvân*-tsiH sent.) (*5 times 50 cents and 10 times 20 cents.*)

If you want to know the postage for an item you're sending to the U.S. — for example, a letter or a postcard — ask the following as you hand your correspondence over the counter:

> **Wie viel kostet es, diesen Brief/diese Ansichtskarte nach Amerika zu schicken?** (vee feel *kos*-tet ês, *deez*-en breef/*deez*-e ahn-ziHts-*kâr*-te nahH â-*mey*-ree-kah tsooh *shik*-en?) (*How much does it cost to send this letter/this picture postcard to the U.S.?*)

Putting your mail in the mailbox

As in the U.S., you can give your mail to a postal worker, drop it into one of the receptacles at the post office (those slits in the wall), or put it into a **Briefkasten** (*breef*-kâst-en) (*mailbox*) found on street corners or in front of post offices (in Germany, mailboxes are yellow, not blue). Sometimes separate mailboxes are available: one for the city you're in and the surrounding area, and another one for other places. So the mailboxes may have signs saying, for example, **Köln und Umgebung** (kerln oont oom-*gey*-boong)

(*Cologne and surrounding area*) and **Andere Orte** (*ân*-de-re *or*-te) (*other places*).

In Germany, you can't put items to mail in your mailbox to be picked up.

Asking for special services

If you want to send an express letter, airmail, certified mail, or a package, you need to be familiar with these words:

- **der Eilbrief** (dêr *ayl*-breef) (*express letter*)
- **das Einschreiben** (dâs *ayn*-shrayb-en) (*registered letter/certified mail*)
- **die Luftpost** (dee *looft*-post) (*airmail*)
- **das Paket** (dâs pâ-*keyt*) (*package*)

To get these pieces of mail on their way, tell the postal worker

> **Ich möchte diesen Brief per Eilzustellung/per Luftpost/per Einschreiben schicken.** (îH *merH*-te *deez*-en breef pêr *ayl*-tsooh-shtêl-oong/pêr *looft*-post/pêr *ayn*-shrayb-en *shik*-en.) (*I would like to send this letter express/by air mail/by registered mail.*)

> **Ich möchte dieses Paket aufgeben.** (iH *merH*-te *deez*-es pâ-*keyt* ouf-gey-ben.) (*I would like to send this package.*)

The following words are helpful when it comes to sending mail (and you also find them on the form you have to fill out when you're sending certified mail):

- **der Absender** (dêr *âp*-zên-der) (*sender*)
- **der Empfänger** (dêr êm-*pfêng*-er) (*addressee*)
- **das Porto** (dâs *por*-toh) (*postage*)

E-mailing

If you want to catch up on your e-mail, your hotel will probably have Wi-Fi Internet access. Otherwise, head for a cybercafé or ask whether a (free) Wi-Fi hotspot is nearby.

The great thing about e-mail and the Internet is that they involve an international language — the language of computers, which is, for the most part, English. However, being aware of the German equivalents for a few words connected with e-mailing is still handy:

- **der Computer** (dêr computer [as in English]) (*computer*)
- **die E-mail** (dee e-mail [as in English]) (*e-mail*)
- **die E-mail-Adresse** (dee e-mail ah-*drês*-e) (*e-mail address*)
- **das Internet** (dâs Internet [as in English]) (*Internet*)

Sending a fax

If you can't conveniently use somebody's **Faxgerät** (*fâx*-ge-rêt) (*fax machine*), you should be able to send a **Fax** (fâx) (*fax*) from most cybercafés, hotels, and some copy shops. Just walk up to the counter and tell the person working there

> **Ich möchte etwas faxen.** (iH *merH*-te êt-vâs *fâx*-en.) (*I would like to fax something.*)

After you find a place that can send your fax, the person operating the machine will ask you for **die Faxnummer** (dee *fâx*-noom-er) (*the fax number*).

Write the fax number on a piece of paper beforehand so that, when you're asked, you can just hand it over with a confident smile.

Talkin' the Talk

Frau Bauer's workday is almost over, and she only has to mail a package at the post office. Listen in on her conversation with **der Postangestellte** (dêr *post*-ân-ge-shtêl-te) (*post office worker*).

Frau Bauer:	**Guten Tag. Ich möchte ein Paket aufgeben.** *gooh*-ten tahk. iH *merH*-te ayn pâ-*keyt* *ouf*-gey-ben. *Hello. I would like to send a package.*
Der Postangestellte:	**Jawohl. Füllen Sie bitte dieses Formular aus.** yah-*vohl*. *fuel*-en zee *bi*-te *deez*-es fohr-moo-*lahr* ous. *Certainly. Please fill out this form.*
Frau Bauer:	**Was für ein Formular ist das?** vâs fuer ayn fohr-moo-*lahr* ist dâs? *What kind of a form is that?*

Der Postangestellte: **Es ist eine Zollerklärung.**
ês ist *ayn*-e *tsol*-êr-klair-oong.
It's a customs declaration.

(Frau Bauer fills out the form and hands it back)

Frau Bauer: **Bitte.**
bi-te
Here you are.

Der Postangestellte: **Also, das macht 12,60 Euro.**
âl-*zoh*, dâs maHt tsverlf *oy*-roh sêH-tsiH.
So, that'll be 12 euros 60.

Getting to Know the Office

When it comes to the workplace, Germans have a reputation for being straightforward, productive, and efficient, but you may be surprised to find out that, statistically speaking, they don't work as many hours as Americans do. Not that people don't work late, but Germans enjoy much more generous vacation time. And on Fridays, many companies close early.

When you're working in a German-speaking **Büro** (*bue*-roh) (*office*), you're assigned various tasks, or **Büroarbeit** (bue-*roh*-âr-bayt) (*office work*).

What do you call all that paraphernalia on your desk or all the stuff in the supply closet? Read on. After you have those terms down, you need to know how to describe what to do with them. Time to get to work!

CULTURAL WISDOM

A vacationer's paradise

Germans get far more vacation time than Americans: 30 workdays of vacation plus paid holidays — and some states of Germany have as many as 12 legal holidays. However, Germans typically have trouble finding the time to actually take vacations. Thus, vacation time is sometimes carried over into the next year.

Office work entails assignments and tasks you may be given or have to give to someone else. Here are a few expressions that come into play in such circumstances. They also come in handy when you need some help:

Wo finde ich den Fotokopierer / das Faxgerät? (voh *fin*-de iH deyn foh-toh-ko-*peer*-er/dâs *fâx*-gê-reyt?) (*Where can I find the copy machine/fax machine?*)

Können Sie mir bitte zeigen, wie das funktioniert? (*kern*-en zee meer *bi*-te *tsay*-gen vee dâs foonk-tsee-oh-*neert?*) (*Could you please show me how that works?*)

Würden Sie bitte diesen Brief für mich übersetzen? (*vuer*-den zee *bi*-te *deez*-en breef fuer miH ue-ber-*zêts*-en?) (*Would you translate this letter for me, please?*)

Mastering your desk and supplies

Typically, you may find — or hope to find — the following items on or around your **Schreibtisch** (*shrayp*-tish) (*desk*):

- **der Brief** (dêr breef) (*letter*)
- **der Bürostuhl** (dêr bue-*roh*-shtool) (*office chair*)
- **der Computer** (dêr computer [as in English]) (*computer*)
- **der Drucker** (dêr *drook*-er) (*printer*)
- **das Faxgerät** (dâs *fâx*-gê-reyt) (*fax machine*)
- **der Fotokopierer** (dêr foh-toh-ko-*peer*-er) (*copy machine*)
- **die Lampe** (dee *lâm*-pe) (*lamp*)
- **die Maus** (dee mouse [as in English]) (*mouse*)
- **das Telefon** (dâs *tê*-le-fohn) (*telephone*)
- **die Unterlagen** (dee *oon*-ter-lah-gen) (*documents, files*)

Don't forget the question **Wo ist . . . ?** (voh ist) (*Where is . . . ?*) if you need to ask someone for help finding something around the office.

Sooner or later, you're likely to need one of the following supplies:

- **der Bleistift** (dêr *blay*-shtift) (*pencil*)
- **der Kugelschreiber** (dêr *kooh*-gel-shray-ber) (*pen*)
- **das Papier** (dâs pâ-*peer*) (*paper*)
- **der Umschlag** (dêr *oom*-shlahk) (*envelope*)

When you need some of these supplies, and you can't find them on your own after rummaging around, ask a colleague to help you find them by saying

> **Haben Sie einen Kugelschreiber/einen Umschlag für mich?** (*hah*-ben zee *ayn*-en *kooh*-gel-shray-ber/*ayn*-en *oom*-shlahk fuer miH?) (*Could you give me a pen/envelope?* Literally: *Do you have a pen/envelope for me?*)

> **Können Sie mir sagen, wo ich Umschläge/Bleistifte/Papier finde?** (*kern*-en zee meer *zah*-gen, voh iH *oom*-shlê-ge/*blay*-shtift-e/pâ-*peer fin*-de?) (*Could you tell me where I would find envelopes/pencils/paper?*)

Doing business in German

Just like everywhere else, German-speaking countries have their own business world with their own culture and specialized language. Non-native speakers study for many years, taking special courses on meetings and negotiations, telephoning, and giving speeches, in order to be successful at doing business in German. This chapter (or book, for that matter) doesn't have the space to provide all the details you need to communicate at the business level — and you probably don't have the time it would take to learn all you'd need to know. But you may find yourself in a situation where a few business terms — and a little advice on how to proceed — can come in pretty handy.

If you plan to perform business with German speakers, you may want to call ahead and ask whether the services of **der Dolmetscher** (dêr *dol*-mêch-er)/**die Dolmetscherin** (dee *dol*-mêch-er-in) (*interpreter*) or **der Übersetzer** (dêr ue-ber-*zêts*-êr)/**die Übersetzerin** (dee ue-ber-*zêts*-êr-in) (*translator*) can be made available to you. Also find out whether the translator will take **die Notizen** (dee noh-*tits*-en) (*notes*) in English during the meeting so that you have a written record of the goings-on. Don't feel the slightest bit shy about asking for an interpreter or a translator. Business people all over the world respect someone who knows when it's time to delegate.

Many German job titles have two versions to show whether a man or a woman is doing that job. Often, the title used for men ends in **-er**, like the term for a male interpreter: **der Dolmetscher**. The women's title ends in **-erin**, as is the case with **die Dolmetscherin**.

Following are a few more steps to take before you start doing business **auf Deutsch** (ouf doych) (*in German*):

- ✔ Study up on the formal introductions in Chapter 3. Nailing the introductions shows your interest in the proceedings, even if you don't understand much more of what's being said.

- ✔ Read the section "Describing your work" in Chapter 6. This will arm you with a few words you need to make small talk about your job.

✔ Acquaint yourself with the following common office terms:

- **anrufen** (*ân*-roohf-en) (*to phone*)

- **die Besprechung** (dee be-*shprêH*-oong) (*meeting*)

- **der Chef/die Chefin** (dêr shêf/die *shêf*-în) (*boss*)

- **der Direktor/die Direktorin** (dêr di-*rêk*-tohr/dee di-rêk-*tohr*-in) (*director*)

- **der Mitarbeiter/die Mitarbeiterin** (dêr *mit*-âr-bay-ter/dee *mit*-âr-bay-ter-in) (*colleague/employee*)

- **der Sekretär/die Sekretärin** (dêr zê-krê-*têr*/dee zê-krê-*têr*-in) (*secretary*).

- **der Termin** (dêr têr-*meen*) (*appointment*)

Talkin' the Talk

Listen in on the following conversation between Frau Seifert and her assistant, Frau. Remmert. Frau Seifert has come to the office early because she has an important meeting.

Frau Seifert: **Guten Morgen, Frau Remmert.**
gooh-ten *mor*-gen, frou *rêm*-ert.
Good morning, Ms. Remmert.

Frau Remmert: **Guten Morgen, Frau Seifert.**
gooh-ten *mor*-gen, frou *zayf*-êrt.
Good morning, Ms. Seifert.

Frau Seifert: **Wissen Sie, ob Herr Krause heute im Hause ist?**
vis-en zee, op hêr *krouz*-e *hoy*-te im *houz*-e ist?
Do you know if Mr. Krause is in the office today?

Frau Remmert: **Ich glaube ja.**
iH *glou*-be yah.
I think so.

Frau Seifert: **Ich muss dringend mit ihm sprechen.**
iH moos *dring*-end mit eem *shprêH*-en.
I have to speak to him urgently.

Frau Remmert: **In Ordnung. Ach ja, Frau Hoffmann von der Firma Solag hat angerufen.**
in *ord*-noong. ahH yah, frou *hof*-mân fon dêr *fir*-mâ *soh*-lahk hât *ân*-gê-roohf-en.
Okay. Oh yes, Ms. Hoffman from (the company) Solag called.

Frau Seifert: **Gut, ich rufe sie gleich an. Und würden Sie bitte diesen Brief für mich übersetzen?**
gooht, iH *roohf*-e zee glayH *ân.* oont *vuer*-den zee *bi*-te *deez*-en breef fuer miH ue-ber-*zêts*-en?
Good, I'll call her right away. And would you translate this letter for me, please?

Frau Remmert: **Wird gemacht, Frau Seifert.**
virt gê-*mâHt* frou *zayf*-êrt
I'll do that, Ms. Seifert.

Words to Know

gleich	glayH	in a moment
sofort	zo-<u>fort</u>	immediately
dringend	<u>drîng</u>-end	urgently
im Hause sein	im <u>houz</u>-e zayn	to be in the building/ office
in Ordnung	in <u>ord</u>-noong	okay
Wird gemacht	virt ge-<u>mâHt</u>	I'll do that. [Literally: It will be done.]

Fun & Games

The following picture shows the kinds of items you would find in a typical office. Write the German terms for each in the blanks provided.

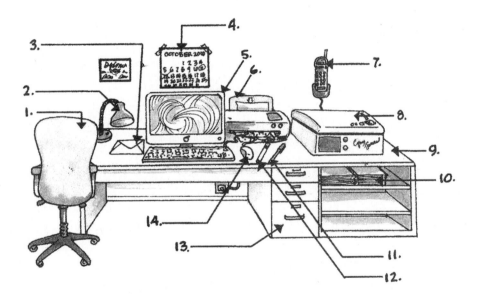

1. Office chair: _____

2. Lamp: _____

3. Envelope: _____

4. Calendar: _____

5. Computer: _____

6. Printer: _____

7. Telephone: _____

8. Copy machine: _____

9. Desk: _____

10. Paper: _____

11. Pen: _____

12. Pencil: _____

13. Files: _____

14. Mouse: _____

Chapter 12

Recreation and the Great Outdoors

- -

In This Chapter

▶ Talking about sports

▶ Understanding reflexive verbs and pronouns

▶ Taking a trip to the mountains, the country, or the sea

- -

This chapter looks at the fun things people do when they're not working. Europeans like to make the most of their time off. Germans in particular are among the world's most seasoned globetrotters, yet they also enjoy visiting the many beautiful spots inside their own country.

Within German-speaking Europe, you can enjoy a vast range of sports and recreation opportunities. Take your pick! You can sail on one of many lakes, ski in the mountains, go mountain biking, relax at the shore, or simply enjoy nature while walking on one of the many well-marked hiking trails, to name just a few possibilities.

Playing Sports

Europeans, like Americans and people all over the world, enjoy participating in and watching a wide variety of indoor and outdoor sports. Traditional favorites include soccer (by far the most popular sport), volleyball, bicycling, skiing, and hiking. Some relative newcomers are tennis, golf, and windsurfing. By using the words and phrases in this section, you can share your interest in sports with other people, **auf Deutsch** (ouf doych) (*in German*)!

Playing around with the verb "spielen"

You can express your general interest in playing many sports by using the verb **spielen** (*shpeel*-en) (to play) together with the noun that describes the sport in the following phrase:

Ich spiele gern. . . . (iH *shpeel*-e gẽrn. . . .) (*I like to play. . . .*)

You can insert the names of the following sports at the end of the sentence, and then let the games begin!

- **Basketball** (basketball [as in English]) (*basketball*)
- **Fußball** (*foohs*-bâl) (*soccer*)
- **Golf** (golf [as in English]) (*golf*)
- **Tennis** (tennis [as in English]) (*tennis*)
- **Volleyball** (volleyball [as in English]) (*volleyball*)

Verbalizing sports you enjoy

Some sports are expressed as verbs, so you don't use the verb **spielen** to talk about them. You can use the following expression to communicate what you're interested in doing:

Ich möchte gern. . . . (iH *merH*-te gêrn. . . .) (*I would like to. . . .*)

To complete the sentence, you simply tack on the verb that expresses the sport — no conjugating necessary — at the end of the expression. For example:

Ich möchte gern segeln. (iH *merH*-te gêrn *zey*-geln.) (*I would like to sail.*)

Here are a few verbs to choose from:

- **Fahrrad fahren** (*fahr*-rât *fahr*-en) (*to ride a bike*)
- **joggen** (*jog*-en) (*to jog*)
- **schwimmen** (*shvim*-en) (*to swim*)
- **segeln** (*zey*-geln) (*to sail*)
- **Ski fahren** (shee *fahr*-en) (*to ski*)
- **windsurfen** (*vint*-soorf-en) (*to windsurf*)

The following construction will get you far when discussing favorite activities:

Ich . . . gern. (iH . . . gêrn.) (*I like to. . . .*)

Here you need to remember to conjugate the verb that you put in the blank. Check out these examples:

Ich schwimme gern. (iH *shvim*-e gêrn.) (*I like to swim.*)

Ich fahre gern Fahrrad. (iH *fahr*-e gêrn *fahr*-rât.) (*I like to bike.*)

Inviting someone to play

To ask someone to join you in an activity, use one of the following expressions and add on either the verb (in infinitive form) that expresses the sport or the noun that expresses the sport plus the verb **spielen**:

Lass uns . . . gehen! (lâs oons . . . *gey*-en!) (*Let's go . . . !*)

Möchtest du . . . ? (*merH*-test dooh . . .) (*Would you like to . . . ?*)

Take a look at these two examples:

Lass uns windsurfen gehen! (lâs oons *vint*-soorf-en *gey*-en!) (*Let's go windsurfing!*)

Möchtest du Volleyball spielen? (*merH*-test dooh volleyball *speel*-en?) (*Would you like to play volleyball?*)

Talkin' the Talk

It's Friday afternoon, and Michael spots his friend Ingo on the subway.

Michael: **Grüß dich Ingo. Was machst du morgen?**
grues dîH *een*-goh. Vâs mâHst dooh *mor*-gên?
Hi Ingo. What are you doing tomorrow?

Ingo: **Nichts Besonderes. Joggen oder schwimmen. Was hast du vor?**
niHts be-*zon*-der-es. *jog*-en *oh*-der *shvim*-en. vâs hâst du for?
Nothing special. Jogging or swimming. What are your plans?

Michael: **Ich möchte gern Fahrrad fahren. Kommst du mit?**
iH *merH*-te gêrn *fahr*-rât *fahr*-en. Komst du mit?
I'd really like to take a bike ride. Want to come along?

Ingo: **Ja, sicher. Wohin fahren wir?**
yâh, *zeeH*-er. voh-*hin fahr*-en veer?
Yes, sure. Where shall we go?

Michael:	**Lass uns zum Starnberger See fahren. Wir können dort in den Biergarten gehen.**
	lâs oons tsoom *shtahrn*-bêr-ger zey *fahr*-en. veer *kern*-en dort in deyn *beer*-gâr-ten *gey*-en.
	Let's ride to Starnberger Lake. We can go to the beer-garden there.
Ingo:	**Abgemacht! Bis morgen!**
	ahp-ge-mâHt. bis *mor*-gen!
	That's a deal! Until tomorrow!

Words to Know

etwas vorhaben	êt-wâs for-hah-ben	to have some plans
mitkommen	mit-kom-en	to come along
ja, sicher	jâh, zeeH-er	yes, sure
wohin	voh-hin	where to
abgemacht	ahp-ge-mâHt	that's a deal
bis morgen	bis mor-gen	until tomorrow

Using Reflexive Verbs to Talk about Plans

You've made vacation plans, and you're excited about participating in activities you're really interested in. How do you tell someone that you're looking forward to something? Germans say

Ich freue mich auf den Urlaub. (iH *froy*-e miH ouf deyn *oor*-loup.)
I'm looking forward to the vacation.

Note that this sentence contains a *reflexive verb*. Reflexive verbs are a lot more commonly used in German than in English. This section explores reflexive verbs a bit more.

Getting reflexive

German verbs have a reputation for acting a bit strangely. They do things that English verbs just don't do. For example, German verbs can be at the end of a sentence. And sometimes they split in two, with only one part of the verb going to the end of a sentence! (See Chapter 14 for more on verbs that split.) You need to flex your German grammar muscles as you read on about reflexive verbs.

Some German verbs just can't work alone and must be accompanied by a helping pronoun in the accusative or the dative case, depending on the pronoun's function in the sentence. The pronoun reflects back (just like a mirror) on the subject. That's why these verbs are commonly called *reflexive verbs,* and the pronouns are called *reflexive pronouns.*

Accusing and dating your pronouns

What are these so-called reflexive pronouns, and what's this about accusing and dating them? Well, many of them may look and sound familiar. Table 12-1 shows you the reflexive pronouns in the accusative and dative cases and, for reference, the corresponding personal pronouns. Note that only two reflexive forms aren't the same in the two cases, namely **mich/mir** (miH/meer) (*me*) and **dich/dir** (diH/deer) (*you*). Accusative and dative reflexive pronouns have the same meanings.

Table 12-1	**Accusative and Dative Reflexive Pronouns**	
Personal Pronoun	*Accusative Reflexive Pronoun*	*Dative Reflexive Pronoun*
ich (iH) (*I*)	**mich** (miH) (myself)	**mir** (meer) (*myself*)
du (dooh) (*you*) (singular, informal)	**dich** (diH) (yourself)	**dir** (deer) (*yourself*)
er, sie, es (êr, zee, ês) (*he,she,it*)	**sich** (ziH) (himself, herself, itself)	**sich** (ziH) (*himself, herself, itself*)
wir (veer) (*we*)	**uns** (oons) (ourselves)	**uns** (oons) (*ourselves*)
ihr (eer) (*you*) (plural, informal)	**euch** (oyH) (yourselves)	**euch** (oyH) (*yourselves*)
sie (zee) (*they*)	**sich** (ziH) (themselves)	**sich** (ziH) (*themselves*)
Sie (zee) (*you*) singular/plural, formal	**sich** (ziH) (*yourself/ yourselves*)	**sich** (ziH) (*yourself/ yourselves*)

The reflexive pronoun goes after the conjugated verb in a normal sentence. In a question starting with a verb, the reflexive pronoun goes after the subject. (See Chapter 2 for more information on forming questions in German.)

Take a look at the following examples of reflexive verbs and reflexive pronouns doing their thing in sentences:

Ich interessiere mich für die Natur. (iH in-te-rê-*see*-re miH fuer dee nâ-*toohr*.) (*I am interested in nature.*) Literally, this sentence translates as *I interest myself in nature.* The subject **ich** (*I*) is reflected in the pronoun **mich** (*myself*).

Freust du dich auf deinen Urlaub? (froyst *dooh* diH ouf *dayn*-en oor-loup?) (*Are you looking forward to your vacation?*)

Herr Grobe hat sich für einen Segelkurs angemeldet. (hêr *groh*-be hât ziH fuer *ayn*-en *zey*-gel-koors *ân*-ge-mêl-det.) (*Mr. Grobe enrolled in a sailing class.*)

Herr und Frau Weber erholen sich im Urlaub an der Küste. (hêr oont frou *vey*-ber êr-*hohl*-en ziH îm *oor*-loup ân dêr *kues*-te.) (*Mr. and Mrs. Weber are relaxing during their vacation on the coast.*)

Some common reflexive verbs

If you're wondering how in the world you're supposed to know which verbs are reflexive and which ones aren't, good for you — it's an excellent question. Unfortunately, the answer may not please you: You have to memorize them.

To give you a leg up, start with some common reflexive verbs that use the accusative reflexive pronouns. Take **sich freuen** (ziH *froy*-en) (*to be glad about, to look forward to*) as an example.

Conjugation	*Pronunciation*
ich freue mich	iH *froy*-e miH
du freust dich	dooh froyst diH
Sie frauen sich	zee *froy*-en ziH
er, sie, es freut sich	êr, zee, ês froyt ziH
wir freuen uns	veer *froy*-en oons
ihr freut euch	eer froyt oyH
Sie freuen sich	zee *froy*-en ziH
sie freuen sich	zee *froy*-en ziH

Some of the most common reflexive verbs with accusative reflexive pronouns include the following:

✔ **sich anmelden** (ziH *an*-mêl-den) (*to enroll in or register for*)

✔ **sich aufregen** (ziH *ouf*-rey-gen) (*to get excited or upset*)

✔ **sich beeilen** (ziH bê-*ay*-len) (*to hurry*)

✔ **sich entscheiden** (ziH ênt-*shay*-den) (*to decide*)

✔ **sich erholen** (ziH êr-*hohl*-en) (*to relax or recover*)

✔ **sich erinnern** (ziH êr-*in*-ern) (*to remember*)

✔ **sich freuen auf** (ziH *froy*-en ouf) (*to look forward to*)

✔ **sich freuen über** (ziH *froy*-en *ue*-ber) (*to be glad about*)

✔ **sich gewöhnen an** (ziH ge-*vern*-en ân) (*to get used to*)

✔ **sich interessieren *für*** (*ziH* in-te-rê-*see*-ren fuer) (*to be interested in*)

✔ **sich setzen** (ziH *zêts*-en) (*to sit down*)

✔ **sich unterhalten** (ziH oon-têr-*hâl*-ten) (*to talk, to enjoy oneself*)

✔ **sich verletzen** (ziH fêr-*lets*-en) (*to get hurt*)

Talkin' the Talk

Anke runs into her friend Jürgen at the supermarket. The two are talking about Anke's vacation plans. (Track 25)

Jürgen:	**Hallo Anke. Wie gehts? Wir haben uns lange nicht gesehen.** *hâ*-lo *ân*-ke. vee geyts? veer *hah*-ben oons lâng-e niHt ge-*zey-en.* *Hello Anke. How are you? We haven't seen each other in a long time.*
Anke:	**Ich hatte viel zu tun. Aber jetzt mache ich endlich Urlaub.** iH *hât*-e feel tsooh toohn. ah-ber yêtst *mâH*-e iH ênt-liH *oor*-loup *I had a lot of work. But now I'm finally going on vacation.*
Jürgen:	**Wie schön. Hast du was vor?** vee shern. hâst dooh vâs for? *How nice. Do you have anything planned?*

Anke: **Ja. Ich fahre in die Schweiz. Ich nehme an einem Snowboardkurs teil.**
            yah. iH *fahr*-e in dee schvayts. iH *ney*-me ân *ayn*-em *snoh-bord*-koors tayl.
            Yes. I'm going to Switzerland. I'm taking part in a snowboarding class.

Jürgen: **Wie lange bleibst du?**
            vee *lâng*-e blaypst dooh?
            How long are you staying?

Anke: **Zwei Wochen. Ich freue mich riesig auf den Kurs.**
            tsvay *voH*-en. iH *froy*-e miH *ree*-ziH ouf deyn koors.
            Two weeks. I'm really looking forward to the course.

Jürgen: **Ich hoffe, du verletzt dich nicht!**
            iH *hof*-e, dooh vêr-*lêtst* diH niHt!
            I hope you don't get hurt!

Words to Know

teilnehmen an	<u>tayl</u>-ney-men ân	to take part in
endlich	<u>ênt</u>-liH	finally
sich auf etwas freuen	ziH ouf <u>êt</u>-vâs <u>froy</u>-en	to be looking forward to something
sich sehen	ziH <u>zey</u>-en	to see each other
bleiben	<u>blay</u>-ben	to stay
der Kurs	dêr koors	class

Reflexive verbs that are flexible

Until this point, you've seen verbs with the accusative reflexive pronouns. In order to strengthen the reputation that German verbs can act strangely, here's yet another aspect to consider. Some verbs — many of them to do with personal hygiene — use dative reflexive pronouns. Look at these examples:

> **Ich putze mir die Zähne.** (iH *poots*-e meer dee *tsai*-ne.) (*I'm brushing my teeth.*)

> **Ich wasche mir die Hände.** (iH *vâsh*-e meer dee *hên*-de.) (*I'm washing my hands.*)

And one more quirk: You can also find verbs that work *three* ways! Without going into too much detail, look at the verb **waschen**. In addition to using the dative reflexive pronoun in the previous sentence, you can use the accusative reflexive pronoun, like this example:

> **Ich wasche mich schnell.** (iH *vâsh*-e miH shnêl.) (*I wash [myself] in a hurry.*)

You can also use **waschen** alone:

> **Ich wasche das Auto morgen.** (iH *vâsh*-e dâs *ou*-toh *mor*-gen.) (*I'm washing my car tomorrow.*)

 If you're the curious type and want to find out more about relative pronouns and verbs, as well as many other details of German grammar, check out the book *Intermediate German For Dummies* (Wiley).

Exploring the Outdoors

Had a hectic week at work? Tired of working out at the gym? Maybe you just want to get away from it all and experience the great outdoors alone or with your family and friends. In that case, lace up your hiking boots and grab your binoculars and guidebook. And don't forget to pack a lunch, because you may not find a snack bar at the end of the trail!

Getting out and going

If you're interested in walking and hiking, the following phrases should get you on your way:

> **Wollen wir spazieren/wandern gehen?** (*vol*-en veer shpâ-*tsee*-ren/ *vân*-dern *gey*-en?) (*Should we take a walk/go hiking?*)

> **Ich möchte spazieren/wandern gehen.** (iH *merH*-te shpâ-*tsee*-ren/ *vân*-dern *gey*-en.) (*I would like to take a walk/go hiking.*)

Things to see along the way

When you return from your tour of the great outdoors, you can tell people about what you saw by saying

> **Ich habe . . . gesehen.** (iH *hah*-be . . . gê-*zey*-en.) (*I saw. . . .*)

> **Ich habe . . . beobachtet.** (iH *hah*-be . . . bê-*oh*-bâH-tet.) (*I was watching. . . .*)

Just fill in the blanks. You may encounter any of the following along the way:

- ✔ **der Baum** (dêr boum) (*tree*)
- ✔ **der Fluss** (dêr floos) (*river*)
- ✔ **die Kuh** (dee kooh) (*cow*)
- ✔ **das Meer** (dâs meyr) (*sea, ocean*)
- ✔ **das Pferd** (dâs pfêrt) (*horse*)
- ✔ **das Reh** (dâs rey) (*deer*)
- ✔ **das Schaf** (dâs shahf) (*sheep*)
- ✔ **der See** (dêr zey) (*lake*)
- ✔ **der Vogel** (dêr *foh*-gel) (*bird*)

Remember that you use the accusative case when completing these sentences. (See Chapter 2 for more information on the accusative case.) For masculine nouns, you phrase your sentences in this way:

> **Ich habe einen Adler gesehen.** (iH *hah*-be *ayn*-en *âd*-ler ge-*zey*-en.) (*I saw an eagle.*)

For feminine nouns, follow this phrasing:

> **Ich habe eine lilafarbene Kuh gesehen!** (iH *hah*-be *ayn*-e *lee*-lâ-fâr-bên-e kooh ge-*zey*-en!) (*I saw a purple-colored cow!*) Well, maybe not in the Alps, but you can see the purple cow on the wrapper of a well-known brand of chocolate.

Express neuter nouns this way:

> **Ich habe ein Reh gesehen.** (iH *hah*-be ayn rey ge-*zey*-en.) (*I saw a deer.*)

Or you may want to use the plural form, which is generally easier:

> **Ich habe viele Vögel gesehen.** (iH *hah*-be *fee*-le *fer*-gel ge-*zey*-en.) (*I saw a lot of birds.*)

The Alps offer a panoply of hiking opportunities for the casual hiker as well as for the expert climber. When you meet German-speaking people in the mountains and strike up a conversation, you're bound to notice that complete strangers may address each other with **du**. Using the familiar form is a means of showing camaraderie with others interested in the experience of hiking.

Talkin' the Talk

 Mr. and Mrs. Paulsen are in a small town in the mountains. Today they want to go hiking. They are speaking with Frau Kreutzer at the local tourist information office to find out about hiking trails in the area. (Track 26)

Frau
Paulsen:
Guten Morgen. Wir möchten eine Wanderung machen.
gooh-ten *mor*-gen. veer *merH*-ten *ayn*-e *vân*-der-oong *mâH*-en.
Good morning. We would like to go hiking.

Frau
Kreutzer:
Ich kann Ihnen eine Wanderkarte für diese Gegend geben.
iH kân *een*-en *ayn*-e *vân*-dêr-*kâr*-te fuer *deez*-e *gey*-gend *gey*-ben.
I can give you a hiking map of this area.

Herr
Paulsen:
Das ist genau das, was wir brauchen.
dâs ist ge-*nou* dâs, vâs veer *brouH*-en.
That's exactly what we need.

Frau
Kreutzer:
Wie wäre es mit dem Hornberg? Wenn Sie Glück haben, können Sie sogar einige Murmeltiere sehen.
vee vair-e ês mit deym *hohrn*-bêrg? vên zee gluek *hah*-ben, *kern*-en zee zoh-*gâr ayn*-ee-ge *moor*-mel-teer-e *zey*-en.
How about Horn mountain? If you're lucky, you can even see some marmots.

Herr
Paulsen:
Das klingt gut. Können Sie uns den Weg auf der Karte markieren?
dâs klinkt gooht. *keer*-en zee oons deyn vêg ouf dêr *kâr*-te mâr-*keer*-en?
Sounds good. Can you mark the trail for us on the map?

Frau
Kreutzer:
Ja, natürlich.
yah, nâ-*tuer*-liH.
Yes, of course.

Frau Paulsen:	**Vielen Dank für ihre Hilfe.**
	fee-len dânk fuer *eer*-e *hil*-fe.
	Thank you very much for your help.

Going to the mountains

Whether you plan to explore the ever-popular Alps or one of the other mountain ranges, you're sure to meet the locals. In fact, you're likely to see whole families out hiking on a Sunday afternoon. Before you join them, fortify yourself with some sustaining vocabulary:

- **der Berg** (dêr bêrg) (*mountain*)

- **das Gebirge** (dâs ge-*bir*-ge) (*mountain range*)

- **der Gipfel** (dêr *gip*-fel) (*peak*)

- **der Hügel** (dêr *hue*-gel) (*hill*)

- **das Naturschutzgebiet** (dâs nâ-*toohr*-shoots-ge-beet) (*nature preserve*)

- **das Tal** (dâs tahl) (*valley*)

Here are a few examples of sentences:

Wir fahren in die Berge. (veer *fahr*-en in dee *bêr*-ge.) (*We're going to the mountains.*)

Wir wollen wandern gehen. (veer *vol*-en *vân*-dern *gey*-en.) (*We want to go hiking.*)

Ich will bergsteigen. (iH vil *bêrg*-shtayg-en.) (*I want to go mountain climbing.*)

Words to Know

wandern	*vân*-dern	to go hiking
spazieren gehen	shpâ-*tsee*-ren *gey*-en	to take a walk
die Wanderung	dee *vân*-der-oong	hike
die Karte	dee *kâr*-te	map
der Weg	dêr veyk	trail, path, way
die Gegend	dee *gey*-gent	area

Talkin' the Talk

Herr Mahler meets Frau Pohl on his way home from work. They start talking about their travel plans.

Frau Pohl: **Tag Herr Mahler. Na, haben Sie schon Urlaubspläne gemacht?**
tahk hêr *mah*-ler. nah, *hah*-ben zee shon *oor*-loups-*plên*-e ge-*mâHt*?
Hello, Mr. Mahler. So, have you made plans for your vacation yet?

Herr Mahler: **Aber ja, meine Frau und ich werden wieder in die Berge fahren.**
ah-ber yah, *mayn*-e frou oont iH *vêr*-den *vee*-der in dee *bêr*-ge *fahr*-en.
Oh yes, my wife and I will go to the mountains again.

Frau Pohl: **Wieder in die Alpen?**
vee-der in dee *âlp*-en?
Back to the Alps?

Herr Mahler: **Nein, diesmal gehen wir in den Pyrenäen wandern. Und Sie?**
nayn, *dees*-mâl *gey*-en veer in deyn per-re-*nê*-en *vân*-dern. oont zee?
No, this time we're going hiking in the Pyrenees. And you?

Frau Pohl: **Wir wollen im Herbst in die Dolomiten zum Bergsteigen.**
veer *vol*-en im hêrpst in dee do-lo-*meet*-en tsoom *bêrg*-shtayg-en.
We want to go mountain climbing in the Dolomite Alps in the fall.

Herr Mahler: **Haben Sie schon ein Hotel gebucht?**
hah-ben zee shohn ayn hotel [as in English] ge-*booHt*?
Did you book a hotel yet?

Frau Pohl: **Nein, wir werden in Berghütten übernachten.**
nayn, veer *vêr*-den în *bêrg*-huet-en ue-ber-*nâH*-ten.
No, we're going to stay in mountain huts.

Going to the country

Mountains not your idea of fun? How about some fresh country air then? Despite a population of around 82 million people in Germany, you can still find quiet rural areas and out-of-the-way places, sometimes surprisingly close to bustling urban centers. And it goes without saying that you can also find peace and quiet in the Austrian and Swiss countryside. All you need to get started is the right language:

- **der Bauernhof** (dêr *bou*-ern-hohf) (*farm*)
- **das Dorf** (dâs dorf) (*village*)
- **das Feld** (dâs fêlt) (*field*)
- **das Land** (dâs lânt) (*countryside*)
- **der Wald** (dêr vâlt) (*forest*)
- **die Wiese** (dee *veez*-e) (*meadow*)

Following are a few sample sentences:

Wir fahren aufs Land. (veer *fahr*-en oufs lânt.) (*We're going to the countryside.*)

Wir machen Urlaub auf dem Bauernhof. (veer *mâH*-en *oor*-loup ouf deym *bou*-ern-hohf.) (*We're vacationing on a farm.*)

Ich gehe im Wald spazieren. (iH *gey*-e im vâlt shpâ-*tsee*-ren.) (*I'm going for a walk in the woods.*)

Talkin' the Talk

Daniel runs into his friend Ellen. After greeting each other, Daniel tells Ellen about his upcoming vacation.

Daniel: **Ich fahre in der letzten Juli Woche aufs Land.**
iH *fahr*-e in dêr *lêts*-te *yooh*-lee *voH*-e oufs lânt.
I'm going to the countryside the last week in July.

Ellen: **Fährst du allein?**
fairst dooh *âl*-ayn?
Are you going alone?

Daniel: **Nein, ich verreise zusammen mit meiner Schwester und ihren Kindern.**
nayn, iH fêr-*ray*-ze tsoo-*zâm*-en mit *mayn*-er *shvês*-ter oont *eer*-en *kin*-dern.
No, I'm traveling together with my sister and her children.

Ellen: **Habt ihr eine Ferienwohnung gemietet?**
hahpt eer *ayn*-e *feyr*-ee-ên-*vohn*-oong ge-*meet*-et?
Did you rent a vacation apartment?

Daniel: **Nein. Wir übernachten auf einem Bauernhof in einem kleinen Dorf.**
nayn. veer ue-bêr-*nâHt*-en ouf *ayn*-em *bou*-ern-hohf in *ayn*-em *klayn*-en dorf.
No. We're staying on a farm in a small village.

Ellen: **Die Kindern freuen sich sicher.**
dee *kin*-der *froy*-en ziH *ziH*-er.
The kids are probably looking forward to that.

Daniel: **Und wie!**
oont vee!
Oh, yes!

Going to the sea

If hiking through the mountains or countryside sounds somewhat dry and tame to you, maybe what you need is a stiff breeze and the cry of gulls overhead. Whether you decide to go to one of the windswept islands in the North Sea or settle for the more serene Baltic Sea, you'll be able to enjoy nature and meet the locals at the same time using the following words:

- ✔ **die Ebbe** (dee *êb*-e) (*low tide*)
- ✔ **die Flut** (dee flooht) (*high tide*)
- ✔ **die Gezeiten** (dee gê-*tsayt*-en) (*tides*)
- ✔ **die Küste** (dee *kues*-te) (*coast*)
- ✔ **das Meer** (dâs meyr) (*sea*)
- ✔ **die Nordsee** (dee *nort*-zey) (*North Sea*)
- ✔ **die Ostsee** (dee *ost*-zey) (*Baltic Sea*)
- ✔ **der Sturm** (dêr shtoorm) (*storm*)
- ✔ **die Wellen** (dee *vêl*-en) (*waves*)
- ✔ **der Wind** (dêr vint) (*wind*)

Talkin' the Talk

Udo and Karin are talking about their holiday trips. They both like the seaside but have different ideas about what's fun.

Udo: **Wir wollen dieses Jahr an die Ostsee.**
veer *vol*-en *deez*-es yahr ân dee *ost*-zey.
We want to go to the Baltic Sea this year.

Karin: **Toll! Und was macht ihr dort?**
Tol! oont vâs mâHt eer dort?
Cool! And what are you going to do there?

Udo: **Wir wollen windsurfen. Und ihr?**
veer *vol*-en *vint*-soorf-en. oont eer?
We want to go windsurfing. And you?

Karin: **Wir werden auf eine Nordseeinsel fahren. Wir wollen im Watt wandern gehen.**
veer *vêr*-den ouf *ayn*-e *nort*-zey-in-zel *fahr*-en. veer *vol*-en im vât *vân*-dern *gey*-en.
We'll go to a North Sea island. We want to go walking in the tidal flats.

Udo: **Ist das nicht gefährlich?**
ist dâs niHt ge-*fair*-liH?
Isn't that dangerous?

Karin: **Nein, man geht bei Ebbe los, und dann hat man einige Stunden Zeit, bevor die Flut kommt.**
nayn, mân geyt bay *êb*-e lohs, oont dân hât mân *ayn*-ee-ge *shtoon*-den tsayt, bê-*fohr* dee flooht komt.
No, you set out at low tide, and then you have several hours before high tide sets in.

Fun & Games

Fill in the boxes with the correct German words.

Across

1. I

3. You (informal, singular)

8. Class

10. Yes

11. Tomorrow

12. Lake

13. She

14. Low tide

15. Mountain

18. And

21. North Sea

Down

2. Hi

3. Article (masculine)

4. Trail

5. Skateboard

6. Article (neuter)

7. Island

9. Skiing

11. Ocean

16. It

17. Good

19. Village

20. a (feminine article)

Part III
German on the Go

The 5th Wave   By Rich Tennant

ACHTUNG!

"It says, children are forbidden from running, touching objects, or appearing bored during the tour of the castle."

In this part . . .

At some point in time, you may very well find yourself doing a bit of traveling in German-speaking parts of Europe, so that's what this part of the book is all about. We cover all aspects of travel, including the planning stages, exchanging money, using public transportation, and reserving a hotel room. **Gute Reise!** (*gooh-*te *ray-*ze!) (*Have a good trip!*)

Chapter 13

Planning a Trip

*W*ould you like to go hiking in the Alps or head to the sea? How about a one-day **Ausflug** (*ous*-floohk) (excursion), perhaps from Munich to the pristine Bavarian lake of **Königsee** (*ker*-nig-zee)**?** Or what about a weeklong vacation **Pauschalreise** (pou-*shahl*-ray-ze) (package) to Turkey? No matter what destination you decide on, every trip requires some preparation. You need to check your calendar and set the dates, make sure your passport is valid for six months past the length of your trip (especially if you're traveling across borders), make reservations, and so on. Whether you prefer gathering information online or having human interaction while planning a trip, you'll find the information in this chapter useful.

Getting Help from a Travel Agent

Booking your trip online is fast and convenient, yet you may find that a travel agent can better serve your needs when you're already in Europe and want to plan a short trip from there. After all, you don't want to get stuck spending five nights at a hotel that blasts ear-splitting music 24/7 from its poolside disco!

When you contact the travel agency, **das Reisebüro** (dâs *ray*-ze-bue-*roh*), tell the employee the following:

   Ich möchte gern . . . (iH *merH*-te gêrn . . .) (*I would like to . . .*)

At the end of this phrase, you can say any of the following to specify what you want them to do for you:

. . . **einen Flug nach . . . buchen.** (*ayn*-en floohk nahH . . . *boohH*-en.) (*book a flight to. . . .*)

. . . **am . . . abfliegen.** (âm . . . *âp*-fleeg-en.) (*depart [fly] on the. . . .*)

. . . **am . . . zurückfliegen.** (âm . . . tsoo-*ruek*-fleeg-en.) (*return [fly back] on the . . . .*)

. . . **eine Pauschalreise nach . . . buchen.** (*ayn*-e pou-*shahl*-ray-ze nahH . . . *boohH*-en.) (*book a vacation package to. . . .*)

. . . **einen Ausflug nach . . . buchen.** (*ayn*-en *ous*-floohk nahH . . . *boohH*-en.) (*book an excursion to. . . .*)

. . . **ein Hotelzimmer reservieren.** (ayn hoh-*têl*-tsi-mer rê-zêr-*vee*-ren.) (*reserve a hotel room.*)

Talkin' the Talk

 Frau Burger wants to book a vacation package to the Spanish island of **Mallorca** (may-*yor*-kâ), a very popular destination for Germans. She calls a travel agency to book her trip. (Track 27)

Angestellter: **Reisebüro Kunze, guten Tag!**
ray-ze-bue-*roh* koon-tse, *gooh*-ten *tahk!*
Travel agency Kunze, hello!

Frau Burger: **Guten Tag. Ich möchte eine Pauschalreise für eine Woche nach Mallorca buchen.**
gooh-ten *tahk.* iH *merH*-te *ayn*-e pou-*shâl-ray*-ze fuer *ayn*-e *woH*-e naH may-*yor*-kâ *boohH*-en.
Hello, I'd like to book a one-week vacation package to Mallorca.

Angestellter: **Gut. Wann möchten Sie hinfliegen?**
gooht. vân *merH*-ten zee *hin*-fleeg-en?
Good. When do you want to fly there?

Frau Burger: **Im Oktober. Aber wie sind die Preise?**
im ok-*toh*-ber. *ah*-ber vee zint dee *pray*-ze?
In October. But what are the prices like?

Angestellter: **Keine Sorge. Oktober ist Nebensaison. Möchten Sie am 5. Oktober abfliegen?**
kayn-e *zohr*-ge. ok-*toh*-ber ist *ney*-ben-zey-zon. *merH*-ten zee âm *fuenf*-ten ok-*toh*-ber *âp*-fleeg-en?
Not to worry. October is the low season. Would you like to leave on the fifth of October?

Frau Burger: **Perfekt. Das passt ausgezeichnet.**
pêr-*fêkt*. dâs pâst *ous*-ge-*tsayH*-nêt.
Perfect. That suits me perfectly.

Angestellter: **Sehr gut. Ich buche den Flug und die Übernachtung für Sie. Ich empfehle Ihnen das fûnf Stern Hotel Eden.**
zeyr gooht. iH *boohH*-e deyn floohk oont dee ue-ber-*nâHt*-oong fuer zee. iH em-*pfey*-le *een*-en dâs fuenf shtêrn hotel [as in English] *ey*-den.
Very good. I'll book the flight and accommodation for you. I recommend the five-star Hotel Eden.

Frau Burger: **Danke.**
dân-ke.
Thank you.

Words to Know

die Reise	dee <u>ray</u>-ze	trip
reisen	<u>ray</u>-zen	to travel
buchen	<u>boohH</u>-en	to book
das Reisebüro	dâs <u>ray</u>-ze-bue-roh	travel agency
die Übernachtung	dee ue-ber-<u>nâHt</u>-oong	accommodation

Planning Ahead: Using the Future Tense

When talking about things that will take place in the future, you use the *future tense*. In English, you create the future tense by adding the word "will" to the verb. Forming the future tense in German is pretty similar to English except that you need to conjugate the German equivalent of the verb "will." You take the appropriate form of the verb **werden** (*veyr*-den) (will) and add the infinitive form of another verb. The conjugated form of **werden** goes in the usual second place for the verb, and the infinitive goes at the very end of the sentence. In this case, **werden** is used as an auxiliary verb meaning "will" (when used on its own, the verb **werden** means "to become").

The proper conjugation of the verb **werden** looks like this:

Conjugation	*Pronunciation*
ich werde	iH *veyr*-de
du wirst	dooh virst
Sie werden	zee *veyr*-den
er, sie, es wird	êr, zee, ês virt
wir werden	veer *veyr*-den
ihr werdet	eer *veyr*-det
Sie werden	zee *veyr*-den
sie werden	zee *veyr*-den

The following sentences show examples of the future tense. Note how the infinitives always go at the end of the sentences and that you create the negative (*will not*) by placing **nicht** directly after **werden**:

Wirst du nächstes Jahr nach Kroatien fahren? (virst dooh *naiH*-stes yahr nahH kroh-*ahts*-ee-en *fahr*-en?) (*Will you go/Are you going to Croatia next year?*)

Wir werden nicht zum Fest kommen. (veer *veyr*-den niHt tsoom fêst *kom*-en.) (*We will not come/we're not coming to the party.*)

Frau Meier wird heute Abend zurückfliegen. (frou *may*-er virt *hoy*-te ah-bent tsoo-*ruek*-fleeg-en.) (*Ms. Meier will fly/is flying back this evening.*)

German speakers are pretty lackadaisical about the future tense; they use it much less frequently than English speakers. Even more important, unlike English, with its various ways of expressing a future meaning, such as "I'm going to visit my parents for Thanksgiving" or "We're taking a trip to Niagara Falls in August," German expresses the future tense only with **werden**. Very often, German speakers prefer to talk about the future using the present tense. Expressions like **morgen** (*mor*-gen) (*tomorrow*) or **nächstes Jahr** (*naiH*-stes yahr) (*next year*) serve to indicate future meaning. The following statements all refer to events that will take place in the future, although the verb in each one of them is in the present tense:

> **Morgen gehe ich wandern.** (*mor*-gen *gey*-e iH *vân*-dêrn.) (*Tomorrow I'll go hiking.*) Literally, *Tomorrow I go hiking.*

> **Fährst du nächstes Jahr wieder zum Filmfest Hamburg?** (fairst dooh *naiH*-stes yahr *vee*-der tsoom *film*-fêst *hâm*-boorg?) (*Are you going to go to the Hamburg film festival next year?*) Roughly translated: *Do you go to the Hamburg film festival next year?*

> **Susanne geht übermorgen zum Konsulat.** (soo-*zân*-e geyt ue-ber-*mor*-gen tsoom kon-zoo-*laht*.) (*Susanne is going to the consulate the day after tomorrow.*) Literally, *Susanne goes to the consulate the day after tomorrow.*

Describing events in specific months

If something takes place in a particular month, you combine the name of the month with the preposition **im** (im) (*in*):

> **Ich fliege im Januar nach Zürich.** (iH *fleeg*-e im *yân*-oo-ahr nahH *tsuer*-iH.) (*I'm flying to Zurich in January.*)

> **Ich fliege im Februar zurück.** (iH *fleeg*-e im *fey*-broo-ahr tsoo-*ruek*.) (*I'm flying back in February.*)

> **Im März werde ich zu Hause sein.** (im mêrts *veyr*-de iH tsooh *houz*-e zayn.) (*In March, I'll be home.*)

Naming specific times in the months

If you need to be more specific about a particular time of the month, the following phrases help narrow down the field:

> **Anfang Januar** (*ân*-fâng *yân*-oo-ahr) (*in the beginning of January*)

> **Mitte Februar** (*mit*-e *fey*-broo-ahr) (*in the middle of February*)
>
> **Ende März** (*ên*-de *mêrts*) (*at the end of March*)

Of course, you can substitute the name of any month after **Anfang**, **Mitte**, and **Ende**:

> **Anfang April fliegen wir nach Berlin.** (*ân*-fâng â-*pril fleeg*-en veer nahH bêr-*leen*.) (*In the beginning of April we're flying to Berlin.*)
>
> **Ich werde Ende Mai verreisen.** (iH *vêr*-de *ên*-de may fêr-*ray*-zen.) (*I'll go traveling at the end of May.*)
>
> **Herr Behr wird Mitte Februar in den Skiurlaub fahren.** (hêr beyr virt *mit*-e *fey*-broo-ahr in deyn *shee*-oor-loup *fahr*-en.) (*Mr. Behr is going on a skiing trip in the middle of February.*)

Rethinking Dates

When talking about the date — **das Datum** (dâs *dah*-toom) — you need to adjust your way of thinking a little bit. In German (and many other languages, for that matter), the day always comes first, and the month comes second. In addition, the day of the month is an ordinal number, and a period is placed after the number, for example: **15. Juni 2011** (*fuenf*-tseyn-ter *yooh*-nee tsvay-*tou*-zênt-êlf) (June 15th, 2011). (Chapter 7 has more info on ordinal numbers.)

That was the long version. You often see or hear a shorter version. For example, you would write **14.10.2000**, and you would say **vierzehnter zehnter zweitausend** (*veer*-tseyn-ter *tseyn*-ter tsvay-*tou*-zênt) ([the] 14th of October, 2000). Again, note the periods after the numerals (both the day and month are ordinals).

If you want to find out what today's date is, ask this way:

> **Welches Datum ist heute?** (*vêlH*-es *dah*-toom ist *hoy*-te?) (*What's today's date?*)

The answer will be one of the following:

> **Heute ist der. . . .** (*hoy*-te ist dêr. . . .) (*Today is the. . . .*)
>
> **Heute haben wir den. . . .** (*hoy*-te *hah*-ben veer deyn. . . .) (*Today we have the. . . .*)

You may hear the name of a year integrated into a sentence in one of two ways. The first, longer way uses the preposition **im** to create the phrase **im Jahr . . .** (im yahr) (*in the year*). The second, shorter way omits this phrase.

The following sentences show you examples of both ways of talking about the year in which an event takes place:

Im Jahr 2010 arbeitete Herr Diebold in den USA. (im yahr tsvay-*tou*-zênt tseyn *âr*-bay-te-te hêr *dee*-bolt in deyn ooh-ês-*ah*.) (*In the year 2010, Mr. Diebold worked in the United States.*)

2008 war er in Kanada. (tsvay-*tou*-zênt-*âHt* vâr êr in *kâ*-nâ-dâ.) (*In 2008 he was in Canada.*)

Words to Know

das Jahr	dâs yahr	year
der Monat	dêr <u>moh</u>-nât	month
die Woche	dee <u>voH</u>-e	week
der Tag	dêr tahk	day
das Datum	dâs <u>dah</u>-toom	date
der Kalender	dêr kâ-<u>lên</u>-der	calendar

Dealing with Passports and Visas

Although the world seems to be shrinking faster and faster thanks to the Internet, you still need paperwork to go places. Specifically, you need a passport (you know, that handy little booklet with the embarrassing picture that you always seem to misplace or let expire just before you're about to leave on a trip?) And then there's the issue of visas.

The all-important passport

Before you leave on a trip, you want to check to make sure that your passport is valid for the entire length of your stay and then some (many countries allow you to stay for between three and six months total). After all, you don't want to spend your time away from home trying to find an American consulate in order to renew your passport. If you forget to take care of this very important task, you'll hear the following when you show your passport at the airline ticket counter, or worse yet, at the border:

Ihr Pass ist abgelaufen! (eer pâs ist *âp*-ge-louf-en!) (*Your passport has expired!*)

At that point, you'll be directed to the nearest American consulate — **das amerikanische Konsulat** (dâs â-mê-ree-*kah*-ni-she kon-zoo-*laht*) — in order to take care of the necessary paperwork.

In the event that you notice your passport is missing, head straight to the American consulate to report it. If necessary, you can stop a policeman or file a report at a police station and say the following in order to get help:

Ich habe meinen Pass verloren. (iH *hah*-be *mayn*-en pâs fêr-*lohr*-en.) (*I lost my passport.*)

Inquiring about visas

Most countries in Europe don't require you to have a visa if you're traveling on vacation and are planning to stay a few weeks or a couple of months. But just in case you like your destination so much that you want to stay longer, or you decide to continue on to a place where you're required to have a visa, the following phrases can come in handy when you apply for one:

Braucht man ein Visum für Reisen nach. . . ? (brouHt mân ayn *vee*-zoom fuer *ray*-zen nahH. . . ?) (*Does one need a visa for trips to. . . ?*)

Wie lange ist das Visum gültig? (vee *lâng*-e ist dâs *vee*-zoom *guel*-tiH?) (*For how long is the visa valid?*)

Ich möchte ein Visum beantragen. (iH *merH*-te ayn *vee*-zoom bê-*ân*-trah-gen.) (*I would like to apply for a visa.*)

Talkin' the Talk

George Beck, an American living in Germany, wants to go on a trip to Phuket (fooh-*ket*), Thailand. As he's making the necessary arrangements at the travel agency, he talks to the agent about entering the country.

George: **Brauche ich ein Visum für Thailand?**
brouH-e iH ayn *vee*-zoom *fuer* tay-lânt?
Do I need a visa for Thailand?

Angestellte: **Nein, für Thailand nicht, aber Sie brauchen natürlich Ihren Reisepass. Ist er noch gültig?**
nayn, fuer tay-lânt niHt, aber zee brouH-en na-tuer-liH eer-en ray-ze-pâs. ist êr noH guel-tiH?
No, not for Thailand, but you need your passport, of course. Is it still valid?

George: **Ja, doch.**
yah, doH.
Yes, it is.

Angestellte: **Prima! Noch irgendwelche Fragen, Herr Beck?**
pree-mâ! noH eer-gênt-velH-ê frah-gen hêr bêk?
Great! Any other questions, Mr. Beck?

George: **Nein, das war's. Vielen Dank.**
nayn, dâs vahrs. *fee*-len dânk.
No, that was it. Thank you very much.

Angestellte: **Gern geschehen. Und, Gute Reise!**
gêrn ge-*shey*-en. oont, *gooh*-te ray-ze!
You're welcome. And have a nice trip!

Words to Know

der Reisepass	dêr <u>ray</u>-ze-pâs	passport
das Visum	dâs <u>vee</u>-zoom	visa
beantragen	bê-<u>ân</u>-trah-gen	to apply for
gültig/ungültig	<u>guel</u>-tiH/<u>oon</u>-guel-tiH	valid/invalid
verlängern	fêr-<u>lêng</u>-ern	to renew, to extend
ablaufen	<u>âp</u>-louf-en	to expire
das Konsulat	dâs kon-zooh-<u>laht</u>	consulate
die Botschaft	dee <u>boht</u>-shâft	embassy

Fun & Games

The following statements all describe events that take place in the future. Your job is to put the verb werden into the appropriate form.

1. Wir _____ ans Meer fahren.

2. _____ du mit deiner Familie in die USA fliegen?

3. Ich _____ meinen Urlaub im Reisebüro buchen.

4. _____ ihr mit dem Zug nach Dänemark fahren?

5. Kai _____ ein Visum für Kanada beantragen.

6. Claudia und Bärbel _____ dieses Jahr nach Polen reisen.

Chapter 14

Making Sense of Euros and Cents

In This Chapter

▶ Exchanging money

▶ Getting money from an ATM

▶ Understanding Euroland

Money does indeed make the world go 'round. And Euroland revolves around its multinational currency, the euro. So what about the good old greenback? In this chapter, we get you up to speed on exchanging your bucks for multicolored, multi-sized euros. Oh, and there's also the matter of those countries such as Switzerland that still have their own respective currencies. Whether you're dealing with a personable teller or an impersonal ATM, a pocketful of the right expressions can get you, well, a pocketful of euros.

Changing Currency

Obtaining local currency in Europe is generally a hassle-free experience. Practically every bank is willing to accept your dollars and provide you with the local cash. And you can easily withdraw cash in the local currency from an ATM machine, provided you're using a major credit card (preferably Visa or Mastercard) and know your PIN.

You usually find a notice posted in or outside the bank with the current *exchange rates* (**Wechselkurse**) (*vêk*-sel-koorz-e). Look for the column marked **Ankauf** (*ân*-kouf) (*purchase/buy*). Then saunter up to the *teller window*, **der Schalter** (dêr *shâl*-ter). The **Bankangestellter** (*bânk*-an-ge-stêl-ter) (*bank teller*) at the counter will either complete your transaction on the spot or send you on to the **Kasse** (*kâs*-e) (*cashier*).

In airports and major train stations, you often find businesses that specialize in exchanging currencies, called **Wechselstube** (*vêk*-sel-stooh-be) in German. No matter where you decide to change your money, the whole process is simple. All you need are the following phrases:

Ich möchte . . . Dollar in Euro wechseln/tauschen. (iH *merH*-te . . . *dol*-âr in *oy*-roh *vêk*-seln/*toush*-en.) (*I would like to change . . . dollars into euros.*) *Note:* Both **wechseln** and **tauschen** can mean *change* or *exchange* — in this case, money.

Wie ist der Wechselkurs? (vee ist dêr *vêk*-sel-koors?) (*What's the exchange rate?*)

Wie hoch sind die Gebühren? (vee hohH zint dee ge-*buer*-en?) (*How much are the transaction fees?*)

Nehmen Sie Reiseschecks? (*ney*-men zee *ray*-ze-shêks?) (*Do you take traveler's checks?*)

When you exchange money, you'll probably be asked for your *passport* (**Reisepass**) (*ray*-ze-pâs). The teller will ask you

Haben Sie ihren Reisepass? (*hah*-ben zee *eer*-en *ray*-ze-pâs?) (*Do you have your passport?*)

After you show your official mug shot — and assuming it appears to be you — the teller may ask you how you want the money:

Welche Scheine hätten Sie gern? (*vêlH*-e *shayn*-e *hêt*-en zee gêrn?) (*What size denominations would you like?*)

You can respond

In Zehnern/in Zwanzigern/in Fünfzigern/in Hundertern, bitte. (in *tseyn*-ern/in *tsvân*-zig-ern/in *fuenf*-tsig-ern/in *hoon*-dert-ern, *bi*-te.) (*In bills of 10/20/50/100, please.*)

German payment system

In Germany, and many European Union (EU) countries, practically all regularly occurring financial transactions are carried out by direct debit, from paychecks to electric bills. When shopping, customers use either paper (that is, hard currency) or plastic. Many Germans prefer to use cash almost exclusively. Plastic, at least for Germans, would mean the electronic cash (EC) card, a debit card. Alternatively, credit cards are used, although many stores and restaurants do not readily accept them. Checks have been relegated to the dinosaur era. It's the EC card that works seamlessly at ATM machines across the EU.

As a non-European, your credit card will work in much the same way as it does at home, but before traveling, you may want to check with the institution that issued your card to find out whether any transaction fees apply. When you want to use your credit card to withdraw cash at an ATM, you need to use your four-digit PIN.

Talkin' the Talk

 Anne, an American tourist, heads to a bank to exchange money. (Track 28)

Bankangestellter:	**Guten Morgen.** *gooh*-ten *mor*-gen. *Good morning.*
Anne:	**Guten Morgen. Ich möchte 300 US-Dollar wechseln. Wie ist der Wechselkurs, bitte?** *gooh*-ten *mor*-gen. iH *merH*-te *dray*-hoon-dert ooh-ês *dol*-âr *vêk*-seln. vee ist dêr *vêk*-sel-koors, *bi*-te? *Good morning. I'd like to change 300 U.S. dollars. What's the exchange rate, please?*
Bankangestellter:	**Einen Moment, bitte. Für einen Dollar bekommen Sie 0,78 Euro.** *ayn*-en moh-*ment*, *bi*-te. fuer *ayn*-en *dol*-âr be-*kom*-en zee nool *kom*-â âHt oont *zeep*-tsiH oy-roh. *One moment, please. One dollar is currently 0.78 euros.*
Anne:	**Können Sie mir bitte Reiseschecks über 300 Dollar in Euro wechseln?** *kern*-en zee meer *bi*-te *ray*-ze-shêks *ue*-ber *dray*-hoon-dêrt *dol*-âr in oy-roh *vêk*-seln? *Could you exchange 300 dollars in traveler's checks into euros, please?*
Bankangestellter:	**Kein Problem. Haben Sie ihren Reisepass?** kayn pro-*bleym*. *hah*-ben zee *eer*-en *ray*-ze-pâs? *No problem. Do you have your passport?*
Anne:	**Ja, hier ist er.** yah, heer ist êr. *Yes, here it is.*
Bankangestellter:	**Für 300 Dollar bekommen Sie 234 Euro. Abzüglich 3,30 Euro Wechselgebühr macht das 230,70 Euro.** fuer *dray*-hoon-dert *dol*-âr bê-*kom*-en zee dâs *tsvay*-hoon-dert-feer-oont-*dray*-siH oy-roh. *âb*-tsueg-liH dray oy-roh *dray*-siH *vêk*-sel-ge-buer mâHt dâs *tsvay*-hoon-dert-*dray*-siH oy-roh *zeep*-tsiH. *For 300 dollars, you get 234 euros. Minus a 3.30 euro transaction fee, that's 230.70 euros.*

Anne:	**Vielen Dank.**
	fee-len dânk
	Thank you very much.

Words to Know

Geld tauschen	gêlt <u>toush</u>-en	to change/ exchange money
Geld wechseln	gêlt <u>vêk</u>-seln	to change/ exchange money
das Bargeld	dâs <u>bâr</u>-gêlt	cash
in bar	in bâr	in cash
einen Reisescheck einlösen	<u>ayn</u>-en ray-ze-shêk <u>ayn</u>-ler-zen	to cash a traveler's check
eine Gebühr bezahlen	<u>ayn</u>-e ge-<u>buer</u> be-<u>tsah</u>-len	to pay a fee
der Wechselkurs	dêr <u>vêk</u>-sel-koors	exchange rate
der Ankauf	dêr <u>ân</u>-kouf	purchase, acquisition
der Verkauf	dêr <u>fêr</u>-kouf	sale

Heading to the ATM

Instead of changing money at the teller window of a bank, you can use a **Geldautomat** (*gêlt*-ou-toh-maht) (*ATM machine*). Just look for your card symbol on the machine to make sure that the machine takes your kind of card.

Many ATM machines give you a choice of languages to communicate in, but just in case German is your only option, you want to be prepared. ATMs use phrases that are direct and to the point — infinitives are the order of the day (see the following section for an explanation). A typical run-through of prompts may look like this:

Karte einführen (kâr-te *ayn*-fuer-en) (*Insert card*)

Sprache wählen (shprahH-e *vai*-len) (*Choose a language*)

Geheimzahl eingeben (ge-*haym*-tsahl *ayn*-gey-ben) (*Enter PIN*)

Betrag eingeben (be-*trahk ayn*-gey-ben) (*Enter amount*)

Betrag bestätigen (be-*trahk* be-*shtê*-ti-gen) (*Confirm amount*)

Karte entnehmen (*kâr*-te ênt-*ney*-men) (*Remove card*)

Geld entnehmen (gêlt ênt-*ney*-men) (*Take cash*)

Transaction completed. Your wallet should now be bulging with local currency — that is, unless something went wrong. The ATM machine may be out of order, in which case, you see the following message:

Geldautomat außer Betrieb. (*gêlt*-ou-toh-maht *ous*-er be-*treep*.) (*ATM out of service.*)

Or the ATM may spit out your card without parting with any of its largesse. In that case, you may receive this message:

Die Karte ist ungültig./Die Karte wird nicht akzeptiert. (dee *kâr*-te ist *oon*-guel-tiH./dee *kâr*-te virt niHt âk-tsep-*teert*.) (*The card is not valid/can't be accepted.*)

The worst case scenario? The ATM machine may swallow your card whole, leaving you with only this message for consolation:

Die Karte wurde eingezogen. Bitte gehen Sie zum Bankschalter. (dee *kâr*-te *voor*-de *ayn*-ge-tsoh-gen. bi-te gey-en zee tsoom *bânk*-shâl-ter.) (*The card was confiscated. Please go to the counter in the bank.*)

Decimal points and commas in numbers

The English and German languages present numbers differently. The use of the comma and decimal point in the numbers are switched. Look at the following examples of German and English numbers to see how it works:

- ✔ **English:**   8.4   20.75   490.99
- ✔ **German:**   8,4   20,75   490,99

And this is how you say one of these numbers: 20,75 = **zwanzig Komma sieben fünf** (*tsvân*-tsiH

kom-â *zee*-ben fuenf). The English equivalent has a decimal point in place of the comma in German, so you'd say the number as *twenty point seven five*.

The next set of numbers shows you one million dollars expressed in both languages:

- ✔ **English:**   1,000,000 dollars
- ✔ **German:**   1.000.000 Dollar

Getting Imperative

ATMs and other machines often use terse-sounding phrases, like **Geheimzahl eingeben** (ge-*haym*-tsahl *ayn*-gey-ben) (*Enter PIN*). Although these phrases may not sound very polite, they're used quite a bit as a way to save space. For example, a more polite way to say **Geheimzahl eingeben** would be

> **Bitte geben Sie Ihre Geheimzahl ein.** (*bi*-te *gey*-ben zee *eer*-e ge-*haym*-tsahl ayn.) (*Please enter your PIN.*)

Grammatically speaking, such terse phrases are infinitives posing as *imperatives* (commands). You encounter these forms wherever language efficiency is of utmost importance to the writer or speaker, or instructions are being given.

When you enter a building, such as a bank, you often find the word **ziehen** (*tsee*-hen) (*Pull*) on the door as you go in and the word **drücken** (*druek*-en) (*Push*) as you leave. Speaking of doors, you may notice a sign asking you to close the doors behind you — **Türen schließen** (*tuer*-en *shlees*-en) (*Close doors*) — when you're entering a building or a train. When you're on a subway, you may hear a similar command that goes something like this: **Vorsicht, die Türen werden geschlossen** (*for*-ziHt, dee *tuer*-en *vêr*-den ge-*shlos*-en) (*Be careful; the doors are closing*).

Talkin' the Talk

Mike is about to meet his girlfriend for a cup of coffee when he realizes that he only has a 200 euro bill in his wallet. He goes to a bank to change his bill into smaller denominations.

Mike:	**Können Sie bitte diesen 200-Euro-Schein in kleinere Scheine wechseln?** *kern*-en zee *bi*-te *deez*-en *tsavy* hoon-dert-*oy*-roh-shayn in *klayn*-er-e *shayn*-e *vêk*-seln? *Could you exchange this 200-euro bill for smaller bills, please?*
Bankangestellte:	**Welche Scheine darf ich Ihnen geben?** *vêlH*-e *shayn*-e *dârf* iH *een*-en *gey*-ben? *What denominations would you like?*
Mike:	**Ich hätte gern einen 50-Euro-Schein, 5 Zwanziger und 5 Zehner.** iH *hêt*-e gêrn *ayn*-en *fuenf*-tsiH-*oy*-roh-shayn, fuenf *tsvân*-tsee-ger oont fuenf *tseyn*-er. *I'd like one 50 euro bill, five 20 euro bills, and five 10 euro bills.*

Bankangestellte:	**Bitte. Haben Sie sonst noch einen Wunsch?**
	bi-te. hah-ben zee sonst noH ayn-en voonsh?
	Here you are. Do you need anything else?
Mike:	**Danke. Das ist alles.**
	dân-ke. dâs ist âl-es.
	Thanks. That's all.

Understanding the Euro and Other Currencies

With the introduction of the European Monetary Union in 2002, the euro became the currency for 12 countries, including Germany and Austria. *Euroland,* the term coined (no pun intended) for countries that have adopted the euro, currently comprises 16 nations, and the numbers are still growing. Switzerland, the UK, Denmark, and Poland are among those countries that still use their respective currencies.

When referring to the plural of **der Euro** (dêr *oy*-roh) (*euro*), you have two choices, **die Euro** or **die Euros**, yet both are pronounced the same, (dee *oy*-roh) (*euros*). Each **Euro** has 100 **Cent(s)** (sênt) (*cents*). The official abbreviation for the euro is EUR. When using the symbol for the euro, €, it appears after the number like this: 47€.

The currencies of other countries are as follows:

- ✔ **Czechoslovakia: die tschechische Krone** (dee *chêH*-ish-e *kroh*-ne) (*Czech crown*)

- ✔ **Denmark: die dänische Krone** (dee *deyn*-ish-e *kroh*-ne) (*Danish crown*)

- ✔ **Poland: der polnische Zloty** (dêr *poln*-ish-e *slo*-tee) (*Polish zloty*)

- ✔ **Switzerland: der schweizer Franken** (dêr *shvayts*-er *frân*-ken) (*Swiss franc*)

- ✔ **U.K.: das Pfund** (dâs pfoont) (*pound*)

- ✔ **United States: der Dollar** (dêr *dol*-âr) (*dollar*)

Fun & Games

Who doesn't like to count money — especially when it's their own? Count up how much money is represented in the following problems and write the correct amount in German words on the blank lines provided.

1.

_____

2.

_____

3.

_____

4.

_____

5.

_____

Chapter 15

Getting Around: Planes, Trains, Taxis, and Buses

. . . .

In This Chapter

▶ Flying: Airport lingo you need to know

▶ Driving: Reading road signs and maps

▶ Traveling by train

▶ Taking a bus, streetcar, subway, or taxi

. . . .

*P*lanes, trains, taxis, streetcars, buses, subways, and automobiles — you have lots of options when it comes to getting around German-speaking countries. In this chapter, we tell you what you need to know to deal with ticket agents, customs officials, car-rental staff, and public transportation personnel. We also show you how to ask the occasional bystander for help, all while keeping a cool head, smiling, and being polite.

Using German at the Airport

Most airline personnel speak several languages, so they're usually able to assist you in English. But in case you need a little backup, this section provides you with enough vocabulary to navigate the airport with confidence and a smile.

For starters, **das Flugticket/der Flugschein** (dâs *floohk*-ti-ket/dêr *floohk*-shayn) is your *airplane ticket*. It's probably a **Rückflugticket** (*ruek*-floohk-ti-ket) (*roundtrip ticket*). When you're checking in, you also need to have **die Bordkarte** (dee *bord*-kâr-te) (*boarding pass*).

Getting your ticket

If you're not able to print out your ticket and boarding pass at home before you get to the airport, you'll need to find the appropriate airline counter. Hopefully the signs at the airport are clear enough, but just in case you're feeling like Alice in Wonderland and don't know which way to go, stop an employee and ask for directions to your airline's ticket counter:

>**Wo ist der . . . Schalter?** (voh ist dêr . . . *shâl*-ter?) (*Where is the . . . counter?*)

When you arrive at the ticket counter, just say the following to inquire about your ticket:

>**Ich möchte mein Ticket abholen.** (iH *merH*-te mayn ticket [as in English] *âp*-hoh-len) (*I would like to pick up my ticket.*)

Checking in

When you're at the check-in counter, the attendant will ask you a few questions to prepare you for boarding the plane:

>**Haben Sie Gepäck?** (*hah*-ben zee ge-*pêk?*) (*Do you have luggage?*)

>**Wo möchten Sie sitzen, am Fenster oder am Gang?** (voh *merH*-ten zee *zits*-en, âm *fêns*-ter *oh*-der âm gâng?) (*Where would you like to sit, by the window or on the aisle?*)

In response to the question about where you want to sit, you can respond simply **am Fenster/am Gang** (âm *fêns*-ter/âm gâng) (*by a window/on the aisle*), according to your preference.

You may also want to ask the following questions to get some details about the flight:

>**Wie lange dauert der Flug?** (vee *lâng*-e *dou*-êrt dêr floohk?) (*How long is the flight?*)

>**Wann fliegt die Maschine ab?** (vân fleekt dee mâ-*sheen*-e âp?) (*When does the plane leave?*)

If you're at the airport to meet somebody who is arriving on another plane, you can ask

>**Wann kommt die Maschine aus . . . an?** (vân komt dee mâ-*sheen*-e ous . . . ân?) (*When does the plane from . . . arrive?*)

Words to Know

das Flugticket/der Flugschein	dâs <u>floohk</u>-ti-ket/dêr <u>floohk</u>-shayn	airplane ticket
das Rückflugticket	dâs <u>ruek</u>-floohk-ti-ket	roundtrip ticket
die Bordkarte	dee <u>bord</u>-kâr-te	boarding pass
das Gepäck/ Handgepäck	dâs ge-<u>pêk</u>/<u>hând</u>-ge-pêk	luggage/hand luggage
das Flugzeug/ die Maschine	das <u>floohk</u>-tsoyk/ dee mâ-<u>shee</u>-ne	airplane
der Flug	dêr floohk	flight
abholen	<u>âp</u>-hoh-len	to pick up
dauern	<u>dou</u>-ern	to last

Talkin' the Talk

 Frau Schöller is flying to Prague. At the airport she's getting her boarding pass at the Lufthansa counter. (Track 29)

Frau Schöller: **Guten Morgen. Ich brauche eine Bordkarte. Hier ist mein Ticket.**
gooh-ten *mor*-gen. iH *brauH*-e *ayn*-e *bord*-kâr-te. Heer ist mayn ticket.
Good morning. I need a boarding pass. Here is my ticket.

Angestellter: **Ihren Pass, bitte.**
eer-en pâs, *bi*-te.
Your passport, please.

Frau Schöller hands the counter agent her passport.

Frau Schöller:	**Bitte schön.** *bi*-te shern. *Here you are.*
Angestellter:	**Danke. Wo möchten Sie sitzen, am Fenster oder am Gang?** *dân*-ke. voh *merH*-ten zee *zits*-en, âm *fêns*-ter *oh*-der âm gâng? *Thank you. Where would you like to sit, by the window or by the aisle?*
Frau Schöller:	**Am Fenster, bitte.** âm *fêns*-ter, *bi*-te. *By the window, please.*
Angestellter:	**Sie haben Platz 15A, einen Fensterplatz. Hier ist Ihre Bordkarte. Haben Sie Gepäck?** zee *hah*-ben plâts *fuenf*-tseyn ah, *ayn*-en *fêns*-ter-plâts. heer ist *eer*-e bord-*kâr*-te. *hah*-ben zee ge-*pêk*? *You have seat 15A, a window seat. Here is your boarding pass. Do you have any luggage?*
Frau Schöller:	**Ich habe nur Handgepäck, diese Tasche.** iH *hah*-be noohr *hând*-ge-pêk, *deez*-e *tâsh*-e. *I only have a carry-on, this bag.*
Angestellter:	**Dann können Sie direkt zum Flugsteig gehen.** dân *kern*-en zee di-*rêkt* tsoom *floohk*-shtayk *gey*-en. *Then you can go straight to the gate.*
Frau Schöller:	**Danke.** *dân*-ke. *Thank you.*

Words to Know

der Abflug	dêr âp-floohk	departure
die Ankunft	dee <u>ân</u>-koonft	arrival
der Flugsteig	dêr <u>floohk</u>-shtayk	gate
mitnehmen	<u>mit</u>-neym-en	to take along
einchecken	<u>ayn</u>-chêk-en	to check in
fliegen	<u>fleeg</u>-en	to fly
abfliegen	<u>âp</u>-fleeg-en	to leave (on a plane)
ankommen	<u>ân</u>-kom-en	to arrive
der Ausweis	dêr <u>ous</u>-vays	ID card
verspätet	fêr-<u>shpey</u>-tet	delayed

Going through immigration

When you're getting off a transatlantic flight, you're directed straight to **die Passkontrolle** (dee *pâs*-kon-*trol*-e) (*passport control*). Make sure that you have your passport handy.

Most of the time you get to choose between two lines: One is for **EU-Bürger** (ey-*ooh-buer*-ger) (*citizens of countries in the European Union*) and the other is for **Nicht-EU-Bürger** (*niHt*-ey-*ooh-buer*-ger) (*citizens of countries outside the EU,* such as the U.S.). After passing through passport control, you claim your baggage and go through **der Zoll** (dêr tsol) (*customs*), where you may have to open your luggage for inspection.

Matters are more laid back when you're traveling from one member country of **die europäische Union** (dee oy-roh-*pey*-i-she oon-ee-*yohn*) (*the European Union*) to another by car or train. With the number of member states currently at 27 — and still counting — you may find yourself crossing many internal borders of the EU without being checked. So when you drive from Germany to France, for example, you may not even notice where the border is until you suddenly discover that the signs are all in French. And you can import virtually unlimited quantities of goods bought from one EU country to another country.

Jet-lagged after a long flight, all you want to do is leave the airport. But first you have two hurdles to overcome. To help you in your foggy state of mind, these are the words you may need to be familiar with when you go through passport control:

> **der Reisepass/der Pass** (dêr *ray*-ze-pâs/dêr pâs) (*passport*)
>
> **EU-Bürger** (ey-*ooh*-buer-ger) (*citizen of a country of the European Union*)
>
> **Nicht-EU-Bürger** (*niHt*-ey-*ooh*-buer-ger) (*citizen of a country outside the EU*)
>
> **Ich bin im Urlaub hier.** (iH bin im *oor*-loup heer.) (*I'm here on vacation.*)
>
> **Ich bin geschäftlich hier.** (iH bin ge-*shêft*-liH heer.) (*I'm here on business.*)
>
> **Ich bin auf der Durchreise nach. . . .** (iH bin ouf dêr *doorH*-ray-ze nâhH. . . .) (*I am on my way to. . . .*)

Going through customs

You passed the first hurdle and are on your way to customs. Are you one of those people who feel guilty even when you have nothing to hide? Customs officers can make you feel that way. It pays to know how to answer their questions succinctly so you can get past them as quickly as possible.

At **der Zoll** (dêr tsol) (*customs*), you usually get to choose between two options: the red exit for people who have to declare goods or the green exit for those people who are carrying only things they don't need to declare.

So far, so good. Customs officers may, of course, use this phrase to ask you personally whether you have anything to declare, in which case you may need to pay duty:

> **Haben Sie etwas zu verzollen?** (*hah*-ben zee *êt*-vâs tsooh fêr-*tsol*-en?) (*Do you have anything to declare?*)

To this question, you can respond with either of the following:

> **Ich möchte . . . verzollen.** (iH *merH*-te . . . fêr-*tsol*-en) (*I would like to declare. . . .*)
>
> **Ich habe nichts zu verzollen.** (iH *hah*-be niHts tsooh fêr-*tsol*-en.) (*I have nothing to declare.*)

Despite your most engaging smile, the customs officer may ask to have a look at your not-so-suspicious-looking stuff by saying

> **Bitte öffnen Sie diesen Koffer/diese Tasche.** (*bi*-te *erf*-nen zee *deez*-en *kof*-er/*deez*-e *tâsh*-e.) (*Please open this suitcase/bag.*)

And when the customs officer asks what you're planning to do with a purchase, you may answer

> **Es ist für meinen persönlichen Gebrauch.** (ês ist fuer *mayn*-en pêr-*sern*-liH-en ge-*brouH.*) (*It's for my personal use.*)

> **Es ist ein Geschenk.** (ês ist ayn ge-*shênk.*) (*It's a gift.*)

Traveling by Car

Before setting out on a European road trip in a rental car, consider acquiring an **internationaler Führerschein** (*in*-têr-nâ-tee-oh-nâ-ler *fuer*-er-shayn) (*international driving permit*). You can apply for one at the local AAA (American Automobile Association) Web site. (You can find your local club at www.aaa.com). Even with an **internationaler Führerschein**, you still need a valid driver's license. Then you're all set to discover new territory.

You're most likely to travel the following types of roads:

- ✔ **die Autobahn** (dee *ou*-toh-bahn) (*freeway, four to six lanes*)

- ✔ **die Bundesstraße** (dee *boon*-des-shtrah-se) or, in Switzerland, **Nationalstrasse** (nâ-tee-oh-*nahl*-shtrah-se) (*two- to four-lane highway*)

- ✔ **die Landstraße** (dee *lânt*-shtrah-se) (*two-lane highway*)

Renting a car

You're likely to find that making car reservations is cheaper and more hassle-free if you do it before leaving for your European trip. However, if you decide to rent a car when you're already in Europe, you need to make your way to the **Autovermietung** (*ou*-toh-fêr-meet-oong) (*car rental agency*). When you arrive at the car rental agency, you can start out by saying

> **Ich möchte ein Auto mieten.** (iH *merH*-te ayn *ou*-toh *meet*-en.) (*I would like to rent a car.*)

The attendant will ask you questions about what kind of car you want by saying something like

> **Was für ein Auto möchten Sie?** (vâs fuer ayn *ou*-toh *merH*-ten zee?) (*What kind of car would you like?*)

You can respond with any of the following:

- **ein zweitüriges/viertüriges Auto** (ayn *tsvay*-tuer-ee-ges/*feer*-tuer-ee-ges *ou*-toh) (*a two-door/four-door car*)

- **einen Kleinwagen** (*ayn*-en *klayn*-wah-gen) (*compact car*)

- **mit Automatik** (mit ou-toh-*mah*-tik) (*car with automatic transmission*)

- **mit Gangschaltung** (mit *gâng*-shâlt-oong) (*car with standard transmission*)

You may also be asked one or more of the following questions:

> **Ab wann möchten Sie den Wagen mieten?** (âp vân *merH*-ten zee deyn *vah*-gen *meet*-en?) (*Starting when would you like to rent the car?*)

> **Wann/Wo möchten Sie den Wagen zurückgeben?** (vân/voh *merH*-ten zee deyn *vah*-gen tsoo-*ruek*-gey-ben?) (*Where/When would you like to return the car?*)

Here are some possible answers:

> **Ich möchte den Wagen ab dem . . . mieten.** (iH *merH*-te deyn *vah*-gen âp deym . . . *meet*-en.) (*I would like to rent the car starting. . . .*)

> **Ich möchte den Wagen am . . . zurückgeben.** (iH *merH*-te deyn *vah*-gen âm . . . tsoo-*ruek*-gey-ben.) (*I would like to return the car on the. . . .*)

> **Ich möchte den Wagen in . . . zurückgeben.** (iH *merH*-te deyn *vah*-gen in . . . tsoo-*ruek*-gey-ben.) (*I would like to return the car in. . . .*)

During the rental process, you'll hear the following words as well:

- **der Führerschein** (dêr *fuer*-er-shayn) (*driver's license*)

- **die Vollkaskoversicherung** (dee *fol*-kâs-koh-fêr-*zeeH*-er-oong) (*comprehensive collision insurance*)

- **inbegriffen** (*in*-be-grif-en) (*included*)

- **ohne Kilometerbegrenzung** (*oh*-ne ki-lo-*mey*-ter-be-*grênts*-oong) (*unlimited mileage*)

Talkin' the Talk

Anke has just arrived in Frankfurt. After going through customs, she heads for a car rental agency where she's talking to an employee.

Anke: **Guten Morgen. Ich möchte ein Auto mieten.**

gooh-ten *mor*-gen. iH *merH*-te ayn *ou*-toh *meet*-en. *Good morning. I would like to rent a car.*

Angestellter:	**Was für ein Auto möchten Sie?**
	vâs fuer ayn *ou*-toh *merH*-ten zee?
	What kind of car would you like?
Anke:	**Einen Kleinwagen mit Automatik.**
	ayn-en *klayn*-vah-gen mit ou-toh-*mah*-tik.
	A compact car with automatic transmission.
Angestellter:	**Wie lange brauchen Sie den Wagen?**
	vee *lâng*-e *brouH*-en zee deyn *vah*-gen?
	How long do you need the car?
Anke:	**Eine Woche.**
	ayn-e *voH*-e.
	For one week.
Angestellter:	**Ein VW Polo kostet für eine Woche ohne Kilometerbregrenzung 299 Euro inklusive Versicherung.**
	ayn vou-*vey poh*-loh *kos*-tet fuer *ayn*-e *voH*-e oh-ne ki-lo-*mey*-ter-be-*grênts*-oong *tsvay*-hoon-dêrt-*noyn*-oont–*noyn*-tsiH *oy*-roh in-kloo-*zee*-ve fêr-*ziH*-er-oong.
	A VW Polo costs 299 euros for one week, including unlimited mileage and insurance.

Making sense of maps

A good map tells you plenty more than how to get from Point A to Point B — and you can mark your route as you travel. Another advantage of maps is that they're primarily visual, so you don't need to know too much of the language in order to read one. However, you may find that knowing the words for different kinds of maps helpful, in case you need to ask for one:

- **die Landkarte** (dee *lânt*-kâr-te) (*map*)
- **der Stadtplan** (dêr *shtât*-plahn) (*map of a city*)
- **die Straßenkarte** (dee *shtrah*-sen-kâr-te) (*road map*)

On a map written in German (and also on road signs), you may see the following words:

- **die Altstadt** (dee *âlt*-shtât) (*historic center*)
- **die Ausfahrt** (dee *ous*-fahrt) (*exit ramp*)

✔ **das Autobahndreieck** (dâs *ou*-toh-bahn-*dray*-êk) (*where one freeway splits off from another freeway*)

✔ **das Autobahnkreuz** (dâs *ou*-toh-bahn-kroyts) (*junction of two freeways*)

✔ **die Einfahrt** (dee *ayn*-fahrt) (*entrance ramp*)

✔ **die Fußgängerzone** (dee *foohs*-gên-ger-*tsohn*-e) (*pedestrian zone*)

✔ **die Kirche** (dee *kirH*-e) (*church*)

✔ **das Parkhaus** (dâs *pârk*-hous) (*parking garage*)

✔ **das Theater** (dâs tey-*ah*-ter) (*theater*)

Wrapping your brain around road signs

You surely don't want to get stopped for driving too fast in the wrong direction down a one-way street that's been closed for construction. To prevent a scenario like this, here are some of the most common road signs that you encounter in German-speaking countries:

✔ **Anlieger frei** (*ân*-lee-ger fray) (*access only; no exit*)

✔ **Baustelle** (*bou*-shtêl-e) (*construction site*)

✔ **Einbahnstraße** (*ayn*-bahn-*shtrah*-se) (*one-way street*)

✔ **Einordnen** (*ayn*-ord-nen) (*merge*)

✔ **50 bei Nebel** (*fuenf*-tsiH bay *ney*-bel) (*50 kilometers per hour when foggy*)

✔ **Gesperrt** (ge-*shpêrt*) (*closed*)

✔ **Licht an/aus** (liHt *ân*/ous) (*lights on/off* — you see these signs at tunnels)

✔ **Umleitung** (*oom*-lay-toong) (*detour*)

✔ **Vorsicht Glätte** (*fohr*-ziHt *glêt*-e) (*slippery when wet*)

Taking a Train

Traveling by rail is a very comfortable way of getting around Europe. No matter whether you'd like to whiz from Stuttgart to Paris on the **Intercity Express (ICE)** (*in*-têr-si-tee-êks-*prês* [ee-tsey-*ey*]) or feel like heading to quaint towns along the Mosel River aboard the (much) slower **Interregio (IR)** (*in*-têr-*rey*-gee-oh [ee-êr]), you can get practically anywhere by train.

Rail travel is very popular among Europeans, so during peak traveling times making a reservation is advisable. You may be interested in a combination ticket that allows you to rent a bicycle or a car from a train station. Or, if you're covering a lot of ground in a short time, go online and check out the various types of rail passes before you leave home.

Interpreting train schedules

Every train station displays schedules for all the trains that run through that particular station. However, with the flood of information, you may find it difficult to figure out what you need to know about the specific train you want to take. The following expressions provide some guidance for demystifying train schedules:

- **die Abfahrt** (dee *âp*-fahrt) (*departure*)
- **die Ankunft** (dee *ân*-koonft) (*arrival*)
- **der Fahrplan** (dêr *fahr*-plahn) (*train schedule*)
- **sonn- und feiertags** (*zon* oont *fay*-er-tâhks) (*Sundays and holidays*)
- **über** (*ue*-ber) (*via*)
- **werktags** (*vêrk*-tâhks) (*workdays*)

Getting information

When you have questions about a train you want to take, head to **die Auskunft** (dee *ous*-koonft) (*the information counter*). There, you may ask any of the following questions:

Von welchem Gleis fährt der Zug nach . . . ab? (fon *vêlH*-Hem glays fairt dêr tsoohk nahH . . . ap?) (*Which track does the train to . . . leave from?*)

Auf welchem Gleis kommt der Zug aus . . . an? (ouf *vêlH*-em glays komt dêr tsoohk ous . . . ân?) (*Which track does the train from . . . arrive on?*)

Hat der Zug Verspätung? (hât dêr tsoohk fêr-*shpêt*-oong?) (*Is the train delayed?*)

Words to Know

der Bahnsteig	dêr <u>bahn</u>-shtayk	platform
das Gleis	dâs glays	track
die Verspätung	dee fêr-<u>shpêt</u>-oong	delay
einsteigen	<u>ayn</u>-shtayg-en	get on
aussteigen	<u>ous</u>-shtayg-en	get off
umsteigen	<u>oom</u>-shtayg-en	change (trains, buses, and so on)
abfahren	<u>âp</u>-fahr-en	leave
ankommen	<u>ân</u>-kom-en	arrive
fahren	<u>fahr</u>-en	go by, travel

Buying tickets

For tickets, you need to go to **der Fahrkartenautomat** (dêr *fahr*-kâr-ten-ou-toh-mât) (*ticket machine*) or **der Fahrkartenschalter** (dêr *fahr*-kâr-ten-*shâl*-ter) (*the ticket counter*). With the help of the words in this section, you can buy a ticket to virtually anywhere you want to go.

The basics

When it's your turn to talk to the ticket agent, just say the following to get yourself a ticket:

> **Eine Fahrkarte nach . . . , bitte.** (*ayn*-e *fahr*-kâr-te nahH . . . , *bi*-te.) (*A train ticket to . . . please.*)

To find out whether you want a one-way or a round-trip ticket, the ticket agent will ask

> **Einfach oder hin und zurück?** (*ayn*-fâH *oh*-der hin oont tsoo-*ruek?*) (*One-way or round-trip?*)

And to find out whether you want a first class or a second class ticket, the ticket agent will ask

Erster oder zweiter Klasse? (*eyrs*-ter *oh*-der *tsvay*-ter klâs-e?) (*In first or second class?*)

Extras

On all trains, there's a set base price per kilometer for first and second class. In addition, you have to pay **der Zuschlag** (dêr *tsooh*-shlahk) (*surcharge*) for the very fast trains marked **ICE** (*Intercity Express*), **IC** (*Intercity*), or **EC** (*Eurocity*). For these trains, the word **Zuschlag** usually appears on the train schedule or the board displaying departures.

On especially busy trains, you may be better off reserving a seat in advance. To do so, simply ask

Ich möchte gern eine Platzkarte für den . . . von . . . nach. . . .
(iH *merH*-te gêrn *ayn*-e *plâts*-kâr-te fuer deyn . . . fon . . . nahH. . . .)
(*I would like to reserve a seat on the . . . from . . . to. . . .*)

Words to Know

die Fahrkarte	dee fahr-kâr-te	train ticket
die erste Klasse	dee êrs-te klâs-e	first class
die zweite Klasse	dee tsvay-te klâs-e	second class
der Zuschlag	dêr tsooh-shlahk	surcharge
die Rückfahrkarte	dee ruek-fahr-kâr-te	round-trip ticket
die Platzkarte	dee plâts-kâr-te	reserved seat
hin und zurück	hin oont tsoo-ruek	round-trip
einfach	ayn-fâH	one-way

Knowing When to Separate Your Verbs

Many German verbs, including many of the verbs used in this chapter, share a peculiar trait. They have prefixes that are detachable from the body (stem) of the verb. When used in the present tense in a sentence, the verb stem and prefix of these verbs separate. The normal verb ending is added to the verb stem, which takes its usual place in the sentence, while the prefix is pushed to the very end of the sentence.

Take a look at this phenomenon in action, using the verb **ankommen** (*ân*-kom-en) (*to arrive*). Notice how the prefix always goes to the end of the sentence, no matter how many words come between it and the verb:

> **Der Zug kommt um 18.15 Uhr an.** (dêr tsoohk komt oom * âHt*-tseyn oohr *fuenf*-tseyn ân.) (*The train arrives at 6:15 p.m.*)

> **Auf welchem Gleis kommt der Zug aus Dessau an?** (ouf *vêlH*-em glays komt dêr tsoohk ous *dês*-ou ân?) (*Which track does the train from Dessau arrive on?*)

How do you know whether a verb is separable? These guidelines indicate that it is:

✔ The verb has a short word at the beginning of the verb to serve as a prefix.

✔ The infinitive is stressed on the first syllable; this is the prefix.

Here are a few verbs that follow this pattern. You encounter several more separable verbs throughout this book. Notice how the first syllable is stressed:

✔ **abfahren** (*âp*-fahr-en) (*to depart* [*train*])

✔ **abfliegen** (*âp*-fleeg-en) (*to depart* [*plane*])

✔ **anfangen** (*ân*-fâng-en) (*to start*)

✔ **ankommen** (*ân*-kom-en) (*to arrive*)

✔ **aufmachen** (*ouf*-mâH-en) (*to open*)

✔ **aufstehen** (*ouf*-shtey-en) (*to get up*)

✔ **aussteigen** (*ous*-shtayg-en) (*to get off*)

✔ **einsteigen** (*ayn*-shtayg-en) (*to get on*)

✔ **zumachen** (*tsoo*-mâH-en) (*to close*)

The honor system

When entering a subway station in a German-speaking country, you won't see any turnstiles. So how do people pay for the ride? They buy tickets first and validate them by inserting the ticket into a validating machine. You find these machines at the entrance to the station or aboard streetcars or buses. So when you purchase a ticket, remember that you have to validate the ticket before getting on a train or subway or when boarding a streetcar or bus. Plainclothes ticket inspectors make frequent checks, and anyone caught without a valid ticket can count on a hefty on-the-spot fine.

When using separable verbs, the main verb stem with the appropriate ending goes in its usual place. The prefix becomes the last word in the sentence. This rule works for the present and simple past tenses.

Navigating Buses, Subways, and Taxis

German cities and towns usually have excellent public transportation systems. A combination of **Bus** (boos) (*bus*), **U-Bahn** (*ooh*-bahn) (*subway*), **Straßenbahn** (*shtrah*-sen-bahn) (*streetcar*), and **S-Bahn** (*ês*-bahn) (*light rail train to the suburbs*) should get you rapidly and safely where you want to go.

Catching the bus

If you need help finding the right bus or train to take, you can ask the agent at the **Fahrkartenschalter** (*fahr*-kâr-ten-shâl-ter) (*ticket window*), or any bus driver (**der Busfahrer**) (dêr *boos*-fahr-er) any of the following questions:

> **Welcher Bus fährt ins Stadtzentrum?** (*vêlH*-er boos fairt ins *shtât*-tsên-troom?) (Which bus goes to the city center?)

> **Ist das die richtige Straßenbahn zum Stadion?** (ist dâs dee *riH*-tee-ge *shtrah*-sen-bahn tsoom *shtah*-dee-on?) (*Is this the right streetcar to the stadium?*)

> **Muss ich umsteigen?** (moos iH *oom*-shtayg-en?) (*Do I have to switch [buses]?*)

> **Hält diese U-Bahn am Hauptbahnhof?** (hêlt *deez*-e *ooh*-bahn âm *houpt*-bahn-hohf?) (*Does this subway stop at the main train station?*)

Words to Know

der Bus	dêr boos	bus
die U-bahn	dee <u>ooh</u>-bahn	subway
die S-Bahn	dee <u>ês</u>-bahn	local train
die Straßenbahn	dee <u>shtrah</u>-sen-bahn	streetcar
die Buslinie/ U-Bahnlinie	dee <u>boos</u>-leen-ye/ <u>ooh</u>-bahn-leen-ye	bus line/subway line
die Haltestelle	dee <u>hâl</u>-te-shtê-le	station, stop
halten	<u>hâl</u>-ten	to stop
die U-Bahnstation	dee <u>ooh</u>-bahn- shtâts-ee-ohn	subway station
das Taxi	dâs <u>tâx</u>-ee	taxi
der Taxistand	dêr <u>tâx</u>-ee-shtânt	taxi stand
der Fahrscheinautomat	dêr fahr-shayn-ou- toh-maht	ticket vending machine

Talkin' the Talk

 Ben wants to take the bus to city hall, but he's not quite sure which bus he should take. So he approaches a teenager who is standing next to him at the bus stop. (Track 30)

Ben: **Entschuldigen Sie bitte, hält hier der Bus Nummer 9?**
ênt-*shool*-dee-gen zee *bi*-te, hêlt heer dêr boos-*noom*-er noyn?
Excuse me please, does the bus number 9 stop here?

Teenager:	**Nein, hier hält nur die Linie 8. Wohin wollen Sie denn?**
	nayn, heer hêlt noohr dee *leen*-ye âHt. *vo*-hin *vol*-en zee dên?
	No, only number 8 stops here. Where do you want to go?
Ben:	**Zum Rathaus.**
	tsoom *raht*-hous.
	To the town hall.
Teenager:	**Fahren Sie mit der Linie 8 bis zum Goetheplatz, und dort steigen Sie in die Linie 9 um.**
	fahr-en zee mit dêr *leen*-ye âHt bis tsoom *ger*-te-plâts, oont dort *shtayg*-en zee in dee *leen*-ye noyn oom.
	Take this bus to Goetheplatz, and switch there to number 9.
Ben:	**Wie viele Haltestellen sind es bis zum Goetheplatz?**
	vee *feel*-e *hâl*-te-shtêl-en zint ês bis tsoom *ger*-te-plâts?
	How many stops are there to Goetheplatz?
Teenager:	**Von hier sind es vier Haltestellen.**
	fon heer zint ês feer *hâl*-te-shtêl-en.
	It's four stops from here.
Ben:	**Vielen Dank für die Auskunft.**
	feel-en dânk fuer dee *ous*-koonft.
	Thank you very much for the information.

Getting a taxi

Taking a taxi isn't hard. Just make your way over to the nearest **Taxistand** (*tâx*-ee-shtânt) (*taxi stand*) and go straight up to the first car in the line. When you get in, the **Taxifahrer** (*tâx*-ee-fahr-er) (*taxi driver*) will turn on the meter and ask you

> **Wohin möchten Sie?** (vo-*hin* merH-ten zee?) (*Where would you like to go?*)

At the end of the trip, you pay the price indicated on the meter, along with a modest tip.

Many Germans taking a taxi alone sit in the passenger seat. You may enjoy doing the same. You have a far greater chance of seeing where you're going, and you can take the opportunity to ask questions.

FUN & GAMES

One part of driving safely is understanding and obeying road signs. To see how well you'd do on a German road, match each German road sign to its English translation.

1._____Exit

2._____Slippery road

3._____One way street

4._____Road closed, no entry

5._____Construction site

6._____Highway

7._____Pedestrians only

8._____Connecting highway

9._____Get in lane

10._____Detour

Chapter 16

Finding a Place to Stay

In This Chapter

▶ Finding accommodations

▶ Making reservations

▶ Checking in and out of your hotel

*R*egardless of whether you're traveling on business or taking a vacation, having a clean and comfortable place to spend the night is an important part of your trip. In this chapter, we help you with the vocabulary and phrases that you need to find accommodations, inquire about facilities, make reservations, and check in and out.

Finding a Hotel

If you're one of those people who like the adventure of doing things on the spur of the moment or if you simply need assistance in finding a hotel, you can get reliable information about all types of accommodations through the tourist information center in any town, which is called **das Fremdenverkehrsbüro** or **Fremdenverkehrsamt** (dâs *frêm*-den-fêr-keyrs-bue-roh/*frêm*-den-fêr-keyrs-âmt). These places are often located conveniently in the center of town or next to the train station.

Perhaps you want to ask other people you know or meet whether they can recommend a hotel. In this case, ask

> **Können Sie mir ein Hotel in . . . empfehlen?** (*kern*-en zee meer ayn hotel [as in English] in . . . êm-*pfey*-len?) (*Can you recommend a hotel in. . . ?*)

You can find a wide range of hotels and hotel-like accommodations in German-speaking countries. Outside urban areas, you're especially likely to see different types of lodging, including the following:

> ✔ **die Ferienwohnung** (dee *feyr*-ree-ên-vohn-oong): A furnished vacation apartment located in a popular tourist destination.

✔ **das Fremdenzimmer** (dâs *frêm*-dên-tsi-mer): A bed and breakfast, often with shared bathroom facilities.

✔ **das Gasthaus/der Gasthof** (dâs *gâst*-hous/dêr *gâst*-hohf): An inn providing food, drinks, and often lodging.

✔ **das Hotel garni** (dâs hotel gâr-*nee*): A hotel that serves only breakfast.

✔ **die Jugendherberge** (die *yooh*-gênt-hêr-bêr-ge): A youth hostel, but not only for the under-25 crowd. This is an inexpensive option, but you generally need a Youth Hostel ID, which you can get before you travel.

✔ **die Pension** (dee pên-zee-*ohn*): A bed-and-breakfast type of place. In addition to breakfast, it may also serve lunch and dinner.

✔ **der Rasthof/das Motel** (dêr *râst*-hohf/dâs motel [as in English]): A roadside lodge or motel located just off a highway.

Reserving Rooms

To avoid last-minute hassles, booking a hotel room in advance is best, especially during the peak season or when a special event in town may mean that hotels are booked solid for months in advance. If you're having difficulty finding a room, you're more likely to find a place outside of towns and city centers. Ask for some assistance at the **Fremdenverkehrsamt** (*frêm*-den-fêr-keyrs-âmt). (See the preceding section for more information on that helpful office with the long name.)

Of course, you can make reservations for hotel rooms online, but if you're using the phone, you may want to read Chapter 11 beforehand. When you call, the following sentence can help you explain the purpose of your call:

Ich möchte gern ein Zimmer reservieren. (iH *merH*-te gêrn ayn *tsi*-mer rê-zêr-*vee*-ren.) (*I would like to reserve a room.*)

If you want to book more than one room, simply substitute the appropriate number — **zwei** (tsvay) (*two*), **drei** (dray) (*three*), and so on — in place of **ein**.

Saying when and how long you want to stay

The person taking your reservation is likely to ask you for some information. Among the first of these questions, you may hear something like

Von wann bis wann möchten Sie das Zimmer reservieren? (fon vân bis vân *merH*-ten zee dâs *tsi*-mer rê-zêr-*vee*-ren?) (*For what dates would you like to reserve the room?*)

To specify how many nights you want to stay or for what dates you want to reserve a room, you can say either of the following, depending on what suits your needs (Chapter 4 gives more details on how to specify the date):

Ich möchte gern ein Zimmer für . . . Nächte reservieren. (iH *merH*-te gêrn ayn *tsi*-mer fuer . . . *naiHt*-e rê-zêr-*vee*-ren.) (*I would like to reserve a room for . . . nights.*)

Ich möchte gern ein Zimmer vom 11. 3. bis zum 15. 3. reservieren. (iH *merH*-te gêrn ayn *tsi*-mer fom *êlf*-ten *drit*-en bis tsoom *fuenf*-tseyn-ten *drit*-en rê-zêr-*vee*-ren.) (*I would like to reserve a room from the 11th to the 15th of March.*)

Specifying the kind of room you want

The person taking your reservation is certain to ask you something like the following in order to find out what kind of room you want:

Was für ein Zimmer möchten Sie gern? (vâs fuer ayn *tsi*-mer *merH*-ten zee gêrn?) (*What kind of room would you like?*)

Or you can take the initiative and state what kind of room you want with the phrase

Ich hätte gern. . . . (iH *hêt*-e gêrn. . . .) (*I would like. . . .*)

At the end of the phrase, add any of the following (or a combination of them) to specify exactly what kind of room you want to rest your weary bones in:

✔ **ein Doppelzimmer** (ayn *dôp*-el-tsi-mer) (*a double room*)

✔ **ein Einzelzimmer** (ayn *ayn*-tsêl-tsi-mer) (*a single room*)

✔ **ein Zimmer mit . . .** (ayn *tsi*-mer mit . . .) (*a room with . . .*) and then choose from the following features:

  • **Bad** (baht) (*bathtub*)

  • **Dusche** (*dooh*-she) (*shower*)

  • **einem Doppelbett** (*ayn*-êm *dôp*-el-bêt) (*one double bed*)

  • **zwei Einzelbetten** (tsvay *ayn*-tsêl-bêt-en) (*two twin beds*)

TIP

A phrase that comes in handy: Was für. . . ?

Was für. . . ? (vâs fuer. . . ?) (*What kind of. . . ?*) is a handy phrase to remember. It can come up whenever you're speaking with customer service people, from a store assistant to someone at the **Fremdenverkehrsbüro**. These questions help people find out exactly what you're looking for. Check out these examples:

Was für eine Ferienwohnung möchten Sie gern? (vâs fuer *ayn*-e *feyr*-ree-ên-vohn-oong *merH*-ten zee gêrn?) (*What kind of vacation apartment would you like?*)

Was für eine Unterkunft suchen Sie? (vâs fuer *ayn*-e *oon*-ter-koonft *zoohH*-en zee?) (*What kind of accommodation are you looking for?*)

Remember that the question **Was für. . . ?** is always used with the indefinite article in the accusative case. (See Chapter 2 for the lowdown on indefinite articles and the accusative case.)

Asking about the price

Even if your last name is Moneybags, you probably want to find out what the hotel room costs. Look at the following variations on the question, depending on whether you want to know the basic price or the price with other features included:

> **Was kostet das Zimmer pro Nacht?** (vâs *kos*-tet dâs *tsi*-mer proh nâHt?) (*What does the room cost per night?*)

> **Was kostet eine Übernachtung mit Frühstück?** (vâs *kos*-tet *ayn*-e ue-ber-*nâHt*-oong mit *frue*-shtuek?) (*What does accommodation including breakfast cost?*)

> **Was kostet ein Zimmer mit Halbpension/Vollpension?** (vâs *kos*-tet ayn *tsi*-mer mit *hâlp*-pân-zee-ohn/*fol*-pân-zee-ohn?) (*What does a room with half board/full board cost?*)

Finalizing the reservation

If the room is available and the price doesn't cause you to faint, you can seal the deal by saying

> **Können Sie das Zimmer bitte reservieren?** (*kern*-en zee dâs *tsi*-mer *bi*-te rê-zêr-*vee*-ren?) (*Could you reserve that room, please?*)

Talkin' the Talk

Klaus und Ulrike Huber want to take a vacation in **Österreich** (*erst*-êr-ayH) (*Austria*), and they've found a hotel on Lake Mondsee where they'd like to stay. Klaus calls the Hotel Alpenhof and talks to the receptionist. (Track 31)

Rezeption:	**Hotel Alpenhof, guten Tag.** hotel [as in English] *âlp*-en-hohf, *gooh*-ten tahk. *Hello, Hotel Alpenhof.*
Klaus:	**Guten Tag. Ich möchte ein Zimmer vom 15. bis zum 23. Juni reservieren.** *gooh*-ten tahk. iH *merH*-te ayn *tsi*-mer fom *fuenf*-tseyn-ten bis tsoom *dray*-oont-tsvân-tsiH-sten *yooh*-nee rê-zêr-*vee*-ren. *Hello. I'd like to book a room from the 15th to the 23rd of June.*
Rezeption:	**Ja, das geht. Was für ein Zimmer möchten Sie?** yah, dâs geyt. vâs fuer ayn *tsi*-mer *merH*-ten zee? *Yes, that's fine. What kind of room would you like?*
Klaus:	**Ein Doppelzimmer mit Bad, bitte. Was kostet das Zimmer pro Nacht?** ayn *dôp*-el-tsi-mer mit baht *bi*-te. vâs *kôs*-tet dâs *tsi*-mer proh nâHt? *A double room with bathroom, please. What does the room cost per night?*
Rezeption:	**129 Euro für die Übernachtung mit Frühstück.** ayn-hoon-dert-noyn-oont-*tsvân*-tsiH *oy*-roh fuer dee ue-ber-*nâHt*-oong mit *frue*-shtuek. *129 euros for accommodation including breakfast.*
Klaus:	**Sehr gut. Können Sie es bitte reservieren? Mein Name ist Huber.** zeyr gooht. *kern*-en zee ês *bi*-te rê-zêr-*vee*-ren? mayn *nah*-me ist *hooh*-ber. *That's very good. Could you please reserve it? My name is Huber.*
Rezeption:	**Geht in Ordnung, Herr Huber.** geyt in *ort*-noong, hêr *hooh*-ber. *Okay, Mr. Huber.*
Klaus:	**Vielen Dank!** *fee*-len dânk *Thank you very much!*

Words to Know

das Fremdenver- kehrsbüro	dâs <u>frêm</u>-den-fêr- keyrs-bue-roh	tourist information center
das Einzelzimmer	dâs <u>ayn</u>-tsêl-tsi-mer	single room
das Doppelzimmer	dâs <u>dôp</u>-el-tsi-mer	double room
das Bad	dâs baht	bathtub
die Dusche	dee <u>dooh</u>-she	shower
Geht in Ordnung!	geyt in <u>ort</u>-noong!	Okay!

Checking In

After you arrive at your hotel, you have to check in at the **Rezeption** (rê-tsêp-tsee-*ohn*)/**Empfang** (êm-*pfâng*) (*reception desk*). To let the receptionist know that you have made reservations, say

> **Ich habe ein Zimmer reserviert.** (iH *hah*-be ayn *tsi*-mer rê-zêr-*veert.*) (*I have reserved a room.*)

Of course, you also have to let the receptionist know what your name is:

> **Mein Name ist. . . .** (mayn *nah*-me ist. . . .) (*My name is. . . .*)

Stating how long you're staying

If you haven't made a reservation or the receptionist wants to double-check the length of your stay, you may hear the question

> **Wie lange bleiben Sie?** (vee *lâng*-e *blay*-ben zee?) (*How long are you going to stay?*)

To the question about how long you want to stay, you can reply with the phrase

> **Ich bleibe/Wir bleiben. . . .** (iH *blay*-be/veer *blay*-ben. . . .) (*I'm going to stay/We're going to stay. . . .*)

Then end the phrase with any of the appropriate lengths of time:

nur eine Nacht (noohr *ayn*-e nâHt) (*only one night*)

bis zum elften (bis tsoom *êlf*-ten) (*until the 11th*)

eine Woche (*ayn*-e *vôH*-e) (*one week*)

Filling out the registration form

At most hotels, you have to fill out **der Meldeschein** (dêr *mêl*-de-shayn) (*reservation form*), commonly referred to as **das Formular** (dâs for-mooh-lahr) (*the form*) as part of the check-in process. The receptionist will hand you the form, saying something like the following:

Bitte füllen Sie dieses Formular aus. (*bi*-te *fuel*-en zee *deez*-ês for-mooh-lahr ous.) (*Please fill out this form.*)

The registration form asks you for all or most of the following information:

- ✔ **Tag der Ankunft** (tahk dêr *ân*-koonft) (*Date of arrival*)
- ✔ **Name/Vorname** (*nah*-me/*fohr*-nah-me) (*Surname/First name*)
- ✔ **Straße/Nummer (Nr.)** (*shtrah*-se/*noom*-er) (*Street/Number*)
- ✔ **Postleitzahl (PLZ)/Wohnort** (*post*-layt-tsahl/*vohn*-ort) (*Zip code/Town*)
- ✔ **Geburtsdatum/Geburtsort** (gê-*boorts*-dah-toohm/gê-*boorts*-ort) (*Birth date/Place of birth*)
- ✔ **Staatsangehörigkeit/Nationalität** (*stahts*-ân-ge-herr-iH-kayt/nâ-tsee-oh-nahl-i-*tait*) (*Nationality*)
- ✔ **Beruf** (bê-*roohf*) (*Occupation*)
- ✔ **Passnummer** (*pâs*-noom-er) (*Passport number*)
- ✔ **Ort/Datum** (ort/*dah*-toohm) (*Place/Date*)
- ✔ **Unterschrift** (*oon*-ter-shrift) (*Signature*)

Getting your luggage in hand

In all likelihood, you'll travel with some kind of **das Gepäck** (dâs ge-*pêk*) (*luggage*). Your luggage could be **der Koffer** (dêr *kof*-er) (*a suitcase*) or maybe even **die Koffer** (dee *kof*-er) (*suitcases*). No, that's not a mistake — the only difference between the singular and plural forms of *suitcase* is the article. (Chapter 2 gives you more details on plural endings for nouns.)

Getting keyed in

After you check in, the receptionist hands you your room key and says something like

> **Sie haben Zimmer Nummer 203.** (zee *hah*-ben *tsi*-mer *noom*-er *tsvay*-hoon-dert-dray.) (*You have room number 203.*)

In some hotels, usually the more tradition-bound, your room key is on a massive, metal key holder. You may be asked to leave your heavy metal key at the reception desk when you go out. When you arrive back at the hotel and need the key to your room, you can use the following phrase:

> **Können Sie mir bitte den Schlüssel für Zimmer Nummer . . . geben?** (*kern*-nen zee meer *bi*-te deyn *shlues*-êl fuer *tsi*-mer *noom*-er . . . *gey*-ben?) (*Could you give me the key for room number. . . ?*)

Asking about amenities and facilities

You may want to find out what kind of services and facilities the hotel offers — does your room have Wi-Fi or a minibar? Does the hotel have a laundry service?

Your room

When you want to ask about specific features of your room, start with the phrase

> **Hat das Zimmer. . . ?** (hât dâs *tsi*-mer. . . ?) (*Does the room have. . . ?*)

Then end the phrase with any of the following items:

> **einen Balkon** (*ayn*-en bâl-*kohn*) (*a balcony*)
>
> **Satellitenfernsehen/Kabelfernsehen** (zâ-tê-*lee*-ten-fêrn-zey-en/*kah*-bel-fêrn-zey-en) (*satellite TV/cable TV*)
>
> **ein Telefon** (ayn *tê*-le-fohn) (*a phone*)
>
> **Wi-Fi** (wee-fee) (*Wi-Fi*)
>
> **eine Minibar** (*ayn*-e minibar [as in English]) (*a minibar*)

The hotel

The hotel may offer a number of services that are outlined in a brochure you find in your room. However, if you need to ask about the hotel's amenities before you arrive or because you misplaced your reading glasses, just ask

> **Hat das Hotel. . . ?** (hât dâs hotel. . . ?) (*Does the hotel have. . . ?*)

Hotel breakfast

Most big hotels offer a breakfast buffet, from which you can usually choose among cereals, eggs, a variety of breads and juices, jam, cheese, and so on. In smaller towns or hotels, however, you may still get the traditional German breakfast: rolls and bread, jam, a soft-boiled egg served in an egg cup, and a choice of cold cuts and cheeses. So if you can't do without your scrambled eggs in the morning, you may have to put in a special order. (See Chapter 8 for help on how to do that.)

You can then ask about any of the following services by ending the preceding phrase with

eine Sauna (*ayn*-e *zou*-nâ) (*a sauna*)

ein Schwimmbad (ayn *shvim*-baht) (*a swimming pool*)

einen Fitnessraum (*ayn*-en *fit*-nes-room) (*a fitness room*)

einen Wäschedienst (*ayn*-en *vêsh*-e-deenst) (*laundry service*)

eine Klimaanlage (*ayn*-e *klee*-mah-ân-lah-ge) (*air-conditioning*)

eine Hotelgarage (*ayn*-e hoh-*têl*-gâ-*rah*-ge [second *g* pronounced as *g* in *genre*]) (*a hotel garage*)

einen Parkplatz (*ayn*-en *pârk*-plâts) (*a parking lot*)

Here are the questions that allow you to inquire about breakfast and room service:

Wann wird das Frühstück serviert? (vân virt dâs *frue*-shtuek zêr-*veert?*) (*At what time is breakfast served?*)

Gibt es Zimmerservice? (gipt ês *tsi*-mer-ser-vis?) (*Is there room service?*)

Talkin' the Talk

 Klaus und Ulrike Huber arrive at the Hotel Alpenhof. They park their car at the entrance and go to the reception desk to check in. (Track 32)

Klaus: **Guten Abend! Mein Name ist Huber. Wir haben ein Zimmer reserviert.**
gooht-en *ah*-bent! mayn *nah*-me ist *hooh*-ber. veer *hah*-ben ayn *tsi*-mer rê-zêr-*veert.*
Good evening! My name is Huber. We've reserved a room.

Rezeption:	**Ja richtig, ein Doppelzimmer mit Bad. Bitte füllen Sie dieses Formular aus.**
	yah *riH*-tiH, ayn *dôp*-el-tsi-mer mit baht. *bi*-te *fuel*-en zee *deez*-es for-mooh-*lahr* ous.
	Yes right, a double room with bath. Please fill out this form.

Klaus:	**Haben Sie eine Garage oder einen Parkplatz?**
	hah-ben zee *ayn*-e gâ-*rah*-ge *oh*-der *ayn*-en *pârk*-plâts?
	Do you have a garage or a parking lot?

Rezeption:	**Jawohl. Der Parkplatz ist hinter dem Hotel. Und hier ist Ihr Zimmerschlüssel, Nummer 203.**
	yah-*vohl.* dêr *pârk*-plâts ist *hin*-ter deym hotel [as in English]. oont heer ist eer *tsi*-mer-*shlues*-êl, *noom*-er *tsavy*-hoon-dert-dray.
	Yes, indeed. The parking lot is behind the hotel. And here is your key, number 203.

Ulrike:	**Wann servieren Sie Frühstück?**
	vân zêr-*vee*-ren zee *frue*-shtuek?
	When do you serve breakfast?

Rezeption:	**Von sieben bis zehn Uhr.**
	fon *zee*-ben bis tseyn oohr.
	From 7 to 10 o'clock.

Ulrike:	**Vielen Dank.**
	fee-len dânk
	Thank you very much.

Tipping at a hotel

Although service charges are usually included in the price of your hotel room, you may want to give a **das Trinkgeld** (dâs *trink*-gêlt) (*tip*) to the porter who brings up your luggage. In this case, 1 or 2 euros per bag is a reasonable amount.

On rare occasions, you also may see a little envelope in your room where you can leave money for the cleaning staff. Depending on the hotel and service, you can give a tip of 10 to 15 euros per week.

Words to Know

bleiben	blay-ben	to stay
das Formular	dâs for-mooh-lahr	form
ausfüllen	ous-fuel-en	to fill out
der Schlüssel	dêr shlues-êl	key
der Zimmerservice	dêr tsi-mer-ser-vis	room service
der Parkplatz	dêr pârk-plâts	parking lot

Checking Out and Paying the Bill

The German language has no exact equivalent for the convenient English term "to check out." The German term you use for checking out of your room is **das Zimmer räumen** (dâs *tsi*-mêr *roy*-men), which literally translates into *to clear out the room*. If you want to ask what time you have to vacate your room, inquire

> **Bis wann müssen wir/muss ich das Zimmer räumen?** (bis vân *mues*-en veer/moos iH dâs *tsi*-mêr *roy*-men?) (*At what time do we/I have to check out of the room?*)

Asking for your bill

When it comes to checking out of the hotel, the word commonly used is **abreisen** (âp-ray-zen) (*to leave,* literally, *to travel on*). When you want to leave, tell the receptionist

> **Ich reise ab./Wir reisen ab.** (iH *ray*-ze âp./veer *ray*-zen âp.) (*I'm leaving./ We're leaving.*)

The preceding phrase will probably be enough to get the receptionist busy preparing your bill. However, if you need to drive home the point that you'd like to have your bill, you can say

Kann ich bitte die Rechnung haben? (kân iH *bi*-te dee *rêH*-noong *hah*-ben?) (*Could I have the bill, please?*)

Chapter 14 tells you all about dealing with bills, paying with a credit card, and asking for a receipt.

Asking small favors

If you have to check out of the hotel before you're actually ready to continue on your trip, you may want to leave your luggage for a couple of hours (most hotels allow you to do this). Simply ask

Können wir unser/Kann ich mein Gepäck bis . . . Uhr hier lassen? (*kern*-en veer *oon*-zer/kân iH mayn ge-*pêk* bis . . . oohr heer *lâs*-en?) (*Could we leave our/Could I leave my luggage here until . . . o'clock?*)

When you return to pick up your luggage, you can say

Können wir/Kann ich bitte unser/mein Gepäck haben? (*kern*-en veer/ kân iH *bi*-te *oon*-zer/mayn ge-*pêk hah*-ben?) (*Could we/Could I get our/my luggage, please?*)

Ready to go to the airport or train station? If you want the receptionist to call you a cab, ask

Können Sie mir bitte ein Taxi bestellen? (*kern*-en zee meer *bi*-te ayn *tâx*-ee be-*shtêl*-en?) (*Could you call a cab for me?*)

The receptionist will need to know where you intend to go before calling for your taxi. The receptionist may ask you

Wo möchten Sie hin? (voh *merH*-ten zee hin?) (*Where would you like to go?*)

Make sure you know the name of the place you want to go to before you approach the receptionist.

Talkin' the Talk

Klaus and Ulrike Huber are ready to move on and explore other parts of the country. They go to the reception desk to check out.

Klaus: **Guten Morgen! Wir reisen heute ab. Kann ich bitte die Rechnung haben?**
gooh-ten *môr*-gen! veer *ray*-zen *hoy*-te âp. kân iH *bi*-te dee *rêH*-noong *hah*-ben?
Good morning! We're leaving today. May I have the bill, please?

Rezeption: **Sicher, einen Moment bitte. Haben Sie gestern abend noch etwas aus der Minibar genommen?**
ziH-er, ayn-en moh-mênt bi-te. hah-ben zee gês-tern ah-bent nôH êt-vâs ous dêr minibar gê-nôm-en?
Sure, one moment please. Did you take anything from the minibar last night?

Klaus: **Ja, zwei Bier.**
yah, tsvay beer.
Yes, two beers.

Rezeption: **Danke. Also, hier ist ihre Rechnung.**
dân-ke. al-zoh, heer ist eer-e rêH-noong.
Thank you. So, here is your bill.

Klaus: **Kann ich mit Kreditkarte bezahlen?**
kân iH mit krê-dit-kâr-te be-tsahl-en?
Can I pay with a credit card?

Rezeption: **Selbstverständlich. Unterschreiben Sie hier, bitte.**
zêlpst-fêr-shtênt-liH. oon-ter-shray-ben zee heer bi-te.
Of course. Please sign here.

Klaus: **Vielen Dank und auf Wiedersehen.**
fee-len dânk oont ouf vee-der-zey-en.
Thank you very much and good-bye.

Rezeption: **Gute Reise!**
gooh-te ray-ze!
Have a good trip!

Words to Know

abreisen	âp-ray-zen	to leave
das Gepäck	dâs ge-pêk	luggage
selbstverständlich	zêlpst-fêr-shtênt-liH	Of course
Gute Reise!	gooh-te ray-ze	Have a good trip!

Fun & Games

Use the correct words to complete the questions:

Wo   Was für   Wie   Wann   Was

1. kostet das Zimmer ? (How much is the room?)

2. lange bleiben Sie? (How long are you going to stay?)

3. wird das Frühstück serviert? (At what time is breakfast served?)

4. möchten Sie hin? (Where would you like to go?)

5. ein Zimmer möchten Sie? (What kind of room would you like?)

You're checking into the Hotel Schlumberger and you need to fill out the following registration form — Meldeschein (mêl-de-shayn). In the blanks provided, write the English equivalents for the requested information showin in German.

Meldeschein

Hotel Schlumberger   Kirchheimstraße 34   83224 Grassau

1) Tag der Ankunft

_____

2) Familienname   3) Vorname   4) Beruf

_____   _____   _____

5) Geburtsdatum   6) Geburtsort   7) Staatsangehörigkeit

_____   _____   _____

8) Straße, Nummer (Nr.)   9) PLZ   10) Wohnort

_____   _____   _____

11) Ort / Datum   12) Unterschrift

_____   _____

Chapter 17

Handling Emergencies

· ·

In This Chapter

▶ Asking for assistance

▶ Getting help for a medical problem

▶ Communicating with the police

· ·

Hopefully, you'll never need to use the vocabulary and information in this chapter, but you never know, so read on. Aside from dealing with accidents and talking to the police, you may need to handle other kinds of emergencies — what if you wake up in the morning with a bout of nausea and stomach cramps? This chapter assists you in dealing with various emergency situations, from seeking medical attention to reporting a theft.

Requesting Help

The hardest part of handling emergencies is keeping your cool so that you can communicate the situation clearly and calmly to someone, be it a police officer, emergency medical technician, or a doctor. So don't panic if you have to express these unpleasant facts in German. In case you really get tongue-tied, we tell you how to ask for someone who speaks English.

Shouting for help

The following expressions come in handy if you need to grab someone's attention to get help in an emergency situation:

Hilfe! (*hilf*-e!) (*Help!*)

Rufen Sie die Polizei! (*roohf*-en zee dee po-li-*tsay!*) (*Call the police!*)

Rufen Sie einen Krankenwagen! (*roohf*-en zee *ayn*-en *krânk*-en-vahg-en!) (*Call an ambulance!*)

Rufen Sie die Feuerwehr! (*roohf*-en zee dee *foy*-er-veyr!) (*Call the fire department!*)

Holen Sie einen Arzt! (*hohl*-en zee *ayn*-en ârtst!) (*Get a doctor!*)

Feuer! (*foy*-êr!) (*Fire!*)

Reporting a problem

If you need to report an accident or let people know that you or other people are hurt, this basic vocabulary can help:

Ich möchte einen Unfall melden. (iH *merH*-te *ayn*-en *oon*-fâl *mêl*-den.) (*I want to report an accident.*)

Ich möchte einen Autounfall melden. (iH *merH*-te *ayn*-en *ou*-toh-oon-fâl *mêl*-den.) (*I want to report a car accident.*)

Ich bin verletzt. (iH bin fêr-*lêtst*.) (*I am hurt.*)

Es gibt Verletzte. (ês gipt fêr-*lêts*-te.) (*There are injured people.*)

Accidents aside, there are other emergencies you should be prepared for, such as robbery or theft:

Ich möchte einen Diebstahl/Raubüberfall melden. (iH *merH*-te *ayn*-en *deep*-shtahl/*roup*-ue-ber-fâl *mêl*-den.) (*I want to report a theft/robbery.*)

Halten Sie den Dieb! (*hâl*-ten zee deyn deep!) (*Catch the thief!*)

Asking for English-speaking help

If you aren't able to get the help you need by speaking German, ask this question:

Spricht hier jemand Englisch? (shpriHt heer *yey*-mânt *êng*-lish?) (*Does anybody here speak English?*)

Words to Know

Hilfe!	hilf-e!	Help!
Rufen Sie die Polizei!	roohf-en zee dee po-li-tsay	Call the police!
Feuer!	foy-êr!	Fire!

Getting Medical Attention

Open your mouth. Say ahhhhhh. Good. Now breathe deeply. Relax. Breathe deeply again. Great! Now you, dear reader, should be relaxed enough to learn how to explain what ails you. Hopefully, you won't need to seek medical assistance, but if you do, this section is exactly what the doctor ordered.

What kind of medical professional do you need? Where do you want to go? Here are a few words you'll need in case you're feeling out of sorts and need medical attention:

- **die Apotheke** (dee ah-poh-*tey*-ke) (*pharmacy*)
- **der Arzt/die Ärztin** (dêr ârtst/dee *êrts*-tin) (*male/female medical doctor*)
- **die Arztpraxis/die Zahnarztpraxis** (dee *ârtst*-prâx-is/dee *tsahn*-ârtst-prax-is) (*doctor's office/dentist's office*)
- **der Doktor** (dêr *dok*-tohr) (*doctor* — profession and form of address)
- **das Krankenhaus** (dâs *krânk*-en-hous) (*hospital*)
- **die Notaufnahme** (dee *noht*-ouf-nah-me) (*emergency room*)
- **der Zahnarzt/die Zahnärztin** (dêr *tsahn*-ârtst/dee *tsahn*-êrts-tin) (*male/female dentist*)

If you need medical help, you can ask for a doctor or find out where the nearest doctor's office, hospital, or pharmacy is located by saying one of the following:

Ich brauche einen Arzt. (iH *brouH*-e *ayn*-en ârtst.) (*I need a doctor.*)

Wo ist die nächste Arztpraxis/das nächste Krankenhaus/die nächste Apotheke? (voh ist dee *naiH*-ste ârtst-prâx-is/dâs *naiH*-ste *krânk*-en-hous/dee *naiH*-ste ah-poh-*tey*-ke?) (*Where is the nearest doctor's office/the nearest hospital/the nearest pharmacy?*)

Describing what ails you

What's up? Got a fever? Shooting pains down your leg? Nausea or worse? Then you've come to the right place. If you want to express that you aren't feeling well and explain where it hurts, use the following sentences:

Ich fühle mich nicht wohl. (iH *fuel*-e miH niHt vohl.) (*I'm not feeling well.*)

Ich bin krank. (iH bin krânk.) (*I am sick.*)

Ich habe Fieber/Durchfall. (iH *hah*-be *feeb*-er/*doorH*-fâl.) (*I have a fever/ diarrhea.*)

Mir tut der Fuß/Bauch/Rücken weh. (meer tooht dêr foohs/bouH/ *ruek*-en vey.) (*My foot/stomach/back hurts.*)

Ich habe Schmerzen im Arm/Bauch. (iH *hah*-be *shmêrts*-en im ârm/ bouH.) (*I feel pain in my arm/stomach.*)

Ich habe (starke) Bauchschmerzen/Kopfschmerzen/Zahnschmerzen. (iH *hah*-be (*shtârk*-e) *bouH*-shmêrts-en/*kopf*-shmêrts-en/*tsahn*-shmêrts-en.) (*I have (a severe) stomachache/headache/toothache.*)

Ich habe Halsschmerzen/Rückenschmerzen. (iH *hah*-be *hâls*-shmêrts-en/ *ruek*-en-shmêrts-en.) (*I have a sore throat/back pain.*)

Telling about any special conditions

An important part of getting treatment is letting the doctor know whether you're allergic to something or have any other medical conditions. To do so, start out by saying

Ich bin . . . . (ih bin . . . .) (*I am . . . .*)

Then finish the sentence with any of the following:

allergisch gegen . . . (â-*lêr*-gish *gey*-gen . . .) (*allergic to . . .*)

behindert (bê-*hin*-dêrt) (*handicapped*)

schwanger (*shvâng*-er) (*pregnant*)

Diabetiker (dee-ah-*bey*-ti-ker) (*a diabetic*)

Epileptiker (ey-pi-*lêp*-ti-ker) (*an epileptic*)

A few specific conditions may require that you begin with the following:

Ich habe . . . . (iH *hah*-be . . . .) (*I have . . . .*)

Then state the condition. Here are some examples:

eine Intoleranz gegen (Penizillin) (*ayn*-e *in*-tol-er-ants *gey*-gen [pê-ni-tsi-*leen*]) (*an intolerance to [penicillin]*)

ein Herzleiden (ayn *hêrts*-layd-en*)* (*a heart condition*)

zu hohen/niedrigen Blutdruck (tsooh *hoh*-en/*need*-reeg-gen *blooht*- drook) (*high/low blood pressure*)

CULTURAL WISDOM

Emergency calls

In case of an emergency, it's always good to have the right phone numbers handy. If you find yourself in an emergency situation while you're in European Union countries, including Germany and Austria, the crucial number you may want to memorize or keep in your wallet is 112. Switzerland and most other non-EU countries in western Europe have also adopted the 112 number for emergencies. When you dial 112, which should work even from a cellphone, your call is routed to the nearest emergency call center. The center is prepared to dispatch the **Polizei** (po-li-*tsay*) (*police*), call the **Feuerwehr** (foy-êr-veyr) (*fire department*),

or contact a **Rettungsdienst** (*rêt*-oongs-deenst) (*emergency service*)

If you're driving on the **Autobahn** and you have to report an accident, the highway systems in Germany, Austria, Switzerland, and many other western European countries have motorist aid call boxes at regular intervals. On the Autobahn in German-speaking countries, such call boxes are labeled **Notruf** or **S.O.S.** (*noht*-roohf or s.o.s. [as in English]) (*emergency call* or *S.O.S.*) You'll also see arrows on guard rails or posts that point in the direction of the nearest emergency phone.

Getting an examination

After you get into the examination room, you want to make sure you understand the doctor's questions and the instructions you need to follow to get the proper diagnosis. The doctor may ask you questions like

> **Was haben Sie für Beschwerden?** (vâs *hah*-ben zee fuer be-*shveyr*-den?) (*What symptoms do you have?*)

> **Haben Sie Schmerzen?** (*hah*-ben zee *shmêrts*-en?) (*Are you in pain?*)

> **Wo tut es weh?** (voh tooht ês vey?) (*Where does it hurt?*)

> **Tut es hier weh?** (tooht ês heer vey?) (*Does it hurt here?*)

> **Wie lange fühlen Sie sich schon so?** (vee *lâng*-e *fuel*-en zee ziH shon zoh?) (*How long have you been feeling this way?*)

> **Sind Sie gegen irgendetwas allergisch?** (zint zee *gey*-gen *ir*-gênt-êt-vâs â-*lêr*-gish?) (*Are you allergic to anything?*)

Here are some (not-so-fun) instructions you may hear from the doctor:

> **Bitte streifen Sie den Ärmel hoch.** (*bi*-te *shtrayf*-en zee deyn *êr*-mel hoH.) (*Please pull up your sleeve.*)

Bitte machen Sie den Oberkörper frei. (*bi*-te *mâH*-en zee deyn *oh*-bêr-kerr-per fray.) (*Please take off your shirt.*)

Bitte legen Sie sich hin. (*bi*-te *ley*-gen zee ziH hin.) (*Please lie down.*)

Machen Sie bitte den Mund auf. (*mâH*-en zee *bi*-te deyn moont ouf.) (*Please open your mouth.*)

Atmen Sie bitte tief durch. (*aht*-men zee *bi*-te teef doorH.) (*Please take a deep breath.*)

Husten Sie bitte. (*hoohs*-ten zee *bi*-te.) (*Please cough.*)

Wir müssen eine Röntgenaufnahme machen. (veer *mues*-en *ayn*-e *rernt*-gên-ouf-nah-me *mâH*-en.) (*We have to take an X-ray.*)

Sie müssen geröntgt werden. (zee *mues*-en ge-*rerngt* *vêr*-den.) (*You have to get an X-ray.*)

Specifying parts of the body

To the question **Wo tut es weh?** (voh tooht ês vey?) (*Where does it hurt?*), you can answer any of the following:

- **der Arm** (dêr ârm) (*arm*)
- **das Auge** (dâs *oug*-e) (*eye*)
- **der Bauch** (dêr bouH) (*stomach*)
- **das Bein** (dâs bayn) (*leg*)
- **die Brust** (dee broost) (*chest*)
- **der Daumen** (dêr *doum*-en) (*thumb*)
- **der Finger** (dêr *fing*-er) (*finger*)
- **der Fuß** (dêr foohs) (*foot*)
- **der Fußknöchel** (dêr *foohs*-knerH-el) (*ankle*)
- **der Hals** (dêr hâls) (*neck*)
- **die Hand** (dee hânt) (*hand*)
- **das Herz** (dâs hêrts) (*heart*)
- **der Kiefer** (dêr *keef*-er) (*jaw*)
- **das Knie** (dâs knee) (*knee*)
- **der Magen** (dêr *mah*-gen) (*stomach*)

✔ **der Mund** (dêr moont) (*mouth*)

✔ **der Muskel** (dêr *moos*-kel) (*muscle*)

✔ **die Nase** (dee *nah*-ze) (*nose*)

✔ **das Ohr** (dâs ohr) (*ear*)

✔ **der Rücken** (dêr *ruek*-en) (*back*)

✔ **die Schulter** (dee *shool*-ter) (*shoulder*)

✔ **der Zahn** (dêr tsahn) (*tooth*)

✔ **der Zeh** (dêr tsey) (*toe*)

✔ **die Zunge** (dee *tsoong*-e) (*tongue*)

You may also need to identify the following parts of the body:

✔ **das Gesicht** (dâs ge-*ziHt*) (*face*)

✔ **das Haar** (dâs hahr) (*hair*)

✔ **der Kopf** (dêr kopf) (*head*)

✔ **die Lippe** (dee *lip*-e) (*lip*)

Getting the diagnosis

After the doctor has gathered the information she needs, she'll tell you what she thinks is wrong. Here are some very useful phrases that keep you from being left in the dark:

die Diagnose (dee dee-âg-*noh*-ze) (*diagnosis*)

Sie haben . . . . (zee *hah*-ben . . . .) (*You have . . . .*)

eine Erkältung (*ayn*-e êr-*kêlt*-oong) (*a cold*)

eine Grippe (*ayn*-e *grip*-e) (*the flu*)

eine Entzündung (*ayn*-e ênt-*tsuend*-oong) (*an inflammation*)

Blinddarmentzündung (*blint*-dârm-ênt-tsuend-oong) (*appendicitis*)

Lungenentzündung (*lung*-en-ênt-tsuend-oong) (*pneumonia*)

Mandelentzündung (*mân*-del-ênt-tsuend-oong) (*tonsillitis*)

Ihr Fußknöchel ist gebrochen/verstaucht/verrenkt. (eer *foohs*-knerH-êl ist ge-*broH*-en/fêr-*shtouHt*/fêr-*rênkt*.) (*Your ankle is broken/sprained/dislocated.*)

Talkin' the Talk

 Ulrich Lempert hasn't been feeling well for a couple days and has made an appointment with his doctor, Dr. Grawen. (Track 33)

Dr. Grawen: **Guten Morgen, Herr Lempert. Was haben Sie für Beschwerden?**
gooht-en *mor*-gen, hêr *lêm*-pêrt. vâs *hah*-ben zee fuer be-*shveyr*-den?
Good morning, Mr. Lempert. What symptoms do you have?

Ulrich: **Ich fühle mich seit ein paar Tagen nicht wohl.**
iH *fuel*-e miH zayt ayn pahr *tah*-gen niHt vohl.
I haven't been feeling well for a couple of days.

Dr. Grawen: **Haben Sie Schmerzen?**
hah-ben zee *shmêrts*-en?
Are you in pain?

Ulrich: **Ja, ich habe starke Kopf- und Magenschmerzen.**
yah, iH *hah*-be *stâr*-ke kopf- oont *mah*-gen-*shmêrts*-en.
Yes, I have a severe headache and stomachache.

Dr. Grawen: **Bitte setzen Sie sich hier hin und machen Sie den Oberkörper frei.**
bi-te *zêts*-en zee ziH heer hin oont *mâH*-en zee deyn *oh*-bêr-kerr-pêr fray.
Please sit down here and take off your shirt.

Dr. Grawen starts examining Ulrich.

Dr. Grawen: **Machen Sie bitte den Mund auf — danke. Atmen Sie bitte tief durch. Husten Sie bitte.**
mâH-en zee *bi*-te deyn moont ouf — *dân*-ke. *aht*-mên zee *bi*-te teef doorH. *hoohs*-ten zee *bi*-te.
Please open your mouth — thank you. Take a deep breath, please. Please cough.

Ulrich: **Und, was stimmt nicht mit mir?**
oont, vâs shtimt niHt mit meer?
And what's wrong with me?

Dr. Grawen: **Sie haben eine Grippe. Ich gebe Ihnen ein Rezept.**
Und bleiben Sie die nächsten Tage im Bett.
zee *hah*-ben *ayn*-e *grip*-e. iH *gey*-be *een*-en ayn rê-
tsêpt. oont *blay*-ben zee dee *naiH*-sten *tah*-ge im bêt.
*You have the flu. I'm giving you a prescription. And
stay in bed for the next few days.*

Words to Know

Ich brauche einen Arzt.	iH <u>brouH</u>-e <u>ayn</u>-en ârtst.	I need a doctor.
Ich bin krank.	iH bin krânk.	I am sick.
Wo tut es weh?	voh tooht ês vey?	Where does it hurt?
Haben Sie Schmerzen?	<u>hah</u>-ben zee <u>shmêrts</u>-en?	Are you in pain?

CULTURAL WISDOM

Getting your medicine

You may be used to getting your prescription medicine at a drugstore. In Germany, however, filling a prescription works a little differently. The German equivalent of the *drugstore* is the **Drogerie** (droh-ge-*ree*), where you get everything from toothpaste to sunblock, as well as non-prescription drugs, such as aspirin and cough syrup. For prescription drugs, however, you have to go to the **Apotheke** (âpoh-*tey*-ke) (*pharmacy*). You'll find that the people working there are very helpful and often as knowledgeable as a doctor. When it comes to prescriptions, the German laws are very strict, which means that a lot of the medicine (such as allergy medication) you can buy over the counter in the United States requires a prescription in Germany (and thus, a trip to the doctor).

Getting treatment

After the doctor tells you what the problem is, he or she will tell you what to do about it. The doctor may ask you one final question before deciding what treatment would be best for you:

Nehmen Sie noch andere Medikamente? (*ney*-men zee noH *ân*-de-re mey-dee-kâ-*mên*-te?) (*Are you taking any other medicine?*)

The doctor may then begin with

Ich gebe Ihnen . . . . /Ich verschreibe Ihnen . . . (iH *gey*-be *een*-en . . ./iH fêr-*shray*-be *een*-en . . . .) (*I'll give you . . . ./I'll prescribe for you . . . .*)

The sentence may be finished with any of the following:

- ✔ **Antibiotika** (ân-tee-bee-*oh*-ti-kâ) (*antibiotics*)
- ✔ **das Medikament/die Medikamente** (pl) (dâs mey-dee-kâ-*mênt*/dee mey-dee-kâ-*mên*-te) (*medicine*)
- ✔ **ein Schmerzmittel** (ayn *shmêrts*-mit-el) (*a painkiller*)
- ✔ **Tabletten** (tâ-*blêt*-en) (*pills*)

Finally, the doctor may indicate that he wants to see you again by saying

Kommen Sie in . . . Tagen/einer Woche wieder. (*kom*-en zee in . . . *tah*-gen/*ayn*-er *voH*-e *vee*-der.) (*Come back in . . . days/one week.*)

The doctor will give you a prescription, **das Rezept** (dâs rê-*tsêpt*), that you take to a pharmacy, called **die Apotheke** (dee âpo-*tey*-ke), to be filled.

The following phrases can help you to understand the instructions for taking your medicine:

Bitte, nehmen Sie . . . Tabletten/Teelöffel . . . (*bi*-te *ney*-men zee . . . tah-*blêt*-en/*tey*-lerf-el . . .) (*Please take . . . pills/teaspoons. . . .*)

dreimal am Tag/täglich (*dray*-mahl âm tahk/*taig*-liH) (*three times a day/daily*)

alle . . . Stunden (*âl*-e . . . *shtoon*-den) (*every . . . hours*)

vor/nach dem Essen (fohr/naH deym *ês*-en) (*before/after meals*)

Talkin' the Talk

After Ulrich gets his diagnosis, he takes the prescription to his neighborhood pharmacy and talks to the pharmacist.

Ulrich: **Guten Morgen. Mein Ärzt hat mir dieses Rezept gegeben.**
gooht-en *mor*-gen. Mayn ârtst hât meer *deez*-es rê-tsêpt ge-*gey*-ben.
Good morning. My doctor has given me this prescription.

Apothekerin: **Einen Moment.**
ayn-en moh-*ment.*
Just a moment.

The pharmacist fills Ulrich's prescription and returns.

So, Herr Lempert. Bitte nehmen Sie dreimal am Tag zwei von diesen Tabletten.
zoh, hêr *lêm*-pêrt. *bi*-te *ney*-men zee *dray*-mahl âm tahk tsavy fon *deez*-en tâ-*blêt*-en.
Okay, Mr. Lempert. Please take two of these pills three times a day.

Ulrich: **Vor oder nach dem Essen?**
fohr *oh*-der nahH deym *ês*-en?
Before or after meals?

Apothekerin: **Nach dem Essen.**
nahH deym *ês*-en.
After meals.

Ulrich: **Wird gemacht.**
virt ge-*mâHt.*
I'll do that.

Apothekerin: **Gute Besserung, Herr Lempert!**
gooh-te *bês*-er-oong, hêr *lêm*-pêrt!
Hope you feel better, Mr. Lempert!

Talking to the Police

You've just discovered that your hotel room has been robbed. The thieves made off with a lot, but fortunately, they left *German For Dummies* behind. Their loss, your gain!

Here are some helpful expressions for handling the situation:

> **Wo ist das nächste Polizeirevier?** (voh ist dâs *naiH*-ste po-li-*tsay*-re-veer?) (*Where is the closest police station?*)

> **Ich möchte einen Diebstahl melden.** (iH *merH*-te *ayn*-en *deep*-shtahl *mêl*-den.) (*I would like to report a theft.*)

Describing what was stolen

To describe a theft, you start out by saying

> **Man hat mir . . . gestohlen.** (mân hât meer . . . ge-*shtohl*-en.) (*Someone has stolen. . . .*)

You can then finish the sentence by inserting any of the following:

- ✔ **mein Auto** (mayn *ou*-toh) (*my car*)
- ✔ **meine Brieftasche/mein Portemonnaie** (*mayn*-e *breef*-tâsh-e/mayn port- mon-*ey*) (*my wallet*)
- ✔ **mein Geld** (mayn gêlt) (*my money*)
- ✔ **meinen Pass** (*mayn*-en pâs) (*my passport*)
- ✔ **meine Tasche** (*mayn*-e *tâsh*-e*) (*my bag*)

If you want to express that someone has broken into your room or office, you use the verb **einbrechen** (*ayn*-brêH-en) (*break into*):

> **Man hat bei mir eingebrochen.** (mân hât bay meer *ayn*-ge-broH-en.) (*Someone has broken into [my room.]*)

If you're talking about your car, however, you use a similar but slightly different verb, **aufbrechen** (*ouf*-brêH-en), which literally means *to break open*:

> **Man hat mein Auto aufgebrochen.** (mân hât mayn *ou*-toh *ouf*-ge-broH-en.) (*Someone has broken into my car.*)

The indefinite pronoun **man** (mân), which means *one, someone,* or *you* (in the sense of people in general), comes in handy. Better yet, it's easy to use because it always has the same form and spelling — **man**. Consider these examples:

> **Man hat seine Tasche gestohlen.** (mân hât *zayn*-e *tâsh*-e ge-*shtohl*-en.) (*Someone has stolen his bag.*)

> **Was macht man jetzt?** (vâs mâHt mân yêtst?) (*What does one do now?*)

Answering questions from the police

So you got a good look at the thug. Was he or she tall or short, thin or fat, hairy or bald? The police will want to know everything. And after you discover how to describe people, you'll also be ready to peruse personal ads.

The police will ask

> **Können Sie die Person beschreiben?** (*kern*-en zee dee pêr-*zohn* be-*shrayb*-en?) (*Can you describe that person?*)

Your answer to this question can begin

> **Die Person/Er/Sie hatte . . .** (dee per-*zohn*/êr/zee hât-e . . .) (*The person/ he/she had . . .*)

Then finish the sentence with any of the following. You can combine traits by saying **und** between any of the following terms:

- ✔ **blonde/schwarze/rote/graue/lange/kurze Haare** (*blon*-de/*shvârts*-e/ *roh*-te/*grou*-e/*lâng*-e/*koorts*-e *hahr*-e) (*blond/black/red/gray/long/short hair*)

- ✔ **einen Bart/einen Schnurrbart/keinen Bart** (*ayn*-en bahrt/*ayn*-en *shnoohr*-bahrt/*kayn*-en bahrt) (*a beard/a mustache/no beard*)

- ✔ **eine Glatze** (*ayn*-e *glâts*-e) (*a bald head*)

- ✔ **eine Brille** (*ayn*-e *bril*-e) (*glasses*)

Alternatively, your answer may begin

> **Die Person/ Er/Sie war . . . .** (dee pêr-*zohn*/êr/zee vahr . . . .) (*The person/ he/she was . . . .*)

You can then end with any of the following:

- **groß/klein** (grohs/klayn) (*tall/short*)
- **schlank/dick** (shlânk/dik) (*thin/fat*)
- **ungefähr . . . Meter . . . groß** (*oon*-ge-fair . . . *mey*-ter . . . grohs) (*approximately . . . meters tall*)
- **ungefähr . . . Jahre alt** (*oon*-ge-fair . . . *yahr*-e âlt) (*approximately . . . years old*)

The police may also ask you the following questions:

Wann ist das passiert? (vân ist dâs pâs-*eert?*) (*When did it happen?*)

Wo waren Sie in dem Moment? (voh *vahr*-en zee in deym moh-*mênt?*) (*Where were you at that moment?*)

Getting legal help

Had enough for the day? If you're really not up to conversing with the law on your own, here are two very important phrases that you should know:

Ich brauche einen Anwalt. (iH *brouH*-e *ayn*-en *ân*-vâlt.) (*I need a lawyer.*)

Ich möchte das Konsulat anrufen. (iH *merH*-te dâs kon-zoo-*laht ân*-roohf-en) (*I would like to call the consulate.*)

Talkin' the Talk

Erika Berger has to drop off some documents at one of her client's offices. When she returns to her car half an hour later, she sees that somebody has broken into it and stolen her bag. Luckily, the nearest police station is right around the corner.

Erika: **Guten Tag. Ich möchte einen Diebstahl melden. Man hat mein Auto aufgebrochen und meine Tasche gestohlen.**
gooht-en tahk. iH *merH*-te *ayn*-en *deep*-shtahl *mêl*-den. mân hât mayn *ou*-toh *ouf*-ge-broH-en oont *mayn*-e *tâsh*-e ge-*shtohl*-en.
Hello. I would like to report a theft. Someone has broken into my car and stolen my bag.

Polizist:	**Moment mal. Wie ist ihr Name?** moh-*mênt* mâl. vee ist eer *nah*-me? *One moment. What is your name?*
Erika:	**Erika Berger.** *êr*-i-kâ *bêr*-ger. *Erika Berger.*
Polizist:	**Wann ist das passiert?** vân ist dâs pâs-*eert?* *When did it happen?*
Erika:	**Zwischen elf und halb zwölf.** *tsvish*-en êlf oont hâlp tsverlf. *Between 11:00 and 11:30.*
Polizist:	**Und wo?** oont voh? *And where?*
Erika:	**Gleich um die Ecke, in der Rothmundstraße.** glayH um dee *êk*-e, în dêr *roht*-moont *shtrah*-se. *Right around the corner, on Rothmundstraße.*
Polizist:	**Was war in Ihrer Tasche?** vâs vahr in *eer*-er *tâsh*-e? *What was in your bag?*
Erika:	**Meine Brieftasche mit ungefähr fünfzig Euro, meine Kreditkarten und mein Führerschein!** *mayn*-e *breef*-tâsh-e mit *oon*-ge-fair *fuenf*-tsiH *oy*-roh, *mayn*-e krê-*deet*-kârt-en oont mayn *fuer*-er-shayn! *My wallet with approximately 50 euros in it, my credit cards, and my driver's license!*
Polizist:	**Nun, ich habe noch einige Fragen. Wir erstatten dann Anzeige.** noon, iH *hah*-be noH *ayn*-ee-ge *frah*-gen. veer êr-*shtât*-en dân *ân*-tsayg-e. *Now I have some more questions. Then we'll file a report.*

FUN & GAMES

Your friend Markus is a daredevil snowboarder, and as fate would have it, you're the first person to find him after he has crashed into a tree. He seems okay, but just to make sure, you ask him about each body part. To make sure you know the German words for the body parts, write them on the corresponding lines.

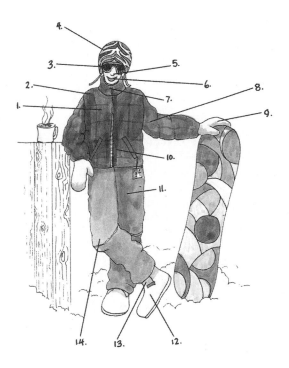

1. chest_____

2. shoulder_____

3. eye_____

4. head_____

5. nose_____

6. mouth_____

7. neck_____

8. arm_____

9. hand_____

10. stomach_____

11. leg_____

12. foot_____

13. ankle_____

14. knee_____

Part IV
The Part of Tens

The 5th Wave   By Rich Tennant

"I'd ask for directions in German, but I don't know how to form a question into the shape of an apology."

In this part . . .

Every *For Dummies* book ends with top-ten lists of handy information, and this book has some very useful ones. In addition to offering tips on how to learn German more effectively, we provide you with German phrases you should avoid, German expressions that make you sound (even more) German, and more. **Viel Spaß!** (feel shpâs!) (*Have fun!*)

Chapter 18

Ten Ways to Pick Up German Quickly

● ●

Getting comfortable with speaking and understanding a new language and its culture can be a really fun and rewarding experience. So what if you find yourself getting bogged down with grammar explanations? Where do you turn if you're feeling overwhelmed by the sheer detail involved in putting the right word in the right place in a sentence? Above all, don't beat yourself up. Instead, be patient with yourself. Take baby steps; after all, that's how you learned to walk, right? Try out some or all these tips for expanding your German. See which ideas work best for you. Whatever you do, we hope you enjoy experimenting with German.

Labeling the World Around You

Get going on some vocabulary around your home, your car, or even your office by labeling the objects around you. This strategy is fun and simple. Use a German/English dictionary (or the dictionary at the back of this book) to find out the German equivalent of words such as *the window* (**das Fenster**) (dâs *fêns*-ter), *the door* (**die Tür**) (dee tuer), *the fridge* (**der Kühlschrank**) (dêr *kuel*-shrânk), or *a cup* (**eine Tasse**) (*ayn*-e *tâs*-e). Write each word on a sticky note and attach it to the thing it describes. When you come across the object, touch it and pronounce the word to yourself. Who knows, maybe your friends and family will join in!

Organizing Useful Expressions

If you want to memorize words within a certain context, compile lists of expressions or entire sentences that have to do with the topic you're interested in. As you go through a chapter in this book, write down no more than ten or so phrases you'd like to pick up quickly. For example, write down the phrases you find most important for asking directions (*How do I get to. . . ? How far is it?*) or dining at a German restaurant (*I'd like the. . . . Could I have the check, please?*).

Then look for one or more convenient spots around the house to post your list; next to the mirror in the bathroom works well, for example. Then every time you preen yourself, practice saying the expressions in a logical sequence. Before long, you'll know all those handy expressions. When you do, it's time to put up a new list.

Writing Shopping Lists

Another way to retain more vocabulary is to make out your shopping lists in German. Write the English equivalents after the German, though, just so you won't get annoyed in the store when you can't remember what you meant. For example, write **Birnen** (*birn*-en) (*pears*), **Karotten** (kâr-*rot*-en) (carrots), or **Zwiebeln** (*tsvee*-beln) (*onions*) on your list. Take this activity one step further by pronouncing the German word to yourself as you pick up each item. You may find yourself making simple sentences as you're shopping, such as the following:

> **Der Käse is sehr teuer.** (dêr *kai*-ze ist zeyr *toy*-er.) (*The cheese is very expensive.*)

> **Wo sind die Kartoffen?** (voh vint dee Kâr-*tof*-en?) (*Where are the potatoes?*)

> **Der Fisch ist sehr frisch.** (dêr fish ist zeyr frish.) (*The fish is very fresh.*)

Thinking in German

Activate your German by formulating your daily routine into phrases as you go through some simple steps. For example, you might say

> **Ich gehe in die Küche.** (iH *gey*-e in dee *kueH*-e.) (I'm going to the kitchen.)

> **Ich mache Kaffee.** (iH *mâH*-e *kâf*-ey.) (*I'm making coffee.*)

> **Das Wetter ist sehr schön.** (das *wêt*-er is zeyr shern.) (*The weather's really beautiful.*)

> **Wie viel Uhr is es? Es ist 20.30.** (vee feel oohr is ês? Es ist *tsvân*-tsiH oohr *drays*-iH.) (*What time is it? It's 8:30 p.m.*)

Using Language CDs and Downloads

On your way to and from work, try listening to language-learning CDs or download German language broadcasts. Just listening to German voices over and over can do wonders to help you retain words and phrases. Get some German music and listen to it when you're in the mood.

Watching German TV and Listening to German Radio Online

The government-funded German television stations **ARD** and **ZDF** are terrific ways to get excellent quality news in German. Simply go to their Web sites — www.ard.de and www.zdf.de — and choose the type of information you're interested in: politics, culture, sports, or, of course, **Nachrichten** (*nâH*-reeH-ten) (*news*). At ARD, you can watch a classic weekly TV series, **Tatort** (*taht*-ort) (*Crime Scene*), a murder mystery/thriller. You may want to try more: **Deutsche Welle** (*doy*-che *vêl*-e) (*German radio*) (www.dw-world.de) broadcasts both radio and TV programs in many languages, including German and English, and quality radio broadcasts are at radioWissen (*rah*-dee-oh *vis*-en) (*radio knowledge*) (www.br-online.de/bayern2/radiowissen). Looking for something else in German? Punch in a major search engine's name, plus the international code: .de for Germany, .at for Austria, and .ch for Switzerland.

Trying an Interactive German Program

To delve deeper into the intricacies of the German language, check out the selection of interactive German courses on the market. Price may be a factor in your budget, but the best ones offer quality visuals, logical language progression, and excellent speech recognition programs.

Watching German Movies

Another fun way to pick up expressions, the accent, cultural habits, and the like is by getting German movies online and watching them several times. Try selecting a movie by genre, director, or actors you're interested in. You may be surprised at how much you can understand. As you watch, enjoy some German **Bier** (beer) (*beer*) or **Wein** (vayn) (*wine*).

Reading German Publications

Buy German magazines, especially those with visuals, or have someone bring you back a few from a trip to a German-speaking country. Start by looking at the captions under the pictures and see whether you can figure out what the picture and its accompanying text are all about. Reading ads is another fun way to discover words. On international flights, you can grab a bilingual in-flight magazine with German on one side and English on the other. German comics for kids are also fun for adults, for example, **Asterix** and **Tim und Struppi**.

Eating German Cuisine

Treat your taste buds to some authentic German food. You may find a German restaurant nearby, but there are plenty of other opportunities to sample German cuisine. Splurge on some imported cheese from Germany or Switzerland. Think humble: The nearby health food store may have out-of-this-world fresh sauerkraut. Go all out and try some German recipes. You'll be delighted to discover that not all German cuisine is your basic meat-and-potatoes fare. Oh, and **Guten Appetit!** (*gooh*-ten â-pê-*teet*) (*Enjoy!*)

Chapter 19

Ten Things Never to Say in German

This chapter's aim is to save you from turning crimson, and we're not talking about a sunburn. You've probably heard non-native English speakers say things that made you want to either crack up or, even worse, hold your breath. Well, making a terrible blunder can happen just when you least expect it, so this chapter offers some pointers to help you avoid the very worst pitfalls!

Using the Right Form of Address

If you've read Chapter 3, you already know that you have to be careful about using the familiar form of address, **du** (dooh) (*you*). If you don't want to be insulting or sound uneducated, never use **du** when speaking to anyone you don't know well who is older than 16. Instead, use the formal **Sie** (zee) (*you*) and say, for example, **Möchten Sie ins Kino gehen?** (*merH*-tên zee ins *kee*-noh *gey*-en?) (*Do you want to go to the movies?*), not **Möchtest du ins Kino gehen?**

In most situations, the correct form to use is probably obvious. If you arrive at a party and everybody addresses you with the familiar form **du**, just go with the flow. And of course, you may be offered the opportunity to use **du**:

> **Wir können uns duzen.** (veer *kern*-en oons *doohts*-en.) (*We can use the familiar form of you.*)

Turning such an offer down would be equally impolite.

Addressing Service People Correctly

When you want to address a waitress or female salesperson, don't call her **Fräulein** (*froy*-layn), which used to be the German version of *Miss*. **Fräulein** literally means *little woman* (the syllable **lein** is a diminutive form). Most women find this form of address offensive. At the very least, they'll suspect that you aren't familiar enough with the German language to know about the word's connotations. No real substitute for it exists, so you have to rely on **Entschuldigen Sie bitte** (ênt-*shool*-di-gen zee *bi*-te) (*Excuse me, please*) or eye contact to get attention.

The same goes for addressing a waiter in a restaurant: Don't call him **Kellner** (*kêl*-ner) (*waiter*). Waiters don't like it, and it's considered patronizing and condescending. Again, eye contact and gestures or a simple **Entschuldigen Sie bitte** are the best way to get attention.

Hot or Cold?

If you'd like to express that you're hot or cold, be sure *not* to say **Ich bin heiß** (iH bin hays) (*I am hot*) or **Ich bin kalt** (iH bin kâlt) (*I am cold*). These expressions mean that you're in heat or have a cold personality! Unless you really want people to think such things about you, remember to use one of the following expressions, both of which use the personal pronoun **mir** (meer) (*me*):

> **Mir ist heiß.** (meer ist hays.) (*I feel hot/I'm hot.*)
>
> **Mir ist kalt.** (meer ist kâlt.) (*I feel cold/I'm cold.*)

I'm Not Loaded

If someone asks you at dinner or lunch whether you want another helping and you're really full, you certainly don't want to translate the word "full" into German. Saying **Ich bin voll** (iH bin fol) (*I am full*) means that you are completely drunk — it's actually the colloquial expression for *I'm loaded.* Unless you want to let the person who's asking know that you've had too many drinks, you should say **Ich bin satt** (iH bin zât) (*I am full*) in an informal situation. Otherwise, a simple **Nein, danke** (nayn *dân*-ke) (*No, thank you*) is appropriate.

Speaking of the Law with Respect

Don't call a police officer **Bulle** (*bool*-e). Although you may hear a lot of people using this word, it's a slang expression that means *bull.* The German words for *policeman* and *policewoman* are **der Polizist** (dêr po-li-*tsist*) and **die Polizistin** (dee po-li-*tsis*-tin), respectively.

Using "Gymnasium" Correctly

If you're trying to tell a German person that you're going to the gym by saying **Ich gehe zum Gymnasium** (iH *gey*-e tsoom germ-*nahz*-ee-oom), you will cause some serious confusion because a **Gymnasium** is not a place to work out; it's a high school. The previous sentence actually says *I'm going to the high school.* Three types of secondary schools exist in Germany, and the **Gymnasium** is the highest level. The German word you want to use for *gym* is **Fitnesscenter** (fitness center [as in English]).

Knowing the Appropriate Form of "Know"

In English, you can use the versatile verb *to know* to express that you know a person, a locality, a fact, and the answer to a question. The German verb you use to express familiarity with people and places is **kennen** (*kên*-en) (*to know/to be acquainted with*); for example, you say

Ich kenne ihn/sie/sie. (iH *kên*-e een/zee/zee.) (*I know him/her/them.*)

When it comes to knowledge of facts, you have to use the verb **wissen** (*vis*-en) (*to know*), which is usually used with a subordinate clause. So, in German you say for example

Ich weiss nicht, wie viel Uhr es ist. (iH vays niHt, vee feel oohr ês ist.) (*I don't know what time it is.*)

A shorter way to say the same thing is

Ich weiss es nicht. (iH vays ês niHt.) (*I don't know [the answer].*)

Going to the Right Closet

Don't mistake the German word **Klosett** (kloh-*zêt*) (*toilet*) for the English *closet.* If you want to find out where the closet is, don't ask **Wo ist das Klosett?** (voh ist dâs kloh-*zêt*?) (*Where is the toilet?*), because people will give you a confused look and then direct you to the bathroom. **Klosett** is the antiquated term for *toilet,* and the right word for *closet* is **der Einbauschrank** (dêr *ayn*-bou-shrânk). If you're at someone's home and you're on informal **du** (dooh) (*you*) terms, the colloquial way to ask where the bathroom is located is

Wo ist das Klo? (voh ist dâs kloh?) (*Where's the bathroom?*)

Otherwise, stick to something like this:

> **Darf ich Ihre Toilette benutzen?** (dârf iH *eer*-e toy-*lêt*-e bê-*noots*-en?)
> (*May I use your bathroom?*)

Using Bekommen Properly

You may conclude that the German verb **bekommen** (be-*kom*-en) corresponds to the English *to become* — a mistake commonly made by English speakers learning the German language and vice versa. Don't try to tell someone that your brother's going to be/become a doctor by saying **Mein Bruder bekommt einen Arzt** (mayn *brooh*-der bê-*komt* ayn-en ârtst). What you're expressing here is *My brother's getting a doctor,* meaning he's getting or receiving a doctor, for example, as a birthday present. The German word for *to become* is **werden** (*veyr*-den), so you have to say

> **Er wird Arzt.** (êr virt ârtst.) (*He's going to be/become a doctor.*)

German speakers use the verb **bekommen** in the sense of *get* to say, for example, *get lots of visitors,* like this:

> **Sie bekommen viel Besuch.** (zee be-*kom*-en feel be-zoohH.) (*They get lots of visitors.*)

When you want to order a glass of white wine, you can say

> **Ich bekomme ein Glas Weisswein, bitte.** (iH be-*kom*-e ayn glâs *vays*-vayn, *bi*-te.) (*I'd like a glass of white wine, please.*)

Using the Right Eating Verb

In Germany, you may hear someone say **Kühe fressen Gras** (*kue*-he *frês*-en grahs) (*Cows eat grass*). But don't conclude that **fressen** (*frês*-en) just means *to eat* and then say something such as **Ich fresse gern Pommes frites** (ih *frês*-e gêrn pom frit.) (*I like to eat French fries*). The German listener may think that you revel in stuffing your face with a super-sized order of fries. The verb **fressen** is reserved for animals. If you're referring to human beings, use **essen** (*ês*-en) (*to eat*): **Ich esse gern Pommes frites** (iH *ês*-e gêrn pom frit). In connection with human beings, **fressen** is used only in a derogatory sense.

Chapter 20

Ten Favorite German Expressions

. . . .

After you get tuned into German a little, you may start noticing that native German speakers use certain expressions frequently, as though they're putting salt and pepper on their thoughts. Indeed, you can think of such words as the flavoring that makes the language more natural, alive, and interesting. Try out the following expressions yourself to give your German a bit of sparkle.

Alles klar!

The literal translation of **Alles klar!** (*âl*-es klahr!) is *everything clear,* but in English you'd actually say *Got it!* You can use this expression to indicate that you understand when somebody explains something to you or to signal your agreement when someone has gone over the details of a plan.

Wirklich

Use the expression **Wirklich** (*virk*-liH) when you want to say *really* to emphasize an adjective, such as "*really* interesting." You can also use the word just the way you say *Really?* or *Really!* in English.

Kein Problem

The literal translation of **Kein Problem** (kayn proh-*bleym*) is *no problem.* Use it to let somebody know that you'll take care of something. You can also agree to a change in plans with this phrase.

Vielleicht

Vielleicht (fee-*layHt*) is the equivalent of *maybe* or *perhaps,* and you can use it, for example, as a short answer to someone's question. Alternatively, this expression comes in handy at the beginning of a sentence when you want to say that something may or may not happen. In the latter case, you say **Vielleicht nicht** (fee-*layHt* niHt) (*maybe not*).

Doch

This simple word has lots of uses. It doesn't have any exact English equivalents, but you use it to express your attitude about a statement. You can use **doch** (doH) to say *indeed, after all, really,* and *however.* When you use it to respond positively to a negative statement or a question, it means roughly *but yes, of course* or *on the contrary.*

Unglaublich!

Unglaublich! (*oon*-gloub-liH!) translates as *Unbelievable!* You can also use it to mean *unbelievably,* adding oomph to the adjective that follows it, for example, **Das Wetter ist unglaublich gut!** (dâs *wêt*-er ist *oon*-gloub-liH gooht!) (*The weather is unbelievably good!*)

Hoffentlich

Hoffentlich (*hof*-ent-liH) means *hopefully,* and you hear people saying it all alone to express optimism. In its negative form, **Hoffentlich nicht,** it's the equivalent of *hopefully not.*

Wie schön!

The literal translation of **Wie schön!** (vee shern!) is *How nice!* It can mean that, but sometimes the phrase is used sarcastically as a way to show annoyance or exasperation.

Genau!

Genau! (ge-*nou!*) means *exactly!* or *precisely!* You use it to show that you agree with what someone is saying.

Stimmt's?

Stimmt's? (shtimts?) translates as *Isn't it true?* or *Don't you agree?* Use this expression when you want your listener to confirm something you just said. It's usually answered with **Stimmt!** (shtimt!) meaning *I agree!* When you want to signal to the server in a restaurant that the amount of money you're handing over includes the tip, you say **Stimmt so** (shtimt zoh) (*That's okay*). In English, you'd probably say *Keep the change.*

Chapter 21

Ten Phrases That Make You Sound German

. . . .

This chapter provides you with some typical German expressions that almost everyone who speaks German knows and uses. These phrases are so very German that you may even pass for a native German speaker when you use them.

Schönes Wochenende!

Schönes Wochenende! (*shern*-es *voH*-en-en-de!) means *Have a good weekend!* You hear people wishing this to one another starting as early as Friday morning if they won't see each other again until the next week.

Gehen wir!

Gehen wir! (*gey*-en veer!) translates to *Let's go!* You can also use this as a question to say *Shall we go?* by ending the phrase with a rising intonation.

Was ist los?

The question **Was ist los?** (vâs ist lohs?) or *What's happening?* is most commonly used in the sense of *What's wrong?*

Das klingt gut!

Das klingt gut! (dâs klinkt gooht!) is the German way of saying *That sounds good!* You can tell someone that his suggestion to do something is a good idea with this phrase.

Keine Ahnung

Keine Ahnung (*kayn-e ahn-*oong) translates to *no idea.* This is the short version of **Ich habe keine Ahnung** (iH *hah-*be *kayn-*e *anh-*oong) (*I have no idea*) and is frequently used to express that you know nothing about the matter in question.

Es zieht!

Use **Es zieht!** (ês tseet!) to declare *There's a draft!* For some reason, Germans are very sensitive about drafts, so if you're feeling cold because the window's open, this expression is for you. Word for word, it actually means *It pulls.*

Nicht zu fassen!

Nicht zu fassen! (niHt tsooh *fâs-*en!) means *I can't believe it!* If you want to express disbelief, concern, or agitation, use this typically German phrase.

Du hast Recht!/Sie haben Recht!

The informal expression **Du hast Recht!** (dooh hâst rêHt!) and it's formal equivalent, **Sie haben Recht!** (zee *hah-*ben rêHt!) translate to *You're right!* This is a typical way of expressing agreement in German.

Lass es!

Lass es! (lâs ês!) is the informal German way of saying *Let it be!* When you want to say *Leave that matter alone,* you can use this phrase.

Nicht schlecht!

Nicht schlecht! (niHt shlêHt!) is the German equivalent of *Not bad!* As in English, this phrase not only means that something is not too bad, but it's also a reserved way of expressing appreciation and approval.

Part V
Appendixes

The 5th Wave   By Rich Tennant

"I think we should arrange to be there for the 'Sauerbraten-Bratwurst-Sauerkraut Week,' and then shoot over to the 'Antacid-Breathmint Festival.'"

In this part . . .

Last but not least, we include the appendixes, which you will no doubt find quite useful. In addition to a pretty comprehensive mini-dictionary, we provide verb tables that show you how to conjugate regular and irregular German verbs. You can also find answer keys for all of the Fun & Games activities that appear throughout the book and a guide to the audio CD that's attached to the book's inside back cover. **Deutsch ist doch leicht, nicht wahr?** (doych ist doH layHt, niHt wahr?) (*German's really easy, isn't it?*)

German-English Mini-Dictionary

A

abbiegen (*âp*-beeg-en): to make a turn
Abend (*ah*-bent) m: evening
Abendessen (*ah*-bent-ês-en) n: dinner
aber (*ah*-ber) but
abfliegen (*âp*-fleeg-en) to depart (by plane)
Abflug (*âp*-floohk) m: departure (by plane)
abreisen (*âp*-rayz-en) to leave
alles (*âl*-es) all
Ampel (*âm*-pel) f: traffic light
an (*ân*) at
Anfang (*ân*-fâng) m: beginning
Ankauf (*ân*-kouf) m: purchase
Ankunft (*ân*-koonft) f: arrival
Anrufbeantworter (*ân*-roohf-be-ânt-for-ter) m: answering machine
anrufen (*ân*-roohf-en) to call (on the phone)
Anwalt (*ahn*-vâlt) m: lawyer
April (â-*pril*) m: April
Arzt (ârtst) m: doctor (male)
Arztpraxis (*ârtst*-prâx-is) f: doctor's office
auch (ouH) also
auf (ouf) on
Auf Wiedersehen (ouf *vee*-der-zey-en) Good-bye
August (ou-*goost*) m: August
Ausfahrt (*ous*-fârt) f: exit
ausfüllen (*ous*-fuel-en) to fill out
ausgezeichnet (*ous*-ge-tsayH-net) excellent
außer (*ous*-er) except

Ausstellung (*ous*-shtel-oong) f: exhibition
Auto (*ou*-toh) n: car
Autobahn (*ou*-toh-bahn) f: highway

B

Bad (baht) n: bath(room)
Bahnhof (*bahn*-hohf) m: train station
Bank (bânk) f: bank
bar (bahr) cash
Bart (bârt) m: beard
Basketball (basketball [as in English]) m: basketball
Bauernhof (*bou*-ern-hohf) m: farm
Baum (boum) m: tree
beginnen (be-*gin*-en) to begin
bei (bay) near, at, by
beim (baym) near, at, by (the)
Berg (bêrk) m: mountain
Beruf (be-*roohf*) m: occupation
beschreiben (be-*shrayb*-en) to describe
besetzt (be-*zêtst*) busy
Besprechung (be-*shprêH*-oong) f: meeting
bestätigen (be-*shtê*-ti-gen) to confirm
Betrag (be-*trahk*) m: amount
bezahlen (be-*tsahl*-en) to pay
Bier (beer) n: beer
bisschen (*bis*-Hen) a little
bitte (*bi*-te) please
bleiben (*blay*-ben) to stay
Bordkarte (*bord*-kâr-te) f: boarding pass
Botschaft (*boht*-shâft) f: embassy

Brief (breef) m: letter

Briefkasten (*breef*-kâs-ten) m: mailbox

Briefmarke (*breef*-mâr-ke) f: stamp

Brieftasche (*breef*-tâsh-e) f: wallet

bringen (*bring*-en) to bring

Brot (broht) n: bread

Brötchen (*brert*-Hên) n: roll

Buch (boohH) n: book

buchen (*boohH*-en) to book

Bus (boos) m: bus

Bushaltestelle (*boos*-hâl-te-shtêl-e) f: bus stop

Butter (*boot*-er) f: butter

D

danke (*dân*-ke) thanks

danke schön (*dân*-ke shern) thank you very much

Datum (*dah*-toom) n: date

dein (dayn) your (familiar, singular)

deutsch (doych) German

Dezember (dey-*tsêm*-ber) m: December

Dienstag (*deens*-tahk) m: Tuesday

Donnerstag (*don*-ners-tahk) m: Thursday

Doppelzimmer (*dop*-el-tsi-mer) n: double room

Dorf (dorf) n: village

dort (dort) there

dritte (*drit*-e) third

drücken (*druek*-en) to push

dürfen (*duerf*-en) to be allowed to, may

durstig (*doors*-tiH) thirsty

Dusche (*dooh*-she) f: shower

E

einfach (*ayn*-fâH) easy, one-way (ticket)

einladen (*ayn*-lah-den) to invite

Einladung (*ayn*-lah-doong) f: invitation

einverstanden (*ayn*-fêr-shtânt-en) agreed

Einzelzimmer (*ayn*-tsêl-tsi-mer) n: single room

E-mail (email [as in English]) f: e-mail

empfehlen (em-*pfey*-len) to recommend

Ende (*ên*-de) n: end

Entschuldigung (ent-*shool*-di-goong) Excuse me

Erkältung (êr-*kêlt*-oong) f: cold

erste (*êrs*-te) first

essen (*ês*-en) to eat

etwas (*êt*-vâs) something

Euro (*oy*-roh) m: euro

F

fahren (*fahr*-en) to go, drive, travel

Fahrkarte (*fahr*-kâr-te) f: ticket (train/bus)

Fahrrad (*fahr*-rât) n: bicycle

Familie (fâ-*mi*-lee-e) f: family

Familienname (fâ-*mi*-lee-en-nâ-me) m: last name

fantastisch (fân-*tâs*-tish) fantastic

faxen (*fâks*-en) to fax

Februar (*fey*-broo-ahr) m: February

Feld (felt) n: field

Fenster (*fêns*-ter) n: window

Feuerwehr (*foy*-er-veyr) f: fire department

Fieber (*fee*-ber) n: fever

Firma (*fir*-mâ) f: company

Fisch (fish) m: fish

Fleisch (flaysh) n: meat

fliegen (*fleeg*-en) to fly

Flug (floohk) m: flight
Flughafen (floohk-hah-fen) m: airport
Flugsteig (floohk-shtayk) m: airport gate
Flugticket (floohk-ti-ket) n: airplane ticket
Flugzeug (floohk-tsoyk) n: airplane
Fluss (floos) m: river
Formular (for-moo-lahr) n: form
fragen (frah-gen) to ask
Freitag (fray-tahk) m: Friday
Fremdenverkehrsbüro (frêm-den-fêr-kêrs-bue-roh) n: tourist information office
Freund (froynt) m: friend (male)
Freundin (froyn-din) f: friend (female)
früh (frue) early
Frühling (frue-ling) m: spring (the season)
Frühstück (frue-shtuek) n: breakfast
für (fuer) for
Fußball (foohs-bâl) m: soccer

G

Gabel (gah-bel) f: fork
Gang (gâng) m: aisle
ganz (gânts) complete(ly)
Garten (gâr-ten) m: garden, lawn
geben (gey-ben) to give
Gebirge (ge-bir-ge) n: mountains
Gebühr (ge-buer) f: fee
gefährlich (ge-fair-liH) dangerous
gefallen (ge-fâl-en) to like
Gegend (gey-gent) f: area
gegenüber (gey-gen-ue-ber) opposite
Geheimzahl (ge-haym-tsahl) f: Personal Identification Number (PIN)
gehen (gey-en) to walk, go
Geld (gêlt) n: money
Geldautomat (gêlt-ou-toh-maht) m: ATM
Gemüse (ge-mue-ze) n: vegetable
genau (ge-nou) exact(ly)

genießen (ge-nees-en) to enjoy
geöffnet (ge-erf-net) open
Gepäck (ge-pêk) n: luggage
geradeaus (ge-rah-de-ous) straight ahead
geschlossen (ge-shlos-en) closed
gestern (gês-tern) yesterday
getrennt (ge-trênt) separate
gewinnen (ge-vin-en) to win
Glas (glahs) n: glass
Gleis (glays) n: track
Glück (gluek) n: luck, fortune
Golf (as in English) n: golf
groß (grohs) tall, big, large
gültig (guel-tiH) valid
gut (gooht) good
Gute Nacht (gooh-te nâHt) good night
Gute Reise (gooh-te ray-ze) have a good trip
Guten Abend (gooh-ten ah-bent) good evening
Guten Morgen (gooh-ten mor-gen) good morning
Guten Tag (gooh-ten tahk) hello (standard greeting, used throughout the day)

H

Haar (hahr) n: hair
haben (hah-ben) to have
Hafen (hah-fen) m: harbor
Halbpension (hâlp-pên-see-ohn) f: room with half board
Hallo (hâ-loh) hello
halten (hâl-ten) to stop
Haltestelle (hâl-te-shtêl-e) f: station, stop
Handy (hên-dee) n: cellphone
Hauptspeise (houpt-shpayz-e) f: main dish
Haus (house [as in English]) n: house
heiß (hays) hot
heissen (hays-en) to be called
helfen (hêlf-en) to help

Herbst (*hêrpst*) m: fall, autumn
heute (*hoy*-te) today
heute Nacht (*hoy*-te nâHt) tonight
hier (heer) here
Hilfe (*hilf*-e) f: help
hin und zurück (hin oont tsoo-*ruek*) round-trip
hinter (*hin*-ter) behind
Hobby (*hob*-ee) n: hobby
hören (*herr*-en) to hear
Hotel (as in English) n: hotel
Hügel (*hue*-gel) m: hill
hungrig (*hoong*-riH) hungry

I

interessant (in-te-re-*sânt*) interesting
Internet (internet [as in English]) n: Internet
Internetanschluß (*in*-ter-nêt-ân-shloos) m: internet connection

J

ja (yah) yes
Jahr (yahr) n: year
Januar (*yahn*-oo-ahr) m: January
jemand (*yey*-mânt) somebody
joggen (*jog*-en [j pronounced as in English]) to jog
Jugendherberge (*yooh*-gent-hêr-bêr-ge) f: youth hostel
Juli (*yooh*-lee) m: July
Juni (*yooh*-nee) m: June

K

Kaffee (*kâf*-ey) m: coffee
Kalender (kâ-*lên*-der) m: calendar
kalt (kâlt) cold

Karte (*kâr*-te) f: map, ticket
Kasse (*kâs*-e) f: cash register
kaufen (*kouf*-en) to buy
kein (kayn) no, not, not any
Kellner (*kêl*-ner) m: waiter
kennen (*kên*-en) to know (a person, place)
kennenlernen (*kên*-en-lêrn-en) to become acquainted with
Kino (*kee*-noh) n: movie theater
Kirche (*kirH*-e) f: church
klasse! (*klâs*-e!) great!
klatschen (*klâch*-en) to clap
klein (klayn) short, small
Klimaanlage (*klee*-mah-ân-lâ-ge) f: air conditioning
Kneipe (*knay*-pe) f: bar, pub
Koffer (*kof*-er) m: suitcase
kommen (*kom*-en) to come
können (*kern*-en) to be able to, can
Konsulat (kon-zoo-*laht*) n: consulate
Konzert (kon-*tsêrt*) n: concert
kosten (*kos*-ten) to cost
krank (krânk) sick
Krankenhaus (*krân*-ken-hous) n: hospital
Krankenschwester (*krân*-ken-shvês-ter) f: nurse
Krankenwagen (*krân*-ken-vah-gen) m: ambulance
Kreditkarte (kre-*deet*-kâr-te) f: credit card
Kreuzung (*kroyts*-oong) f: intersection
Kuchen (*koohH*-en) m: cake
Kuh (kooh) f: cow
kurz (koorts) short (in length)
Küste (*kues*-te) f: coast

L

lachen (*lâH*-en) to laugh
Land (lânt) n: countryside, country
lang (lâng) long (in length)

langweilig (*lâng*-vay-liH) boring
laufen (*louf*-en) to run, walk, go
leben (*ley*-ben) to live
legen (*ley*-gen) to lay
leider (*lay*-der) unfortunately
Leitung (*lay*-toong) f: line
lesen (*ley*-zen) to read
letzte (*lets*-te) last (opposite of first)
links (links) left
Liter (*lee*-ter) m: liter
Löffel (*lerf*-el) m: spoon
Luftpost (*looft*-post) f: airmail

M

machen (*mâH*-en) to do
macht nichts (mâHt niHts) never mind
Mai (may) m: May
Mannschaft (*mân*-shâft) f: team
Markt (mârkt) m: market
März (mêrts) m: March
Meer (meyr) n: sea, ocean
mein (mayn) my
Messer (*mês*-er) n: knife
Milch (milH) f: milk
Minute (mi-*nooh*-te) f: minute
mit (mit) with
mitbringen (*mit*-bring-en) to bring (along)
Mittag (*mi*-tahk) m: noon
Mittagessen (*mi*-tahk-ês-en) n: lunch
Mitte (*mit*-e) f: middle
Mittwoch (*mit*-voH) m: Wednesday
möchten (*merH*-ten) would like
mögen (*mer*-gen) to like
Moment (moh-*mênt*) m: moment
Monat (*moh*-nât) m: month
Montag (*mohn*-tahk) m: Monday
Morgen (*mor*-gen) m: morning

morgen (*mor*-gen) tomorrow
Museum (mooh-*zey*-oom) n: museum
müssen (*mues*-en) must, to have to

N

nach (nahH) to
Nachmittag (*nahH*-mi-tahk) m: afternoon
Nachricht (*nahH*-reeHt) f: message
nächste (*naiH*-ste) nearest
Nacht (nâHt) f: night
Nachtisch (*nahH*-tish) m: dessert
nah (nah) close, near
Name (*nah*-me) m: name
Nationalität (nâ-tsee-oh-nâ-li-*tait*) f: nationality
natürlich (nâ-*tuer*-liH) naturally
Naturschutzgebiet (nâ-*toohr*-shoots-ge-beet) n: nature reserve
neben (*ney*-ben) next to
nehmen (*ney*-men) to take
nein (nayn) no (opposite of yes)
nicht (niHt) not
nie (nee) never
Norden (*nor*-den) m: north
Notaufnahme: (*noht*-ouf-nah-me) f: emergency room
November (noh-*vêm*-ber) m: November
nur (noohr) just, only

O

Obst (ohpst) n: fruit
öffnen (*erf*-nen) to open
Oktober (ok-*toh*-ber) m: October
Oper (*oh*-per) f: opera
Osten (*os*-ten) m: east
Ozean (*oh*-tsê-ân) m: ocean

P

Paket (pâ-*keyt*) n: package
Park (pârk) m: park
Parkplatz (*pârk*-plâts) m: parking lot
passen (*pâs*-en) to suit
Pferd (pfêrt) n: horse
Polizei (po-li-*tsay*) f: police
Portier (por-tee-*ey*) m: doorman
Post (post) f: post office, mail
Postamt (*post*-âmt) n: post office
Postkarte (*post*-kâr-te) f: postcard
Postleitzahl (*post*-layt-tsahl) f: zip code
prima! (*pree*-mâ!) great!
pro (proh) per
Prost! (prohst!) Cheers!
pünktlich (*puenkt*-liH) on time

Q

Quittung (*kvit*-oong) f: receipt

R

Rathaus (*rât*-hous) n: town hall
Rechnung (*rêH*-noong) f: check, bill
rechts (rêHts) right
reden (*rey*-den) to talk
Regen (*rey*-gen) m: rain
regnen (*reyk*-nen) to rain
Reh (rey) n: deer
Reise (*ray*-ze) f: trip
Reisebüro (*ray*-ze-bue-roh) n: travel agency
reisen (*ray*-zen) to travel
Reisepass (*ray*-ze-pâs) m: passport
Reisescheck (*ray*-ze-shêk) m: traveler's check
reservieren (rê-zêr-*veer*-en) to reserve

Restaurant (rês-tuh-*ron*) n: restaurant
Rezeption (rey-tsêp-tsee-*ohn*) f: reception desk
Rückflugticket (*ruek*-floohk-ti-ket) n: round-trip ticket

S

Saft (zâft) m: juice
sagen (*zah*-gen) to say
Samstag (*zâms*-tahk) m: Saturday
Sänger (*zêng*-er) m: singer
S-Bahn (*ês*-bahn) f: local train
Schaf (shahf) n: sheep
Schalter (*shâl*-ter) m: teller window, counter
Schauspieler (*shou*-shpeel-er) m: actor
Scheck (shêk) m: check
Schein (shayn) m: bill
schicken (*shik*-en) to send
Schlüssel (*shlues*-el) m: key
Schmerz (shmêrts) m: pain
Schnee (shney) m: snow
schneien (*shnay*-en) to snow
schön (shern) pretty
Schule (*shooh*-le) f: school
Schwimmbad (*shvim*-baht) n: swimming pool
schwimmen (*shvim*-en) to swim
See (zey) m: lake; f: sea
segeln (*zey*-geln) to sail
sehen (*zey*-en) to see
sehr (zeyr) very
sein (zayn) to be
Sekunde (sê-*koon*-de) f: second
selbstverständlich (zêlpst-fêr-*shtênt*-liH) of course, certainly
September (zêp-*têm*-ber) m: September
sich auskennen (ziH *ous*-kên-en) to know one's way around
sich erinnern (ziH êr-*in*-ern) to remember

sich freuen (ziH *froy*-en) to be happy

sich freuen auf (ziH *froy*-en ouf) to look forward to

sich freuen über (ziH *froy*-en *ue*-ber) to be glad about

sich interessieren für (ziH in-te-rê-*seer*-en fuer) to be interested in

sich setzen (ziH *zêts*-en) to sit down

sich treffen (ziH *trêf*-en) to meet

sich unterhalten (ziH oon-têr-*hâl*-ten) to talk, enjoy oneself

sich vorstellen (ziH *fohr*-shtêl-en) to introduce oneself, imagine

singen (*zing*-en) to sing

Ski fahren (*shee* fahr-en) to ski

Sommer (*zom*-er) m: summer

Sonnabend (*zon*-ah-bent) m: Saturday

Sonne (*zon*-e) f: sun

Sonntag (*zon*-tahk) m: Sunday

spannend (*shpân*-ent) suspenseful

spazieren gehen (shpâ-*tsee*-ren *gey*-en) to take a walk

Speisekarte (*shpayz*-e-kâr-te) f: menu

Spiel (shpeel) n: game

spielen (*shpeel*-en) to play

sprechen (*shprêH*-en) to speak

Stadt (shtât) f: city

stattfinden (*shtât*-fin-den) to take place

Straße (*shtrah*-se) f: street

Straßenbahn (*shtrah*-sen-bahn) f: streetcar

Stunde (*shtoon*-de) f: hour

Süden (*zue*-den) m: south

Suppe (*zoop*-e) f: soup

T

Tag (tahk) m: day

Tal (tahl) n: valley

tanzen (*tân*-tsen) to dance

Tasche (*tâsh*-e) f: bag

Tasse (*tâs*-e) f: cup

Taxi (*tâx*-ee) n: taxi

Taxistand (*tâx*-ee-shtânt) m: taxi stand

Tee (tey) m: tea

teilnehmen (*tayl*-ney-men) to participate

Telefon (*tê*-le-fohn) n: phone

Telefonbuch (tê-le-*fohn*-booH) n: phone book

telefonieren (tê-le-fohn-*eer*-en) to make a call

Telefonnummer (tê-le-*fohn*-noom-er) f: phone number

Telefonzelle (tê-le-*fohn*-tsêl-e) f: phone booth

Teller (*têl*-er) m: plate

Tennis (tennis [as in English]) n: tennis

Termin (têr-*meen*) m: appointment

Theater (tey-*ah*-ter) n: theater

Tisch (tish) m: table

Toast (tohst) m: toast

Toilette (toy-*lêt*-e) f: toilet (bathroom)

toll! (tol!) great!

tragen (*trah*-gen) to carry, wear

trinken (*trink*-en) to drink

Trinkgeld (*trink*-gêlt) n: tip

Tschüs (chues) bye (informal)

Tür (tuer) f: door

U

U-Bahnhaltestelle (*ooh*-bahn-hâl-te-shtêl-e) f: subway station

U-Bahnstation (*ooh*-bahn-shtâts-ee-ohn) f: subway station

Übernachtung (ue-ber-*nâHt*-oong) f: accommodation

Uhr (oohr) f: clock, o'clock

und (oont) and

Unfall (*oon*-fâl) m: accident

ungefähr (*oon*-ge-fair) approximately

ungültig (*oon*-guel-tiH) invalid
Unterschrift (*oon*-ter-shrift) f: signature
Urlaub (*oohr*-loup) m: vacation

V

Verbindung (fêr-*bin*-doong) f: connection
Verkauf (fêr-*kouf*) m: sale
verletzt (fêr-*lêtst*) hurt
verlieren (fêr-*leer*-en) to lose
verreisen (fêr-*ray*-zen) to travel
verspätet (fêr-*shpai*-tet) delayed
Verspätung (fêr-*shpai*-toong) f: delay
verstehen (fêr-*shtey*-en) to understand
vielen Dank (*fee*-len dânk) thank you very much
vielleicht (fee-*layHt*) perhaps
Visum (*vee*-zoom) n: visa
Vogel (*foh*-gel) m: bird
Vollpension (*fol*-pên-see-ohn) f: room with full board
vor (fohr) in front of
Vormittag (*fohr*-mi-tahk) m: morning
Vorname (*fohr*-nâ-me) m: first name
Vorsicht (*fohr*-ziHt) f: caution
vorstellen (*fohr*-shtêl-en) to introduce
Vorstellung (*fohr*-shtêl-oong) f: show
Vorwahl (*fohr*-vâl) f: area code

W

Wald (vâlt) m: forest
walk (gehen) *gey*-en
wandern (*vân*-dern) hike
wann (vân) when
warm (vârm) warm
was (vâs) what

Wasser (*vâs*-er) n: water
Wechselkurs (*vêk*-sel-koors) m: exchange rate
Weg (veyg) m: trail, path, way
Wein (vayn) m: wine
weit (vayt) far
wer (vêr) who
werden (*vêr*-den) to become, will
Westen (*vês*-ten) m: west
wie (vee) how
wieder (*vee*-der) again
wiederholen (vee-der-*hoh*-len) to repeat
Wind (vint) m: wind
windsurfen (*vint*-soorf-en) to windsurf
Winter (*vin*-ter) m: winter
wirklich (*virk*-liH) really
wissen (*vis*-en) to know (a fact)
wo (voh) where
Woche (*voH*-e) f: week
wohin (voh-*hin*) where . . . to
wollen (*vol*-en) to want to
Wurst (voorst) f: sausage

Z

Zeit (tsayt) f: time
Zentrum (*tsên*-troom) n: center
ziehen (*tsee*-hen) to pull
Zimmer (*tsi*-mer) n: room
Zimmerservice (*tsi*-mer-ser-vis) m: room service
Zoll (tsol) m: customs
zu Hause (tsooh *hou*-ze) at home
Zug (tsoohk) m: train
Zugabe (*tsooh*-gâ-be) f: encore
zusammen (tsoo-*zâm*-en) together
zweite (*tsvay*-te) second (ordinal number)

English-German Mini-Dictionary

A

accident: **Unfall** (*oon*-fâl) m

accommodation: **Übernachtung** (ue-ber-*nâHt*-oong) f

actor: **Schauspieler** (*shou*-shpeel-er) m

afternoon: **Nachmittag** (*nahH*-mi-tahk) m

again: **wieder** (*vee*-der)

agreed: **einverstanden** (*ayn*-fêr-shtânt-en)

air conditioning: **Klimaanlage** (*klee*-mah-ân-lâ-ge) f

airmail: **Luftpost** (*looft*-post) f

airplane: **Flugzeug** (*floohk*-tsoyk) n

airplane ticket: **Flugticket** (*floohk*-ti-ket) n

airport: **Flughafen** (*floohk*-hah-fen) m

airport gate: **Flugsteig** (*floohk*-shtayk) m

aisle: **Gang** (gâng) m

all: **alles** (*âl*-es)

allowed to: **dürfen** (*duerf*-en)

also: **auch** (ouH)

ambulance: **Krankenwagen** (*krân*-ken-vah-gen) m

amount: **Betrag** (be-*trahk*) m

and: **und** (oont)

answering machine: **Anrufbeantworter** (*ân*-roohf-be-ânt-for-ter) m

appointment: **Termin** (têr-*meen*) m

approximately: **ungefähr** (*oon*-ge-fair)

April: **April** (â-*pril*) m

area: **Gegend** (*gey*-gent) f

area code: **Vorwahl** (*fohr*-vâl) f

arrival: **Ankunft** (*ân*-koonft) f

ask: **fragen** (*frah*-gen)

at: **an** (ân)

at home: **zu Hause** (tsooh *hou*-ze)

ATM: **Geldautomat** (*gêlt*-ou-toh-maht) m

August: **August** (ou-*goost*) m

B

bag: **Tasche** (*tâsh*-e) f

bank: **Bank** (bânk) f

bar, restaurant: **Kneipe** (*knay*-pe) f

basketball: **Basketball** [as in English] m

bath(room): **Bad** (baht) n, **Toilette** (toy-*let*-e) f

be: **sein** (zayn)

be called: **heißen** (*hays*-en)

be glad about: **sich freuen über** (ziH *froy*-en *ue*-ber)

be happy: **sich freuen** (ziH *froy*-en)

be interested in: **sich interessieren für** (ziH in-te-rê-*seer*-en fuer)

beard: **Bart** (bârt) m

become: **werden** (*vêr*-den)

become acquainted with: **kennenlernen** (*kên*-en-lêrn-en)

beer: **Bier** (beer) n

begin: **beginnen** (be-*gin*-en)

beginning: **Anfang** (*ân*-fâng) m

behind: **hinter** (*hin*-ter)

between: **zwischen** (*tsvish*-en)

bicycle: **Fahrrad** (*fahr*-rât) n

big: **groß** (grohs)

bill: **Schein** (shayn) m

bird: **Vogel** (*foh*-gel) m

boarding pass: **Bordkarte** (*bord*-kâr-te) f

book: **Buch** (boohH) n

book (verb): **buchen** (*boohH*-en)

boring: **langweilig** (*lâng*-vay-liH)

bread: **Brot** (broht) n

breakfast: **Frühstück** (*frue*-shtuek) n

bring: **bringen** (*bring*-en)

bring along: **mitbringen** (*mit*-bring-en)

bus: **Bus** (boos) m

bus stop: **Bushaltestelle** (*boos*-hâl-te-shtêl-e) f

busy: **besetzt** (be-*zêtst*)

but: **aber** (*ah*-ber)

butter: **Butter** (*boot*-er) f

buy: **kaufen** (*kouf*-en)

by: **bei** (bay)

bye (informal): **Tschüs** (chues)

C

cake: **Kuchen** (*koohH*-en) m

calendar: **Kalender** (kâ-*lên*-der) m

call (to telephone): **anrufen** (*ân*-roohf-en)

can: **können** (*kern*-en)

car: **Auto** (*ou*-toh) n

carry: **tragen** (*trah*-gen)

cash: **bar** (bahr)

cash register: **Kasse** (*kâs*-e) f

caution: **Vorsicht** (*fohr*-ziHt) f

cellphone: **Handy** (*hên*-dee) n

center: **Zentrum** (*tsên*-troom) n

certainly: **selbstverständlich** (zêlpst-fêr-*shtênt*-liH)

check: **Scheck** (shêk) m

check (bill): **Rechnung** (*rêH*-noong) f

cheers!: **Prost!** (prohst!)

church: **Kirche** (*kirH*-e) f

city: **Stadt** (shtât) f

clap: **klatschen** (*klâch*-en)

clock: **Uhr** (oohr) f

close: **nah** (nah)

closed: **geschlossen** (ge-*shlos*-en)

coast: **Küste** (*kues*-te) f

coffee: **Kaffee** (*kâf*-ey) m

cold: **Erkältung** (êr-*kêlt*-oong) f

cold: **kalt** (kâlt)

come: **kommen** (*kom*-en)

company: **Firma** (*fir*-mâ) f

complete(ly): **ganz** (gânts)

concert: **Konzert** (kon-*tsêrt*) n

confirm: **bestätigen** (be-*shtê*-ti-gen)

connection: **Verbindung** (fêr-*bin*-doong) f

consulate: **Konsulat** (kon-zoo-*laht*) n

cost: **kosten** (*kos*-ten)

country(side): **Land** (lânt) n

cow: **Kuh** (kooh) f

credit card: **Kreditkarte** (krê-*deet*-kâr-te) f

cup: **Tasse** (*tâs*-e) f

customs: **Zoll** (tsol) m

D

dance: **tanzen** (*tân*-tsen)

dangerous: **gefährlich** (ge-*fair*-liH)

date: **Datum** (*dah*-toom) n

day: **Tag** (tahk) m

December: **Dezember** (dey-*tsêm*-ber) m

deer: **Reh** (rey) n

delay: **Verspätung** (fêr-*shpai*-toong) f

delayed: **verspätet** (fêr-*shpai*-tet)

depart (by plane): **abfliegen** (*âp*-fleeg-en)

departure (by plane): **Abflug** (*âp*-floohk) m

describe: **beschreiben** (be-*shrayb*-en)

dessert: **Nachtisch** (*nahH*-tish) m

dinner: **Abendessen** (*ah*-bent-ês-en) n

do: **machen** (*mâH*-en)

doctor: **Arzt** (ârtst) m

doctor's office: **Arztpraxis** (*ârtst*-prâx-is) f

door: **Tür** (tuer) f

doorman: **Portier** (por-tee-*ey*) m

double room: **Doppelzimmer** (*dop*-el-tsi-mer) n

drink: **trinken** (*trink*-en)

drive: **fahren** (*fahr*-en)

E

early: **früh** (frue)

east: **Osten** (*os*-ten) m

easy: **einfach** (*ayn*-fâH)

eat: **essen** (*ês*-en)

e-mail: **E-mail** (email [as in English]) f

embassy: **Botschaft** (*boht*-shâft) f

emergency room: **Notaufnahme** (*noht*-ouf-nah-me) f

encore: **Zugabe** (*tsooh*-gâ-be) f

end: **Ende** (*ên*-de) n

enjoy: **genießen** (ge-*nees*-en)

enjoy oneself: **sich unterhalten** (ziH oon-têr-*hâl*-ten)

euro: **Euro** (*oy*-roh) m

evening: **Abend** (*ah*-bent) m

exact(ly): **genau** (ge-*nou*)

excellent: **ausgezeichnet** (*ous*-ge-tsayH-net)

except: **außer** (*ous*-er)

exchange rate: **Wechselkurs** (*vêk*-sel-koors) m

excuse me: **Entschuldigung** (ent-*shool*-di-goong)

exhibition: **Ausstellung** (*ous*-shtel-oong) f

exit: **Ausfahrt** (*ous*-fârt) f

F

fall: **Herbst** (hêrpst) m

family: **Familie** (fâ-*mi*-lee-e) f

fantastic: **fantastisch** (fân-*tâs*-tish)

far: **weit** (vayt)

farm: **Bauernhof** (*bou*-ern-hof) m

fax: **faxen** (*fâks*-en)

February: **Februar** (*fey*-broo-ahr) m

fee: **Gebühr** (ge-*buer*) f

fever: **Fieber** (*fee*-ber) n

field: **Feld** (fêlt) n

fill out: **ausfüllen** (*ous*-fuel-en)

fire department: **Feuerwehr** (*foy*-er-veyr) f

first: **erste** (*êrs*-te)

first name: **Vorname** (*fohr*-nâ-me) m

fish: **Fisch** (fish) m

flight: **Flug** (floohk) m

fly: **fliegen** (*fleeg*-en)

for: **für** (fuer)

forest: **Wald** (vâlt) m

fork: **Gabel** (*gah*-bel) f

form: **Formular** (for-moo-*lahr*) n

fortune: **Glück** (gluek) n

Friday: **Freitag** (*fray*-tahk) m

friend: **Freund** (froynt) m

friend: **Freundin** (*froyn*-din) f

fruit: **Obst** (ohpst) n

G

game: **Spiel** (shpeel) n

garden: **Garten** (*gâr*-ten) m

gate (airport): **Flugsteig** (*floohk*-shtayk) m

German: **deutsch** (doych)

give: **geben** (*gey*-ben)

glass: **Glas** (glahs) n

go: **gehen** (*gey*-en)

golf: **Golf** [as in English] n

good: **gut** (gooht)

good-bye: **Auf Wiedersehen** (ouf *vee*-der-zey-en)

good evening: **Guten Abend** (*gooh*-ten *ah*-bent)

good morning: **Guten Morgen** (*gooh*-ten *mor*-gen)

good night: **Gute Nacht** (*gooh*-te nâHt)

great!: **prima!/klasse!/toll!** (*pree*-mâ!/ *klâs*-e!/tol!)

H

hair: **Haar** (hahr) n

harbor: **Hafen** (*hah*-fen) m

have: **haben** (*hah*-ben)

have to: **müssen** (*mues*-en)

have a good trip: **Gute Reise** (*gooh*-te *ray*-ze)

hear: **hören** (*herr*-en)

hello (standard greeting, used throughout the day): **Guten Tag** (*gooh*-ten tahk)

hello (informal): **Hallo** (*hâ*-loh)

help: **helfen** (*hêlf*-en)

help: **Hilfe** (*hilf*-en) f

here: **hier** (heer)

highway: **Autobahn** (*ou*-toh-bahn) f

hike: **wandern** (*vân*-dern)

hill: **Hügel** (*hue*-gel) m

hobby: **Hobby** (*hob*-ee) n

horse: **Pferd** (pfêrt) n

hospital: **Krankenhaus** (*krân*-ken-hous) n

hot: **heiß** (hays)

hotel: **Hotel** (hotel [as in English]) n

hour: **Stunde** (*shtoon*-de) f

house: **Haus** (house [as in English]) n

how: **wie** (vee)

hungry: **hungrig** (*hoong*-riH)

hurt: **verletzt** (fêr-*lêtst*)

I

imagine: **sich vorstellen** (ziH *fohr*-shtêl-en)

in front of: **vor** (fohr)

interesting: **interessant** (in-te-re-*sânt*)

internet: **Internet** [as in English] n

internet connection: **Internetanschluss** (*in*-ter-nêt-ân-shloos) m

intersection: **Kreuzung** (*kroyts*-oong) f

introduce: **vorstellen** (*fohr*-shtêl-en)

introduce oneself: **sich vorstellen** (ziH *fohr*-shtêl-en)

invalid: **ungültig** (*oon*-guel-tiH)

invitation: **Einladung** (*ayn*-lah-doong) f

invite: **einladen** (*ayn*-lah-den)

J

January: **Januar** (*yahn*-oo-ahr) m

jog: **joggen** (*jog*-en [*j* pronounced as in English])

juice: **Saft** (zâft) m

July: **Juli** (*yooh*-lee) m

June: **Juni** (*yooh*-nee) m

just: **nur** (noohr)

K

key: **Schlüssel** (*shlues*-el) m

knife: **Messer** (*mês*-er) n

know (a fact): **wissen** (*vis*-en)

know (a person, place): **kennen** (*kên*-en)

know one's way around: **sich auskennen** (ziH *ous*-kên-en)

L

lake: **See** (zey) m

large (in size): **groß** (grohs)

last (opposite of first): **letzte** (*lets*-te)

last name: **Familienname** (fâ-*mi*-lee-en-nâ-me) m

laugh: **lachen** (*lāH*-en)

lawyer: **Anwalt** (*ahn*-vâlt) m

lay: **legen** (*ley*-gen)

leave: **abreisen** (*âp*-ray-zen)

left: **links** (links)

letter: **Brief** (breef) m

like: **mögen** (*mer*-gen), **gefallen** (ge-*fâl*-en)

line: **Leitung** (*lay*-toong) f

liter: **Liter** (*lee*-ter) m

little (a little): **bisschen** (*bis*-Hen)

live: **leben** (*ley*-ben)

local train: **S-Bahn** (*ēs*-bahn) f

long (in length): **lang** (lâng)

look forward to: **sich freuen auf** (ziH *froy*-en ouf)

lose: **verlieren** (fêr-*leer*-en)

luck: **Glück** (gluek) n

luggage: **Gepäck** (ge-*pêk*) n

lunch: **Mittagessen** (*mi*-tahk-ēs-en) n

M

mail: **Post** (post) f

mailbox: **Briefkasten** (*breef*-kâs-ten) m

main dish: **Hauptspeise** (*houpt*-shpayz-e) f

make: **machen** (*māH*-en)

make a call: **telefonieren** (tê-le-fohn-*eer*-en)

make a turn: **abbiegen** (*âp*-beeg-en)

map: **Karte** (*kâr*-te) f

March: **März** (mêrts) m

market: **Markt** (mârkt) m

may: **dürfen** (*duerf*-en)

May: **Mai** (may) m

meat: **Fleisch** (flaysh) n

meet: **sich treffen** (ziH *trêf*-en)

meeting: **Besprechung** (be-*shprēH*-oong) f

menu: **Speisekarte** (*shpayz*-e-kâr-te) f

message: **Nachricht** (*nahH*-reeHt) f

middle: **Mitte** (*mit*-e) f

milk: **Milch** (milH) f

minute: **Minute** (mi-*nooh*-te) f

Monday: **Montag** (*mohn*-tahk) m

money: **Geld** (gêlt) n

month: **Monat** (*moh*-nât) m

morning: **Morgen** (*mor*-gen) m

morning (forenoon): **Vormittag** (*fohr*-mi-tahk) m

mountain: **Berg** (bêrg) m

mountains: **Gebirge** (ge-*bir*-ge) n

movie theater: **Kino** (*kee*-noh) n

museum: **Museum** (mooh-*zey*-oom) n

must: **müssen** (*mues*-en)

my: **mein** (mayn)

N

name: **Name** (*nah*-me) m

nationality: **Nationalität** (nâ-tsee-oh-nâ-li-*tait*) f

naturally: **natürlich** (nâ-*tuer*-liH)

nature reserve: **Naturschutzgebiet** (nâ-*toohr*-shoots-ge-beet) n

near: **bei** (bay)

near (the): **beim** (baym)

nearest: **nächste** (*naiH*-ste)

never: **nie** (nee)

never mind: **macht nichts** (mâHt niHts)

next to: **neben** (*ney*-ben)

night: **Nacht** (nahHt) f

no (opposite of yes): **nein** (nayn)

no, not, not any: **kein** (kayn)

noon: **Mittag** (*mi*-tahk) m

north: **Norden** (*nor*-den) m

not: **nicht** (niHt); **kein** (kayn)

November: **November** (noh-*vêm*-ber) m

nurse: **Krankenschwester** (*krân*-ken-shvês-ter) f

O

occupation: **Beruf** (be-*roohf*) m

ocean: **Ozean** (*oh*-tsê-ân) m

o'clock: **Uhr** (oohr) f

October: **Oktober** (ok-*toh*-ber) m

of course: **selbstverständlich** (zêlpst-fêr-*shtênt*-liH)

on: **auf** (ouf)

one-way (ticket): **einfach** (*ayn*-fâH)

on time: **pünktlich** (*puenkt*-liH)

open (adjective): **geöffnet** (ge-*erf*-net)

open (verb): **öffnen** (*erf*-nen)

opera: **Oper** (*oh*-per) f

opposite: **gegenüber** (gey-gen-*ue*-ber)

P

package: **Paket** (pâ-*keyt*) n

pain: **Schmerz** (shmêrts) m

park: **Park** (pârk) m

parking lot: **Parkplatz** (*pârk*-plâts) m

participate: **teilnehmen an** (*tayl*-ney-men ân)

passport: **Reisepass** (*ray*-ze-pâs) m

pay: **bezahlen** (be-*tsahl*-en)

per: **pro** (proh)

perhaps: **vielleicht** (fee-*layHt*)

Personal Identification Number (PIN): **Geheimzahl** (ge-*haym*-tsahl) f

phone: **Telefon** (*tê*-le-fohn) n

phone book: **Telefonbuch** (tê-le-*fohn*-booH) n

phone booth: **Telefonzelle** (tê-le-*fohn*-tsêl-e) f

phone number: **Telefonnummer** (tê-le-*fohn*-noom-er) f

plate: **Teller** (*têl*-er) m

play: **spielen** (*shpeel*-en)

please: **bitte** (*bi*-te)

police: **Polizei** (po-li-*tsay*) f

post office: **Post** (post) f; **Postamt** (*post*-âmt) n

postcard: **Postkarte** (*post*-kâr-te) f

pretty: **schön** (shern)

pull: **ziehen** (*tsee*-hen)

purchase: **kaufen** (*kouf*-en)

push: **drücken** (*druek*-en)

R

rain: **Regen** (*rey*-gen) m

rain (to rain): **regnen** (*reyk*-nen)

read: **lesen** (*ley*-zen)

really: **wirklich** (*virk*-liH)

receipt: **Quittung** (*kvit*-oong) f

reception desk: **Rezeption** (rey-tsêp-tsee-*ohn*) f

recommend: **empfehlen** (em-*pfey*-len)

remember: **sich erinnern** (ziH êr-*in*-ern)

repeat: **wiederholen** (vee-der-*hoh*-len)

reserve: **reservieren** (rê-zêr-*veer*-en)

restaurant: **Restaurant** (rês-tuh-*ron*) n

right: **rechts** (rêHts)

river: **Fluss** (floos) m

roll: **Brötchen** (*brert*-Hên) n

room: **Zimmer** (*tsi*-mer) n

room service: **Zimmerservice** (*tsi*-mer-ser-vis) m

room with full board: **Vollpension** (*fol*-pên-see-ohn) f

room with half board: **Halbpension** (*hâlp*-pên-see-ohn) f

round-trip: **hin und zurück** (hin oont tsoo-*ruek*)

round-trip ticket: **Rückflugticket** (*ruek*-floohk-ti-ket) n

run: **laufen** (*louf*-en)

S

sail: **segeln** (*zey*-geln)

sale: **Verkauf** (fêr-*kouf*) m

Saturday (in northern Germany): **Samstag** (*zâms*-tahk) m

Saturday (in southern Germany, Austria, German-speaking Switzerland): **Sonnabend** (*zon*-ah-bent) m

sausage: **Wurst** (voorst) f

say: **sagen** (*zah*-gen)

school: **Schule** (*shooh*-le) f

sea, ocean: **Meer** (meyr) n

second: **Sekunde** (sê-*koon*-de) f

second (ordinal number): **zweite** (*tsvay*-te)

see: **sehen** (*zey*-en)

send: **schicken** (*shik*-en)

separate: **getrennt** (ge-*trênt*)

September: **September** (zêp-*têm*-ber) m

sheep: **Schaf** (shahf) n

short (in size): **klein** (klayn)

short (in length): **kurz** (koorts)

show: **Vorstellung** (*fohr*-shtêl-oong) f

shower: **Dusche** (*dooh*-she) f

sick: **krank** (krânk)

signature: **Unterschrift** (*oon*-ter-shrift) f

sing: **singen** (*zing*-en)

singer: **Sänger** (*zêng*-er) m

single room: **Einzelzimmer** (*ayn*-tsêl-tsi-mer) n

sit down: **sich setzen** (ziH *zêts*-en)

ski: **Ski fahren** (*shee* fahr-en)

small: **klein** (klayn)

snow: **Schnee** (shney) m

snow (to snow): **scheien** (*shnay*-en)

soccer: **Fußball** (*foohs*-bâl) m

somebody: **jemand** (*yey*-mânt)

something: **etwas** (*êt*-vâs)

soup: **Suppe** (*zoop*-e) f

south: **Süden** (*zue*-den) m

speak: **sprechen** (*shprêH*-en)

spoon: **Löffel** (*lerf*-el) m

spring: **Frühling** (*frue*-ling) m

stamp: **Briefmarke** (*breef*-mâr-ke) f

station, stop: **Haltestelle** (*hâl*-te-shtêl-e) f

stay: **bleiben** (*blay*-ben)

stop: **halten** (*hâl*-ten)

straight ahead: **geradeaus** (ge-rah-de-*ous*)

street: **Straße** (*shtrah*-se) f

streetcar: **Straßenbahn** (*shtrah*-sen-bahn) f

subway station: **U-Bahnhaltestelle** (*ooh*-bahn-hâl-te-shtêl-e) f; **U-Bahnstation** (*ooh*-bahn-shtâts-ee-ohn) f

suit: **passen** (*pas*-en) (to fit)

suitcase: **Koffer** (*kof*-er) m

summer: **Sommer** (*zom*-er) m

sun: **Sonne** (*zon*-e) f

Sunday: **Sonntag** (*zon*-tahk) m

suspenseful: **spannend** (*shpân*-ent)

swim **schwimmen** (*shvim*-en)

swimming pool: **Schwimmbad** (*shvim*-baht) n

T

table: **Tisch** (tish) m

take: **nehmen** (*ney*-men)

take a walk: **spazieren gehen** (shpâ-*tsee*-ren *gey*-en)

take place: **stattfinden** (*shtât*-fin-den)

talk: **reden** (*rey*-den)

talk, to enjoy oneself: **sich unterhalten**
(ziH oon-têr-*hâl*-ten)

tall: **groß** (grohs)

taxi: **Taxi** (*tâx*-ee) n

taxi stand: **Taxistand** (*tâx*-ee-shtânt) m

tea: **Tee** (tey) m

team: **Mannschaft** (*mân*-shâft) f

teller window: **Schalter** (*shâl*-ter) m

tennis: **Tennis** [as in English] n

thanks: **danke** (*dân*-ke)

theater: **Theater** (tey-*ah*-ter) n

there: **dort** (dort)

third: **dritte** (*drit*-e)

thirsty: **durstig** (*doors*-tiH)

Thursday: **Donnerstag** (*don*-ers-tahk) m

ticket: **Karte** (*kâr*-te) f

ticket (train/bus): **Fahrkarte** (*fahr*-kâr-te) f

time: **Zeit** (tsayt) f

tip: **Trinkgeld** (*trink*-gêlt) n

to: **nach** (nahH)

toast: **Toast** (tohst) m

today: **heute** (*hoy*-te)

together: **zusammen** (tsoo-*zâm*-en)

tomorrow: **morgen** (*mor*-gen)

tonight: **heute Nacht** (*hoy*-te nâHt)

tourist information office:
Fremdenverkehrsbüro
(frêm-den-fêr-*kêrs*-bue-roh) n

town hall: **Rathaus** (*rât*-hous) n

track: **Gleis** (glays) n

traffic light: **Ampel** (*âm*-pel) f

trail, path, way: **Weg** (veyg) m

train: **Zug** (tsoohk) m

train station: **Bahnhof** (*bahn*-hohf) m

travel: **reisen** (*ray*-zen)

travel (to go/be away [on a trip]):
verreisen (fêr-*ray*-zen)

travel agency: **Reisebüro** (*ray*-ze-bue-roh) n

traveler's check: **Reisescheck**
(*ray*-ze-shêk) m

tree: **Baum** (boum) m

trip: **Reise** (*ray*-ze) f

Tuesday: **Dienstag** (*deens*-tahk) m

turn: **abbiegen** (*ap*-beeg-en)

U

understand: **verstehen** (fêr-*shtey*-en)

unfortunately: **leider** (*lay*-der)

V

vacation: **Urlaub** (oor-loup) m

valid: **gültig** (*guel*-tiH)

valley: **Tal** (tahl) n

vegetable: **Gemüse** (ge-*mue*-ze) n

very: **sehr** (zeyr)

village: **Dorf** (dorf) n

visa: **Visum** (*vee*-zoom) n

W

waiter: **Kellner** (*kêl*-ner) m

wallet: **Brieftasche** (*breef*-tâsh-e) f

want to: **wollen** (*vol*-en)

warm: **warm** (vârm)

water: **Wasser** (*vâs*-er) n

wear: **tragen** (*trah*-gen)

Wednesday: **Mittwoch** (*mit*-voH) m

week: **Woche** (*voH*-e) f

west: **Westen** (*vês*-ten) m

what: **was** (vâs)

when: **wann** (vân)

where: **wo** (voh)

where . . . to: **wohin** (voh-*hin*)

who: **wer** (vêr)

will: **werden** (*vêr*-den)

win: **gewinnen** (ge-*vin*-en)

wind: **Wind** (vint) m

window: **Fenster** (*fêns*-ter) n
windsurf: **windsurfen** (*vint*-soorf-en)
wine: **Wein** (vayn) m
winter: **Winter** (*vin*-ter) m
with: **mit** (mit)
woods: **Wald** (vâlt) m
would like: **möchten** (*merH*-ten)

Y

year: **Jahr** (yahr) n
yes: **ja** (yah)
yesterday: **gestern** (*gês*-tern)
your: **dein** (dayn) (familiar, singular)
youth hostel: **Jugendherberge** (*yooh*-
gênt-hêr-bêr-ge) f

Z

zip code: **Postleitzahl** (*post*-layt-tsahl) f

Appendix B

Verb Tables

· ·

***N**ote:* Many German verbs fall into multiple categories, but in general, they break down into two groups: regular, also known as *weak* verbs, and irregular, also described as *strong* verbs. Irregular verbs have a stem vowel change in one or more tenses. Some irregular verbs are conjugated with **haben,** others with **sein** in the present perfect tense. This appendix is arranged to accommodate these idiosyncrasies of the German language.

Regular Verbs (No Stem Vowel Change)

Note: To form the future tense of such verbs, use the infinitive form of another verb and the conjugated form of the verb **werden** (*will*). The past is conjugated with **haben** (*to have*).

For example: bezahlen (to pay)
Past Participle: bezahlt (paid)

	Present	Past
ich (I)	bezahle	
du (you, sing. inf.)	bezahlst	
er/sie/es (he/she/it)	bezahlt	bezahlt
wir (we)	bezahlen	(conjugate with haben)
ihr (you, pl. inf.)	bezahlt	
sie/Sie (they/ you, form.)	bezahlen	

Special Conjugations

Verb *haben* (to have)

(Note: The present tense of *haben* is used as an auxiliary verb with
the past participle of another verb to form the past tense.)

Past Participle: gehabt (had)

	Present	Past	Future
ich (I)	habe	habe gehabt	werde haben
du (you, sing. inf.)	hast	hast gehabt	wirst haben
er/sie/es (he/she/it)	hat	hat gehabt	wird haben
wir (we)	haben	haben gehabt	werden haben
ihr (you, pl. inf.)	habt	habt gehabt	werdet haben
sie/Sie (they/ you, form.)	haben	haben gehabt	werden haben

Verb *sein* (to be)

(Note: The present tense of *sein* is used as an auxiliary verb with
the past participle of another verb to form the past tense.)

Past Participle: gewesen (been)

	Present	Past	Future
ich (I)	bin	bin gewesen	werde sein
du (you, sing. inf.)	bist	bist gewesen	wirst sein
er/sie/es (he/she/it)	ist	ist gewesen	wird sein
wir (we)	sind	sind gewesen	werden sein
ihr (you, pl. inf.).	seid	seid gewesen	werdet sein
sie/Sie (they/ you, form.)	sind	sind gewesen	werden sein

Note: For more information on the verb **sein**—for example, how to use it in the past tense—see Chapters 2 and 10.

Auxiliary Verb *werden* (will)
(The present tense of *werden* is used as an auxiliary verb with the infinitive of another verb to form the future tense.)

	Present
ich (I)	werde
du (you, sing. inf).	wirst
er/sie/es (he/she/it)	wird
wir (we)	werden
ihr (you, pl. inf.)	werdet
sie/Sie (they/ you, form.)	werden

Note: For more information on how to use the future tense, see Chapter 13.

Separable Verbs
For example: anrufen (to phone)
Past Participle: angerufen (phoned)

	Present	Past	Future
ich (I)	rufe an	habe angerufen	werde anrufen
du (you, sing. inf.)	rufst an	hast angerufen	wirst anrufen
er/sie/es (he/she/it)	ruft an	hat angerufen	wird anrufen
wir (we)	rufen an	haben angerufen	werden anrufen
ihr (you, pl. inf.)	ruft an	habt angerufen	werdet anrufen
sie/Sie (they/ you, form.)	rufen an	haben angerufen	werden anrufen

Note: For more information on how to use separable verbs and a list of separable verbs, go to Chapter 15.

Reflexive Verbs Dative
For example: sich etwas kaufen (to buy [oneself] something)
Past Participle: gekauft (bought)

	Present	Past	Future
ich (I)	kaufe mir	habe mir gekauft	werde mir kaufen
du (you, sing. inf.)	kaufst dir	hast dir gekauft	wirst dir kaufen
er/sie/es (he/she/it)	kauft sich	hat sich gekauft	wird sich kaufen
wir (we)	kaufen uns	haben uns gekauft	werden uns kaufen
ihr (you, pl. inf.)	kauft euch	habt euch gekauft	werdet euch kaufen
sie/Sie (they/ you, form.)	kaufen sich	haben sich gekauft	werden sich kaufen

Reflexive Verbs Accusative
For example: sich freuen (to be glad about, look forward to)
Past Participle: gefreut (was happy about, looked forward to)

	Present	Past	Future
ich (I)	freue mich	habe mich gefreut	werde mich freuen
du (you, sing. inf.)	freust dich	hast dich gefreut	wirst dich freuen
er/sie/es (he/she/it)	freut sich	hat sich gefreut	wird sich freuen
wir (we)	freuen uns	haben uns gefreut	werden uns freuen
ihr (you, pl. inf.)	freut euch	habt euch gefreut	werdet euch freuen
sie/Sie (they/ you, form.)	freuen sich	haben sich gefreut	werden sich freuen

Note: For more details on dative and accusative reflexive verbs, look at Chapter 12.

Irregular and Modal Verbs

Note: To form the future tense of the verbs in this list, use the infinitive form of another verb and the conjugated form of the verb **werden** (*will*). Most of these verbs are conjugated in the present perfect tense with **haben** (to have); some are conjugated with **sein** (to be).

		Present	Past Participle
beginnen to begin	ich	beginne	
	du	beginnst	
	er/sie/es	beginnt	begonnen
	wir	beginnen	(conjugate with haben)
	ihr	beginnt	
	sie/Sie	beginnen	
bleiben to stay, remain	ich	bleibe	
	du	bleibst	
	er/sie/es	bleibt	geblieben
	wir	bleiben	(conjugate with sein)
	ihr	bleibt	
	sie/Sie	bleiben	
bringen to bring	ich	bringe	
	du	bringst	
	er/sie/es	bringt	gebracht
	wir	bringen	(conjugate with haben)
	ihr	bringt	
	sie/Sie	bringen	
denken to think	ich	denke	
	du	denkst	
	er/sie/es	denkt	gedacht
	wir	denken	(conjugate with haben)
	ihr	denkt	
	sie/Sie	denken	
dürfen may, to be allowed to (modal verb)	ich	darf	
	du	darfst	
	er/sie/es	darf	gedurft
	wir	dürfen	(conjugate with haben)
	ihr	dürft	
	sie/Sie	dürfen	

		Present	**Past Participle**
essen to eat	ich	esse	
	du	isst	
	er/sie/es	isst	gegessen
	wir	essen	(conjugate with haben)
	ihr	esst	
	sie/Sie	essen	

fahren to drive, travel, ride, go	ich	fahre	
	du	fährst	
	er/sie/es	fährt	gefahren
	wir	fahren	(conjugate with sein)
	ihr	fahrt	
	sie/Sie	fahren	

fliegen to fly	ich	fliege	
	du	fliegst	
	er/sie/es	fliegt	geflogen
	wir	fliegen	(conjugate with sein)
	ihr	fliegt	
	sie/Sie	fliegen	

geben to give	ich	gebe	
	du	gibst	
	er/sie/es	gibt	gegeben
	wir	geben	(conjugate with haben)
	ihr	gebt	
	sie/Sie	geben	

gehen to go	ich	gehe	
	du	gehst	
	er/sie/es	geht	gegangen
	wir	gehen	(conjugate with sein)
	ihr	geht	
	sie/Sie	gehen	

		Present	**Past Participle**
halten	ich	halte	
to hold, keep,	du	hälst	
stop, consider	er/sie/es	hält	gehalten
	wir	halten	(conjugate with haben)
	ihr	haltet	
	sie/Sie	halten	
helfen	ich	helfe	
to help, assist	du	hilfst	
	er/sie/es	hilft	geholfen
	wir	helfen	(conjugate with haben)
	ihr	helft	
	sie/Sie	helfen	
kennen	ich	kenne	
to know (by	du	kennst	
acquaintance), be	er/sie/es	kennt	gekannt
familiar with	wir	kennen	(conjugate with haben)
	ihr	kennt	
	sie/Sie	kennen	
kommen	ich	komme	
to come	du	kommst	
	er/sie/es	kommt	gekommen
	wir	kommen	(conjugate with sein)
	ihr	kommt	
	sie/Sie	kommen	
können	ich	kann	
can, to be able to	du	kannst	
(modal verb)	er/sie/es	kann	gekonnt
	wir	können	(conjugate with haben)
	ihr	könnt	
	sie/Sie	können	

		Present	**Past Participle**
laufen	ich	laufe	
to run, walk	du	läufst	
	er/sie/es	läuft	gelaufen
	wir	laufen	(conjugate with sein)
	ihr	lauft	
	sie/Sie	laufen	

lesen	ich	lese	
to read	du	liest	
	er/sie/es	liest	gelesen
	wir	lesen	(conjugate with haben)
	ihr	lest	
	sie/Sie	lesen	

liegen	ich	liege	
to lie, be	du	liegst	
situated	er/sie/es	liegt	gelegen
	wir	liegen	(conjugate with haben)
	ihr	liegt	
	sie/Sie	liegen	

mögen	ich	mag	
to like (to),	du	magst	
to want	er/sie/es	mag	gemocht
(modal verb)	wir	mögen	(conjugate with haben)
	ihr	mögt	
	sie/Sie	mögen	

müssen	ich	muss	
to have to, must	du	musst	
(modal verb)	er/sie/es	muss	gemusst
	wir	müssen	(conjugate with haben)
	ihr	müsst	
	sie/Sie	müssen	

		Present	**Past Participle**
nehmen	ich	nehme	
to take	du	nimmst	
	er/sie/es	nimmt	genommen
	wir	nehmen	(conjugate with haben)
	ihr	nehmt	
	sie/Sie	nehmen	
schreiben	ich	schreibe	
to write	du	schreibst	
	er/sie/es	schreibt	geschrieben
	wir	schreiben	(conjugate with haben)
	ihr	schreibt	
	sie/Sie	schreiben	
sehen	ich	sehe	
to see	du	siehst	
	er/sie/es	sieht	gesehen
	wir	sehen	(conjugate with haben)
	ihr	seht	
	sie/Sie	sehen	
sitzen	ich	sitze	
to sit	du	sitzt	
	er/sie/es	sitzt	gesessen
	wir	sitzen	(conjugate with haben)
	ihr	sitzt	
	sie/Sie	sitzen	
sollen	ich	soll	
to be supposed to,	du	sollst	
should	er/sie/es	soll	gesollt
(modal verb)	wir	sollen	(conjugate with haben)
	ihr	sollt	
	sie/Sie	sollen	

		Present	**Past Participle**
sprechen	ich	spreche	
to speak	du	sprichst	
	er/sie/es	spricht	gesprochen
	wir	sprechen	(conjugate with haben)
	ihr	sprecht	
	sie/Sie	sprechen	

stehen	ich	stehe	
to stand, be located	du	stehst	
	er/sie/es	steht	gestanden
	wir	stehen	(conjugate with haben)
	ihr	steht	
	sie/Sie	stehen	

tragen	ich	trage	
to carry, wear	du	trägst	
	er/sie/es	trägt	getragen
	wir	tragen	(conjugate with haben)
	ihr	tragt	
	sie/Sie	tragen	

treffen	ich	treffe	
to meet	du	triffst	
	er/sie/es	trifft	getroffen
	wir	treffen	(conjugate with haben)
	ihr	trefft	
	sie/Sie	treffen	

trinken	ich	trinke	
to drink	du	trinkst	
	er/sie/es	trinkt	getrunken
	wir	trinken	(conjugate with haben)
	ihr	trinkt	
	sie/Sie	trinken	

		Present	**Past Participle**
verlieren to lose	ich	verliere	
	du	verlierst	
	er/sie/es	verliert	verloren
	wir	verlieren	(conjugate with haben)
	ihr	verliert	
	sie/Sie	verlieren	

verstehen to understand	ich	verstehe	
	du	verstehst	
	er/sie/es	versteht	verstanden
	wir	verstehen	(conjugate with haben)
	ihr	versteht	
	sie/Sie	verstehen	

wissen to know (a fact)	ich	weiß	
	du	weißt	
	er/sie/es	weiß	gewusst
	wir	wissen	(conjugate with haben)
	ihr	wisst	
	sie/Sie	wissen	

wollen to want, to intend (modal verb)	ich	will	
	du	willst	
	er/sie/es	will	gewollt
	wir	wollen	(conjugate with haben)
	ihr	wollt	
	sie/Sie	wollen	

Appendix C
On the CD

. . . .

Track Listing

*T*he following is a list of the tracks that appear on this book's audio CD. Note that this is an audio-only CD — it'll play in any standard CD player or in your computer's CD-ROM drive. **Viel Spaß!** (feel shpahs!) (*Have fun!*).

Track 1: The German alphabet (Chapter 3)

Track 2: Pronouncing German vowels (Chapter 3)

Track 3: Pronouncing vowels with umlauts (Chapter 3)

Track 4: Pronouncing diphthongs (Chapter 3)

Track 5: Pronouncing German consonants (Chapter 3)

Track 6: Pronouncing the German "r" and "l" (Chapter 3)

Track 7: Pronouncing consonant combinations (Chapter 3)

Track 8: Formal greetings (Chapter 3)

Track 9: Informal greetings between old friends (Chapter 3)

Track 10: Saying goodbye at the train station (Chapter 3)

Track 11: Buying food, using the metric system (Chapter 4)

Track 12: Chatting about family (Chapter 5)

Track 13: Discussing jobs (Chapter 6)

Track 14: Chatting about plans and the weather (Chapter 6)

Track 15: Asking for directions to a taxi stand (Chapter 7)

Track 16: Finding a friend's hotel (Chapter 7)

Track 17: Being seated at a restaurant (Chapter 8)

Track 18: Ordering a meal (Chapter 8)

Track 19: Paying the check and tipping (Chapter 8)

Track 20: Buying a ladies' shirt (Chapter 9)

Track 21: Trying on a blouse (Chapter 9)

Track 22: Making a date to go to the movies (Chapter 10)

Track 23: Talking about the ballet (Chapter 10)

Track 24: Making a business call (Chapter 11)

Track 25: Talking about vacation plans (Chapter 12)

Track 26: Getting information at the tourist office (Chapter 12)

Track 27: Booking a flight with a travel agent (Chapter 13)

Track 28: Exchanging money (Chapter 14)

Track 29: Checking in at the airport (Chapter 15)

Track 30: Asking which bus to take (Chapter 15)

Track 31: Reserving a room (Chapter 16)

Track 32: Checking into a hotel (Chapter 16)

Track 33: Discussing symptoms with a doctor (Chapter 17)

Customer Care

If you have trouble with the CD, please call Wiley Product Technical Support at 877-762-2974. Outside the United States, call 317-572-3993. You can also contact Wiley Product Technical Support at support.wiley.com. Wiley Publishing will provide technical support only for installation and other general quality control items.

To place additional orders or to request information about other Wiley products, please call 877-762-2974.

Appendix D

Answer Key

The following pages provide you with the answer keys to the Fun & Games activities that you find at the end of the chapters.

Chapter 3: Hallo! Pronunciation and Basic Expressions

1. geht, Ihnen, gut, ist, freut, auch; 2. hallo, geht's, mir, selbst, auch; 3. heißt, heiße, du, bin, wer, meine

Chapter 4: Getting Numbers, Time, and Measurements Straight

1, Montag, acht Uhr, anrufen (*call*) Herr Hegele; 2. Montag, zehn Uhr dreißig–elf Uhr dreißig, Meeting; 3. Dienstag, neun Uhr fünfundvierzig, Golf; 4. Mittwoch, ICE Zug (*train*) nach (*to*) Dortmund, vierzehn Uhr einundzwanzig; 5. Donnerstag, fliegen (*fly*) nach (*to*) Innsbruck, sieben Uhr vierzig; 6. Freitag, Abendessen (*dinner*), zwanzig Uhr; 7. Samstag, Museum Haus der Kunst, zwölf Uhr; 8. Samstag, Theater Faust, neunzehn Uhr dreißig; 9. Sonntag, Cocktail mit (*with*) Andrea, achtzehn Uhr

Chapter 5: Talking about Home and Family

A. Bad; B. Schlafzimmer; C. Esszimmer; D. Küche; E. Wohnzimmer

Chapter 6: Getting to Know You: Making Small Talk

1. Unwetter, donnert; 2. unter Null, schneit; 3. Temperatur, regnen; 4. Regen

Chapter 7: Asking for Directions

1. D; 2. G; 3. E; 4. C; 5. H; 6. B; 7. A; 8. F

Chapter 8: Guten Appetit! Dining Out and Going to the Market

A. die Suppe; B. die Serviette; C. die Gabel; D. der Teller; E. das Steak; F. das Kartoffelpüree; G. das Messer; H. die Tasse Kaffee; I. das Glas Wasser; J. der Löffel. (The waiter forgot der Salat.)

Chapter 9: Shopping Made Easy

7th floor: Restaurant; 6th floor: Computer; 5th floor: TV/Telekommunikation; 4th floor: Schuhe; 3rd floor: Kinderabteilung; 2nd floor: Herrenabteilung; 1st floor: Damenabteilung; Erdgeschoss: Schmuckabteilung; Untergeschoss: Supermarkt

Chapter 10: Going Out on the Town

1. Museum; 2. Sinfonie; 3. Film; 4. Ballet; 5. Oper; 6. Party

Chapter 11: Taking Care of Business and Telecommunications

1. der Bürostuhl; 2. die Lampe; 3. der Umschlag; 4. der Kalender; 5. der Computer; 6. der Drucker; 7. das Telefon; 8. der Fotokopierer; 9. der Schreibtisch; 10. das Papier; 11. der Kugelschreiber; 12. der Bleistift; 13. die Unterlagen; 14. die Maus

Chapter 12: Recreation and the Great Outdoors

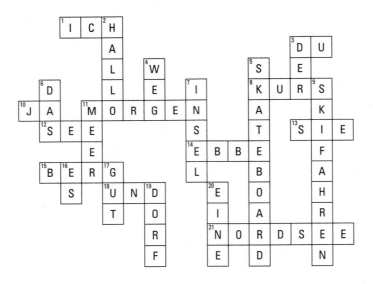

Chapter 13: Planning a Trip

1. werden; 2. Wirst; 3. werde; 4. Werdet; 5. wird; 6. werden

Chapter 14: Making Sense of Euros and Cents

1. fünfhundertzehn Euro, dreißig Cent; 2. zweihundertsechs Euro, sechzig Cent; 3. sechshundert Euro, fünfzig Cent; 4. zwölf Euro; 5. zwei Euro, fünfzig Cent

Chapter 15: Getting Around: Planes, Trains, Taxis, and More

1. G; 2. D; 3. B; 4. E; 5. A; 6. F; 7. J; 8. H; 9. I; 10. C

Chapter 16: Finding a Place to Stay

First Activity: 1. Was; 2. Wie; 3. Wann; 4. Wo; 5. Was für

Second Activity: 1. Date of Arrival; 2. Last name; 3. First name; 4. Occupation; 5. Birth date; 6. Place of birth; 7. Nationality; 8. Street Number; 9. Zip Code; 10. City; 11. Town/Date; 12. Signature

Chapter 17: Handling Emergencies

1. die Brust; 2. die Schulter; 3. das Auge; 4. der Kopf; 5. die Nase; 6. der Mund; 7. der Hals; 8. der Arm; 9. die Hand; 10. der Bauch/der Magen; 11. das Bein; 12. der Fuß; 13. der Fußknöchel; 14. das Knie

Index

• F •

• *M* •

Notes

Apple & Macs

iPad For Dummies
978-0-470-58027-1

iPhone For Dummies,
4th Edition
978-0-470-87870-5

MacBook For Dummies, 3rd
Edition
978-0-470-76918-8

Mac OS X Snow Leopard For
Dummies
978-0-470-43543-4

Business

Bookkeeping For Dummies
978-0-7645-9848-7

Job Interviews
For Dummies,
3rd Edition
978-0-470-17748-8

Resumes For Dummies,
5th Edition
978-0-470-08037-5

Starting an
Online Business
For Dummies,
6th Edition
978-0-470-60210-2

Stock Investing
For Dummies,
3rd Edition
978-0-470-40114-9

Successful
Time Management
For Dummies
978-0-470-29034-7

Computer Hardware

BlackBerry
For Dummies,
4th Edition
978-0-470-60700-8

Computers For Seniors
For Dummies,
2nd Edition
978-0-470-53483-0

PCs For Dummies,
Windows
7 Edition
978-0-470-46542-4

Laptops For Dummies,
4th Edition
978-0-470-57829-2

Cooking & Entertaining

Cooking Basics
For Dummies,
3rd Edition
978-0-7645-7206-7

Wine For Dummies,
4th Edition
978-0-470-04579-4

Diet & Nutrition

Dieting For Dummies,
2nd Edition
978-0-7645-4149-0

Nutrition For Dummies,
4th Edition
978-0-471-79868-2

Weight Training
For Dummies,
3rd Edition
978-0-471-76845-6

Digital Photography

Digital SLR Cameras &
Photography For Dummies,
3rd Edition
978-0-470-46606-3

Photoshop Elements 8
For Dummies
978-0-470-52967-6

Gardening

Gardening Basics
For Dummies
978-0-470-03749-2

Organic Gardening
For Dummies,
2nd Edition
978-0-470-43067-5

Green/Sustainable

Raising Chickens
For Dummies
978-0-470-46544-8

Green Cleaning
For Dummies
978-0-470-39106-8

Health

Diabetes For Dummies,
3rd Edition
978-0-470-27086-8

Food Allergies
For Dummies
978-0-470-09584-3

Living Gluten-Free
For Dummies,
2nd Edition
978-0-470-58589-4

Hobbies/General

Chess For Dummies,
2nd Edition
978-0-7645-8404-6

Drawing
Cartoons & Comics
For Dummies
978-0-470-42683-8

Knitting For Dummies,
2nd Edition
978-0-470-28747-7

Organizing
For Dummies
978-0-7645-5300-4

Su Doku For Dummies
978-0-470-01892-7

Home Improvement

Home Maintenance
For Dummies,
2nd Edition
978-0-470-43063-7

Home Theater
For Dummies,
3rd Edition
978-0-470-41189-6

Living the
Country Lifestyle
All-in-One
For Dummies
978-0-470-43061-3

Solar Power Your Home
For Dummies,
2nd Edition
978-0-470-59678-4

Internet

Blogging For Dummies,
3rd Edition
978-0-470-61996-4

eBay For Dummies,
6th Edition
978-0-470-49741-8

Facebook For Dummies,
3rd Edition
978-0-470-87804-0

Web Marketing
For Dummies,
2nd Edition
978-0-470-37181-7

WordPress
For Dummies,
3rd Edition
978-0-470-59274-8

Language & Foreign Language

French For Dummies
978-0-7645-5193-2

Italian Phrases
For Dummies
978-0-7645-7203-6

Spanish For Dummies,
2nd Edition
978-0-470-87855-2

Spanish
For Dummies,
Audio Set
978-0-470-09585-0

Math & Science

Algebra I
For Dummies,
2nd Edition
978-0-470-55964-2

Biology For Dummies,
2nd Edition
978-0-470-59875-7

Calculus For Dummies
978-0-7645-2498-1

Chemistry For Dummies
978-0-7645-5430-8

Microsoft Office

Excel 2010 For Dummies
978-0-470-48953-6

Office 2010 All-in-One
For Dummies
978-0-470-49748-7

Office 2010 For Dummies,
Book + DVD Bundle
978-0-470-62698-6

Word 2010 For Dummies
978-0-470-48772-3

Music

Guitar For Dummies,
2nd Edition
978-0-7645-9904-0

iPod & iTunes For
Dummies, 8th Edition
978-0-470-87871-2

Piano Exercises
For Dummies
978-0-470-38765-8

Parenting & Education

Parenting For Dummies,
2nd Edition
978-0-7645-5418-6

Type 1 Diabetes
For Dummies
978-0-470-17811-9

Pets

Cats For Dummies,
2nd Edition
978-0-7645-5275-5

Dog Training For Dummies,
3rd Edition
978-0-470-60029-0

Puppies For Dummies,
2nd Edition
978-0-470-03717-1

Religion & Inspiration

The Bible For Dummies
978-0-7645-5296-0

Catholicism For Dummies
978-0-7645-5391-2

Women in the Bible
For Dummies
978-0-7645-8475-6

Self-Help & Relationship

Anger Management
For Dummies
978-0-470-03715-7

Overcoming Anxiety
For Dummies,
2nd Edition
978-0-470-57441-6

Sports

Baseball
For Dummies,
3rd Edition
978-0-7645-7537-2

Basketball
For Dummies,
2nd Edition
978-0-7645-5248-9

Golf For Dummies,
3rd Edition
978-0-471-76871-5

Web Development

Web Design
All-in-One
For Dummies
978-0-470-41796-6

Web Sites
Do-It-Yourself
For Dummies,
2nd Edition
978-0-470-56520-9

Windows 7

Windows 7
For Dummies
978-0-470-49743-2

Windows 7
For Dummies,
Book + DVD Bundle
978-0-470-52398-8

Windows 7 All-in-One
For Dummies
978-0-470-48763-1

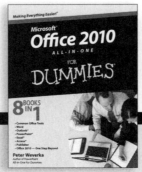

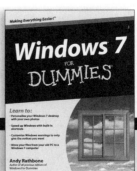

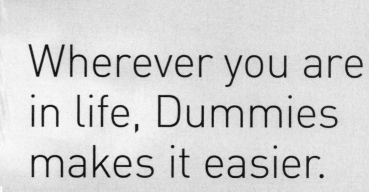

Wherever you are
in life, Dummies
makes it easier.

From fashion to Facebook®,
wine to Windows®, and everything in between,
Dummies makes it easier.

Visit us at Dummies.com

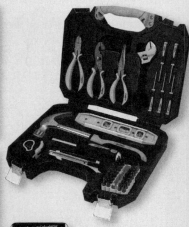